AROUND THE WORLD

Submerged

Captain Edward L. Beach

UNITED STATES NAVY

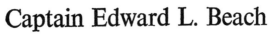

AROUND

Books by Edward L. Beach

Around the World Submerged
Run Silent, Run Deep
Submarine!

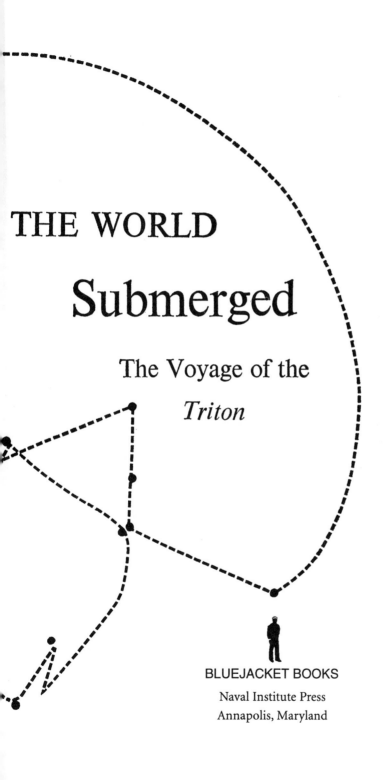

THE WORLD

Submerged

The Voyage of the

Triton

BLUEJACKET BOOKS

Naval Institute Press
Annapolis, Maryland

Naval Institute Press
291 Wood Road
Annapolis, MD 21402

First Bluejacket Books printing, 2001

Library of Congress Cataloging-in-Publication Data
Beach, Edward Latimer, 1918–
    Around the world submerged : the voyage of the Triton / Edward L. Beach.
        p.   cm.
    Originally published: New York : Holt, Rinehart and Winston, 1962.
    ISBN 1-55750-215-3 (alk. paper)
    1. Triton (Submarine) 2. Voyages around the world. 3. Beach, Edward Latimer, 1918– I. Title.
VA65.T7B38   2001
910.4'5—dc21   00-052445

Printed in the United States of America on acid-free paper ∞
08 07 06 05 04 03 02 01   8 7 6 5 4 3 2 1

The man whose inspiration, genius, and perseverance created the power plant without which *Triton*'s voyage could not have been conceived has never been categorized as easy to deal with, nor is his high resolve entirely without problems for himself and others. But his single-minded determination, his idealism, his relentless insistence upon the right, and his love for the United States of America distinguish him as one of the great men of our time.

To Vice-Admiral H. G. Rickover, United States Navy, who made *Triton* possible, and without whom the fantastic power of the nuclear reaction would still, in my opinion, be harnessed only for atomic explosives, this book, without his permission, is very respectfully dedicated.

IN GRATEFUL ACKNOWLEDGMENT

Ship's Company During Submerged Circumnavigation

OFFICERS

LCDR Will Mont Adams, Jr.	Executive Officer
CDR James Ellis Stark, MC	Medical Officer
LCDR Robert Dean Fisher, SC	Supply Officer
LCDR Robert William Bulmer	Operations Officer
LT Donald Gene Fears	Engineer Officer
LT Robert Brodie III	Communications Officer
LT Robert Patrick McDonald	Reactor Control Officer
LT Tom Brobeck Thamm	Auxiliary Division Officer
LT George John Troffer	Electrical Officer
LT Curtis Barnett Shellman, Jr.	Machinery Division Officer
LT George Albert Sawyer, Jr.	Gunnery Officer
LT Richard Adams Harris	CIC/ECM Officer
LT Milton Robert Rubb	Electronics Officer
LT James Cahill Hay	Assistant A Division
MACH Phillip Brown Kinnie, Jr.	Assistant M Division

CHIEF PETTY OFFICERS

Chester Raymond Fitzjarrald, TMC Chief of the Ship
Alfred E. Abel, ENCA
Hugh M. Bennett, Jr., ICC
Joseph H. Blair, Jr., EMCA
James J. DeGange, EMCA
John F. Faerber, ENCA
Loyd [sic] L. Garlock, FTC
William L. Green, SDCA
William R. Hadley, CTC

Harry W. Hampson, ETCA
Herbert F. Hardman, EMCS
Clarence M. Hathaway, Jr., ENCA
Robert L. Jordan, ICC
Jack R. Judd, ETCS
Ralph A. Kennedy, ENCA
James T. Lightner, ENCA
Lynn S. Loveland, MMCA
William J. Marshall, QMC
George W. McDaniel, SOCA

In Grateful Acknowledgment

Walter H. O'Dell, EMCA
Mack Parker, EMCA
Richard N. Peterson, ICCA
Bernard E. Pile, RDCS
"L" "E" [sic] Poe, EMC
*John R. Poole, RDCA
Edwin C. Rauch, ENCS
Joseph Rosenblum, EMCS

Fred Rotgers, ENC
Frank W. Snyder, ENC
Joseph W. Walker, YNC
Joseph E. Walsh, RMC
Hosie Washington, ENCA
Roy J. Williams, Jr., HMC
Marion A. Windell, RMCA

ENLISTED

Walter J. Allen, ET1
Ronald Everett Almeida, RM2
Erland N. Alto, EN1
Edward G. Arsenault, RM2
Ramon D. Baney, CS2
Robert F. Barrila, EN3
Horace H. Bates, EN2
Curtis K. Beacham, QM1
Lawrence W. Beckhaus, SO1
James C. Bennett, RM2
Nathan L. Blaede, ET1
George M. Bloomingdale, EM1
David E. Boe, SN
John S. Boreczky, Jr., EN3
Robert U. Boylan, ETNSN
Richard L. Brown, EM1
Earl E. Bruch, Jr., CS2
Franklin D. Caldwell, EMFN
Edward C. Carbullido, SD2
Robert M. Carolus, EN1
Robert C. Carter, MM1
Leslie R. Chamberlin, Jr., CS3
Gerald J. Clark, RD3
Charles E. Cleveland, EM1
Colvin R. Cochrane, MM1
Raymond J. Comeau, Jr., EM2
William E. Constantine, FT1
William J. Crow, CS1

Bertram Cutillo, DK3
Raymond R. Davis, EN1
James Obie Dixon, Jr., YN2
Martin F. Docker, ET1
Gary L. Dowrey, SOSSN
Ralph F. Droster, EN2
Alan T. Ferdinandsen, IC3
Richard R. Fickel, HM1
James A. Flaherty, RM1
Joseph R. Flasco, EN1
Fred J. Foerster, FN
René C. Freeze, RD1
Gerald W. Gallagher, IC1
Bruce F. Gaudet, IC3
Adrian D. Gladd, HM1
Edward R. Hadley, EN3
Carl C. Hall, QM3
Lawrence C. Hankins, Jr., EN1
Carlus G. Harris, EN2
Ralph W. Harris, EN2
David L. Hartman, EN2
Gene R. Hoke, IC1
William C. Holly, RD2
Floyd W. Honeysette, QM2
Berten J. Huselton, IC1
Wilmot A. Jones, TM2
Edward K. Kammer, EM1
Fred Kenst, SN

* Did not complete voyage.

Ronald D. Kettlehake, EMFN
Richard R. Knorr, ENFN
Peter P. J. Kollar, GM1
John F. Kuester, CS3
Raymond R. Kuhn, Jr., FN
Leonard F. Lehman, EM1
Larry N. Mace, EM1
Ross S. MacGregor, FT2
Edward J. Madden, EN2
Anton F. Madsen, QM3
Robert M. Maerkel, FN
Harry A. Marenbach, MM1
Harold J. Marley, Jr., RM1
Arlan F. Martin, EN3
George W. Mather, ET1
Boyd L. McCombs, EN1
Douglas G. McIntyre, EN1
William A. McKamey, SN
"J" "C" [sic] Meaders, HM1
Charles F. Medrow II, ETN3
Roger A. Miller, QM3
Philip P. Mortimer, Jr., EN2
John Moulton, FA
Larry E. Musselman, MM1
Bruce H. Nelson, FN
Ronald D. Nelson, EN1
Rudolf P. Neustadter, IC3
Raymond J. O'Brien, SK1
Harry Olsen, EN2
Charles S. Pawlowicz, ETRSN
Charles P. Peace, ET2
Robert C. Perkins, Jr., RM2
Richard H. Phenicie, IC3
Russell F. Pion, ET1
George V. Putnam, TM2

Donald R. Quick, EN1
Kenneth J. Remillard, SO1
Max L. Rose, SN
Richard M. Rowlands, TM1
Jerry D. Saunders, RD2
Russell K. Savage, QM2
Paul K. Schulze, EN1
Thomas J. Schwartz, TM3
Stanley L. Sieveking, TM1
Donald P. Singleton, EN3
Gordon E. Simpson, ET1
James H. Smith, Jr., SN
Peter F. Springer, EN1
Allen W. Steele, TM3
Richard W. Steeley, EN3
James A. Steinbauer, EN3
Gerald Royden Stott, ET1
Leonard H. Strang, EN3
Robert R. Tambling, TM1
Joseph W. Tilenda, SN
Jessie L. Vail, EM1
James O. Ward, SD3
William R. Welch, MM1
Henry H. Weygant, EN1
Robert W. Whitehouse, EN1
Lamar "C" Williams, EN2
William Williams, EN1
Audley R. Wilson, RD1
Donald R. Wilson, SD3
John W. Wouldridge, RM1
Gordon W. Yetter, EN1
Raymond F. Young, YNSN
Robert C. Zane, YN2
Herbert J. Zeller, EM1
Ernest O. Zimmerman, RD2

TECHNICAL AND SCIENTIFIC PERSONNEL

CDR Joseph B. Roberts, USNR, Office of Information, Navy Department
Earnest R. Meadows, PH1

Dr. Benjamin B. Weybrew, Psychologist, Naval Medical Research
    Laboratory, Submarine Base, New London
Mr. Michael Smalet, Geophysicist, USN Hydrographic Office
Mr. Gordon E. Wilkes, Civil Engineer, USN Hydrographic Office
Mr. Nicholas R. Mabry, Oceanographer, USN Hydrographic Office
Mr. Frank E. McConnell, Engineer, General Dynamics
Mr. Eldon E. Good, Inertial Guidance Division, Sperry

In the account of *Triton*'s voyage which follows, I have drawn
freely upon the narrative section of the official report of our trip. When
assembled, this report formed a tome about three inches thick. It contained many detailed tabulations and much succinctly presented raw
information, and all the officers of the ship participated in its preparation. My contribution was the narrative section, which was made
public when we arrived back in the United States.

Here, interspersed between the sections of the "Log" and forming
the major portion of this book, are my own personal thoughts and
observations as later reconstituted at my typewriter at home after all
the excitement had died down.

All portions of this manuscript have been submitted to the Navy
Department for clearance, and each chapter bears the stamp "no objection to publication on grounds of military security." Over and above
this, the entire responsibility for everything which appears in these
pages obviously must be my own.

—Edward L. Beach
Captain, United States Navy
Mystic, Connecticut

PROLOGUE

As a small boy, I had the good fortune of being a Navy Junior while living a settled life in a small community, without the frenetic shifts of locale inherent in a Service life. My father, as a Captain, after a long and rewarding career in the Navy, retired when I was four years old to accept the post of Professor of Military and Naval History at Stanford University. He had served the Navy thirty-seven-and-a-half years, and his sea duty had culminated with command of the American flagship in the European war zone during World War I.

During the course of his career, Dad had written thirteen books about naval life, most of them for teen-aged youths, plus several others aimed at a more mature audience. He had made a lifetime avocation of the study of history, with a natural inclination, of course, toward naval history; he had fought in three minor and two major wars (and was fond of saying that the minor ones were far more dangerous, so far as he personally was concerned, than the major). He had commanded one repair ship, two armored cruisers, and two battleships; I was born while he skippered the new "superdreadnaught" *New York,* in 1918.

My formative youth was spent in Palo Alto, California, where, after his years as a professor at Stanford, Father held the combined posts of City Clerk and Assessor. Among my childhood recollections were the stories Father used to tell about his experiences in the Philippines during and after the Spanish-American War, at the Naval Academy as a midshipman and

xii   Prologue

later as an instructor, and particularly about that dreadful
day in 1916 when his ship, the armored cruiser *Memphis,* was
engulfed and destroyed by a tidal wave. The latter was my
favorite yarn, and I never wearied of forcing my poor father
to repeat all the details of the catastrophe which had blighted
his career.

Father said that I would do well to study medicine, but I
felt his heart wasn't in it. My only thoughts were of going to
the Naval Academy and becoming, like him, an officer in the
US Navy.

The long-sought fulfillment of my ambitions came in 1935.
So great was my anticipation I couldn't understand why
Mother was crying when my parents took me to the train station, nor the meaning behind Father's faraway look. I was
then just seventeen years old.

Four years at the Naval Academy had more ups than
downs and were most satisfying, but when I graduated on the
first of June, 1939, it was with the sad knowledge that Father
was slipping away from me. His long and interesting letters
had become increasingly difficult to read. The thoughts in
them of late had begun to wander, and I noticed that more
and more he relived the past, particularly the loss of his old
Memphis and the crew members he had had to watch drown.

Father used to say that the place for a young officer was in
a big ship; so upon graduation from Annapolis, I applied for
the ten thousand ton cruiser *Chester.* I had been aboard about
two months when the war in Europe broke out. Because of a
surname beginning early in the alphabet I found myself transferred to the *Lea,* destroyer number 118.

The *Lea* was tiny, one-tenth the displacement of the *Chester,*
and she had been "permanently" retired to mothballs some
years before. The brass plate on her varnished wooden mast revealed her age as being the same as my own. There were
only five officers in the *Lea,* and I was the most junior. Later
on, when the "Third" was transferred, I automatically rose

to the high eminence of Fourth, but this, under the circumstances, had little effect on my unofficial title of "George."

"George," the traditional name of the most junior officer on board, always served as the ship's commissary officer, communications officer, ship's service officer, torpedo officer, gunnery officer, and first lieutenant. In addition, I had to insert a three-year stack of corrections into the ship's allotment of classified books and pamphlets—a horrendous job—was in charge of the landing party (luckily it seldom got an opportunity to go ashore), stood two four-hour watches a day on the bridge while under way, and while in port stood a twenty-four-hour "day's duty" every third day (except for a short period when I had the duty every other day).

There was also a Destroyer Officers Qualification Course of some twenty lengthy assignments, which I was required to complete within a year's time; and the Bureau of Navigation, evidently afraid that Ensigns might neglect their leisure time reading, had decided that we should submit a two thousand word book report each month.

The ship also had a skipper, an engineer, and an executive officer, but I never had time to discover what any of them did.

After two years on the *Lea,* in September, 1941, a message arrived directing me to submarine school in New London for instruction in submarine duty. By this time, I loved that slender four-stacked race horse of a destroyer, and didn't want to leave; but my skipper, an old submariner himself, would not send the protest I drafted, so off I went.

The course of instruction at the submarine school, originally six months long, had been curtailed to three by the war emergency, and on December 20, 1941, I was one of fifty-one graduates who heard the officer in charge of the school deliver a graduation address. In the course of it he said, "Many of you will command your own ships before this war is over."

None of us believed we could achieve such greatness, but

a little later we all noted the other side of the coin, when the first of our group went to eternity in the shattered submarine to which he had reported only a couple of weeks before.

My first submarine was USS *Trigger* (SS237), then under construction at the Navy Yard, Mare Island, California. During my two years on the *Lea*, I had finally bequeathed the "George" spot to someone else, but in the *Trigger* I found myself with that familiar title again. As before, I was greeted by a huge stack of uncorrected confidential and secret publications. The similarity, however, ended here; for *Trigger*, a first-line ship of war, was designed to operate in an entirely new and unfamiliar medium. The amount of highly technical equipment crammed into her sturdy hull amazed me.

I reported to *Trigger* on New Year's Day, 1942, but it wasn't until May that we arrived at Pearl Harbor. No one in *Trigger* had ever heard a shot fired in anger. We were all new, green as grass—even the skipper. A feeling of trepidation crept over us as we approached our recently desecrated Pacific bastion.

A short leave during an overhaul period in mid-1943 had great personal significance. I saw Father for the last time, I met Ingrid Schenck, and when I returned to *Trigger* I became second-in-command.

When I was detached, a year later, Dad had been gone six months and *Trigger,* now top-ranking submarine in the force, had less than a year to live. With orders to report to Portsmouth, New Hampshire, as Executive Officer of the not-yet-launched submarine *Tirante,* I used authorized delay time to take a ten-day honeymoon with the girl I had courted during three hectic weeks of leave the year before.

Tirante was a very successful submarine, earning Lieutenant Commander George L. Street, her skipper, a Congressional Medal of Honor. In June of 1945, the prediction of three and one half years was fulfilled when I was given command of my own ship, the *Piper*. The war, however, was drawing to a close. I strove mightily to get *Piper* into action, but the bombs of Hiroshima and Nagasaki got there first. Instead of killing and destroying, we rescued six bombed or torpedoed Japanese (we could never determine what had sunk their ship) from the middle of the Sea of Japan, and I have since felt grateful, after all the depth charges and torpedoes, that this, instead of destruction of my fellow man, is my last memory of the war.

Life in the peacetime Navy was, of course, very different from the war years. I spent periods in the Navy Department in Washington and periods at sea. There was a moment of deep grief when our first child, little Inga, aged three years and a week, died suddenly in Key West, Florida. There was a period of professional triumph when my ship, the *Amberjack,* pioneering new tactics to exploit her revolutionary streamlined shape, was for a time the most battle-worthy submarine in the force.

Happily, we had more children; two boys and another little girl. I spent some time on the staff of General Omar N. Bradley while he was Chairman of the Joint Chiefs of Staff, and then went to sea in command of the newly constructed submarine, *Trigger* (SS564). Despite the heritage of her name, this ship, named after my old destroyed *Trigger,* was a great sorrow. Her engines, poorly designed and put into service after insufficient testing, were not dependable.

My indignation ran high. Diesel engines had long since been perfected. At one time submariners had assisted in their development, but that job had been done, the principles proven. Now, our job, as I saw it, was to operate the ships, develop tactics for them, and test their combat capabilities—not help to build diesel engines any more. One of the three types of diesel engines with which we had fitted our boats before the war had proved to be an inglorious failure, thus endangered the lives of the crews. The most worth-while contribution *Trigger* II could make, I felt, was to prevent this from happening again by being forthright about the deficiencies. But condemnation of the new engines was not well-received in the Navy Department, where a more popular view was that submarine skippers should spend their time stoically trying to make their boats run instead of documenting their faults. Vainly, I argued that glossing over its manifest undependability for war service was precisely what had been done with the pre-war HOR engine (sometimes, with a deep tone of disgust, the initials were pronounced as a word), with the result that it was not taken off the line soon enough. Ultimately all of them were replaced, but not before men had fought the enemy in defective ships and come back in passionate anger. It was one lesson we had learned well: no operational commander would send a ship like the new *Trigger* on any important mission in war, I said.

The controversy was still going on when we had occasion to put *Trigger* in dry dock one day in January, 1953. During dry-dock operations, there is a short time when your ship is completely out of communication with the outside world. It is impossible for anyone to go ashore, and telephones are not yet hooked up. Temporarily, you are entirely incommunicado. It was while *Trigger* was in this condition that a large overhead crane swung toward us from the dock, and someone noticed a telephone hanging from the crane's hook. Seconds later, the crane, capable of lifting twenty tons, laid the five-pound telephone gently on our afterdeck. It was ringing steadily.

"It's for you, Captain." The sailor answering the phone still wore the surprised look with which he had picked it up. The caller was an officer in the Bureau of Naval Personnel. He wanted me to come to Washington as soon as possible, but would not say why. I spent the next several hours worrying. The only reason anyone would want me in Washington, so far as I could guess, was to be unpleasant about my attitude toward the Navy's new submarine diesel engines.

I caught the night train, was in Washington early the next morning, and was directed to report to the headquarters of the President-elect of the United States at a downtown hotel. There, after several minutes of aimless conversation with busy people, a singularly pleasant, soft-spoken, and slender gentleman, whom I later discovered to be Major General Wilton B. Persons, USA (ret.), suddenly asked, "Would you like to be the President's Naval Aide?"

The question caught me by surprise, as no doubt it was intended to do. What I knew about naval aiding a President was not impressive. I remember wondering whether it would be anything like working for General Bradley, and, in virtually the same thought, whether he might have had anything to do with suggesting me. And I remember also thinking quickly that coming ashore meant I would no longer be "attached to and serving on board a submarine." This would automatically result in a pay cut amounting to $180.00 a month.

But that is about all I recall of the interview, for the next thing I found myself saying was that I would like the job, if Mr. Eisenhower wanted me. A friendly Army colonel by the name of Pete Carroll introduced me to a few more people and then showed me out. "When do I start?" I asked him.

"You've started," he replied.

The four years I served as Naval Aide to the President are, of course, among the most precious recollections my wife and I have. To be associated in any capacity with the President of the United States and to have had the opportunity to earn his regard is a piece of good fortune which cannot fall to many.

I soon found that a tremendous amount of official paper flows every day between the White House and the Pentagon. About ninety-five percent of this paper is routine—and the Navy's portion of this reaches the President through the Naval Aide. Naturally, there were other duties, too.

One of the more pleasant tasks which fell to me was that of making the arrangements for Mrs. Eisenhower's christening of the *Nautilus*. The affair burgeoned from a rather simple expedition to an elaborate operation, involving special trains, special protocol arrangements, and all sorts of intricate details in New London.

During a moment of leisure after the 1956 campaign, I communicated to the President my feeling that as a career naval officer I should not remain longer than four years in the position I then held. His ready understanding has been one of my warm memories of him.

The Navy Department concurred in my desire for sea duty, and since I had recently attained the rank of Captain, I was assigned to command one of the fast fleet oilers serving our forces in the Mediterranean. *Salamonie*, or "Old Sal" as we dubbed her, had been built for the Standard Oil Company as a so-called "super-tanker" just before the war. Taken over by the Navy before completion, she had been a part of the fleet ever since, and when I saw her, she bore the scars of many years of strenuous operations.

Almost all my time on board was spent at sea in the Mediterranean, fueling ships and fighting rust, and as we prepared to leave that strategic area, I was amazed at the tabulated number of ships we had refueled and the quantity of fuel oil, gasoline, and jet fuel we had pumped through our tanks. We had serviced an average of four ships per day, and on some days we counted as many as twenty-four ships alongside during a twenty-four-hour period.

During the *Salamonie*'s return trip to the United States, in December of 1957, she had a brief moment of distinction when three destroyers, caught in a lengthy period of bad weather at sea, began to run perilously low on fuel. We were the only ship in the vicinity, and after three days of struggle at the tail end of a North Atlantic hurricane, we managed to get fuel to the three ships and save the situation. It was a strenuous operation from the heaving, pitching deck of the *Salamonie*, and it must have been even more so from the destroyers' point of view.

During the first day, a heavy sea swept a man overboard from one of them; snatched him, in fact, from the boat deck, a full deck higher than the ship's main deck. To launch a life-boat was impossible; we were all pitching too violently, and even "Old Sal" was rolling her decks under. By good fortune, I happened to be looking at the *Gearing* through my binoculars at the very moment her signal searchlight began to spell out the words, "MAN OVERBOARD," and read the electrifying message direct. In this situation *Salamonie,* being the biggest ship present, had the advantage; and we were able to maneuver into position to pick the man up by sending a strong swimmer with a line fastened to his waist into the fifty-foot seas after him. The volunteer who thus risked his life to save another was Lawrence W. Beckhaus, then a Gunner's Mate Second Class.

"Old Sal" reached the United States on December 22, 1957. On arrival, Beckhaus received a medal for heroism; and I was home for Christmas. In the mail were orders detaching me from command of *Salamonie* and directing me to report to the "Director of Naval Reactors, Atomic Energy Commission, Washington, D.C., for duty under instruction in nuclear power."

AROUND THE WORLD

Submerged

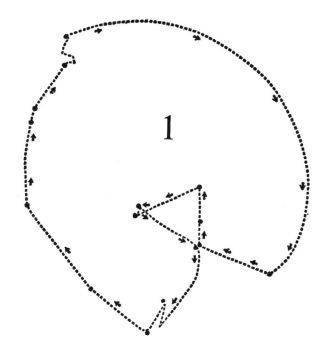

1

If there is anything about the redoubtable Vice-Admiral Rick-over which is predictable, it must be his insistence upon the most thorough training, the most complete familiarity with operational and design procedures, the most meticulously care-ful engineering practice by the designers, builders, and per-sonnel who operate nuclear machinery. A magnificent record of trouble-free operation of his nuclear power plants is one of the results. It is attained by vigilance on the part of all per-sonnel involved—and of all of them, the most vigilant is Vice-Admiral Rickover himself.

In the case of the *Triton,* by the time the ship first put to sea in September, 1959, some of her crew had been training for a period of two years or more. Officers and enlisted men

alike had to go through a rigorous program, carefully tailored
for the needs of each individual case.

Executive Officer Will Adams and I, for instance, received
what we later decided was the most strenuous and yet the
most satisfying period of training, testing, and qualification
either of us had ever experienced. Before we were finished, we
had mapped out the entire power plant of the *Nautilus* prototype near Arco, Idaho, and had done the same thing for
Triton's own prototype, more recently completed at West
Milton, New York. We spent eight weeks in Idaho, during the
hot summer of 1958, studying from sixteen to eighteen hours
a day, seven days a week, Sundays and holidays included. At
the conclusion of this period Adams and I took a comprehensive written examination which, in my case at least, took
fourteen hours to complete (Will, to my dismay, walked out
of the examination room two hours before me). At West Milton, our eight weeks of training was split up, partly because the
prototype had barely begun to operate; but here, too, we made
the same slow careful checkout of all systems.

By the time we arrived at the Electric Boat Division of the
General Dynamics Corporation, in Groton, Connecticut, to
participate in the launching of our new ship, which took place
on August 19, 1958, we had received the best possible training
in the techniques of operating her highly complicated machinery and handling all conceivable functions and malfunctions.

As time went on, and we came to know them intimately,
Adams and I developed a deep admiration for the designers
of our fantastic power plant, and it is probably proper at this
point to state that Lieutenant Commander David Leighton,
USN, stands second only to Admiral Rickover in our appreciation of the job done. We also developed a strong regard for the
officers and men of *Triton*'s crew, who had already spent so
many days learning how to man her.

Already, she had created difficulties because of her great
size. Among the problems faced by the builders was that her

huge bow blocked the space reserved for the railroad which ran just forward of the building ways. This railroad was needed to haul regular loads of ship-building supplies which were needed in the Yard. It had to be kept operating. The problem was solved by cutting away a part of the lower section of *Triton*'s bow to clear the trains, and replacing it barely a few days before the launching.

At the other end of the ship, her stern projected so far out over the Thames River that efficient construction was not possible. Therefore, to the considerable consternation of the people on the New London side of the river, who could see only a great unfinished cavern where *Triton*'s stern should have been, her last fifty-foot section was constructed on the adjoining ways. After the stern was built, a pair of tremendous overhead cranes hauled it into its proper place. (Before this was done, Electric Boat was many times playfully reminded of the importance of finishing a ship before launching her.)

One segment of the ship could not, however, be installed before the launching ceremony. *Triton* stood on the ways about seven stories above the ground, too high to slide under the giant overhead cranes of the building ways; the top twelve feet of her sail (the great vertical structure carrying her periscopes and retractable masts) had to be cut off and reinstalled after launching.

The outstanding feature of *Triton,* responsible for her unprecedented length and displacement, was that for the first time not one but two reactors were included in a nuclear submarine. The forward reactor would supply steam to the forward engine room and drive the starboard propeller; number two reactor would supply steam to the after engine room and drive the port propeller. The two plants, identical in design, were entirely independent and separate, but could, of course, be cross-connected if necessary. Designed for high speed on the surface as well as beneath it, she had a long slender hull in contrast to the short, fat shape best suited to underwater speed alone. *Triton* was 447½ feet long, more than a hundred feet longer than any previous US submarine, almost as long as Dad's lost *Memphis* of some forty years before. But where the *Memphis* had over sixty feet of beam, *Triton* had only thirty-seven. Her surface displacement was approximately six thousand tons; submerged, she would displace eight thousand tons, about twice as much as any other submarine.

As *Triton* stood ready for launching, her mammoth hull equaled in size a light cruiser of World War II. Inside, her reactors and machinery were of the most sophisticated design and development yet achieved by any nuclear power plant.

Her underwater body showed a dull olive green when the scaffolding was cleared and she stood in solitaire on two ribbons of shiny tan-colored wax. Around her towered the black skeletonlike framework of the overhead cranes, and crowning her entire length was a double-strength steel superstructure, painted a brilliant orange. Perched on top of this was the bulky lower section of the sail, truncated by removal of the upper half but still seeming high enough to strike the cranes above.

Launching a ship is an important point in her construction program. Contrary to the impression some people may have, a ship is far from fully constructed when she is launched. With the exception of small pleasure craft, no ship can be completed before she is floating in the water, for even the most careful calculations cannot foretell the precise manner in which the hull will take up the stresses of being waterborne. Certain extremely precise technical work, such as final boring of the propeller-shaft tubes and lining up turbines and reduction gears on their foundations, cannot be accomplished until after the ship is afloat. Otherwise, a tiny deflection of a sixteenth or a thirty-second of an inch—easily possible in a hull the length of ours—might throw the reduction gears or propeller shafting out of line.

On the nineteenth of August, 1958, a warm New England summer day, thirty-five thousand guests had come to the Electric Boat Division to see *Triton* launched—the biggest crowd ever assembled at EB, so the papers said, for the biggest submarine ever built. It was a great day for *Triton,* for Electric Boat, for *Triton*'s crew, and for me.

About half our crew were aboard for the ceremony, in close formation on the forecastle, resplendent in their dress-white uniforms. Also in whites, I waited above them on a makeshift platform provided at the half-level of the decapitated bridge. A few planks had been nailed together to make a platform near the forward end, and this was where I stood. Unfortunately, it was so low I could barely see over the side, but I found that by standing on top of the ship's whistle, built into the forward section of the sail, and holding onto a girder at its edge, I was able to get a pretty good view of the ceremonies. I could not, however, see the launching platform or the festivities going on there beneath the *Triton*'s bow.

The gaily dressed crowd on the ground below spread out in all directions, spilled over the temporary barriers erected by Electric Boat, crowded on top of the stacked lumber and building materials on both sides. Some of them even stood on the roofs of nearby buildings. As I watched, I was amused to see an Electric Boat officer climb to the top of one of the buildings and chase away a number of teen-agers. Most of the uniforms were whites, the prescribed attire for the occasion. There were sailors from other ships acting as ushers; a sprinkling of blue and gray-green-uniformed police officers scattered about, preserving order. Nearly half the crowd were women; and there were a number of children about, too, most of them clutching the hands of their parents. One or two of the smaller tots perched on the shoulders of a uniformed father, and a few raced around in games of tag or follow-the-leader.

My own children were somewhere in the crowd, I knew, but I searched for them without success. They were supposed to be up near the launching platform in the care of a secretary of Electric Boat, for Ingrid, my wife, could not be here. She was in Boston with her father, whose postoperative condition had suddenly become critical.

Excited, high-pitched chatter wafted up to me, but soon the crowd grew silent, and I heard the loudspeakers rumble with the voice of one of the presiding dignitaries. Not a word of what was being said could be distinguished, but from the timetable I had studied that morning, I knew that Admiral Jerauld Wright, Commander in Chief of the United States Atlantic Fleet and Supreme Allied Commander, Atlantic, was about to deliver the principal address. After Admiral Wright finished, there would be an invocation, and then *Triton* would be christened by Louise Will, wife of Vice-Admiral John Will, USN (ret.), with the traditional shattering of a bottle of champagne. Then, at long last, the trigger holding the launching cradle would be released, and we would slide backward into the water.

There was a scattering of applause from below, then silence again. The drone of the loudspeakers went on and off several times. Some people near the invisible launching platform bowed their heads. Still not an intelligible word came through the loudspeakers, and I could only assume that the launching was drawing closer. Instinctively, I took a firmer grip on the handrail.

There is always a little apprehension when a ship is launched. Will she start when the trigger is released? Will the motion be accompanied by a jolt which might knock personnel off their feet or over the side? Poised only on two slender slides for her entry into water, our ship was in its most vulnerable condition. Any miscalculation, any error in fixing the location of the stresses, could easily result in damage. Unthinkable, but conceivable—she might even topple over. Surface ships, usually broader than they are tall and essentially flat-bottomed, are not prone to such mishaps, but submarines are taller than they are wide and their bottoms are round. The catastrophe of rolling over on the crowds below would be appalling. A fine time for me to come up with this, I thought; surely the Electric Boat people ought to know how to launch a submarine, even one as big as *Triton*.

Being idle, I also had time to concern myself over how the new ship would behave when she entered the water. Were the many hull openings all closed? Submarines are designed to lie low in the water. Might *Triton* not partially submerge as she entered her element? It had happened before.

The speakers went off again. There was a moment's interruption, then the blare of a steam whistle and a siren, joined immediately by several others. I felt nothing: no tremor, no shift of weight, no indication of motion—nothing. And then the steel General Dynamics sign on the structure of one of the crane tracks began to glide away. For a long moment I watched it, wondering whether it was really moving or whether it was simply that I wanted it to move. But the sign was actually receding, and within seconds, the vertical stanchions that lined the building ways were flying by.

I turned around just in time to see our stern enter the water with a great froth of white spray, as the propellers dug in. An insignificant amount of water came up over the turtle back and part of the main deck aft—not far. On either side of us, long streamers of white wake marked our dash. And now we were in the river; small boats and pleasure craft of all sorts, heretofore maintaining a cautious distance, raced toward us for a closer look. Up ahead was water, and the naked ways. *Triton* was fully waterborne.

In reporting the ceremony and the launching, the New London *Day* commented that as she slid down the ways, *Triton* attained a speed higher than she would ever see again. Having spent the past seven months studying the power-packed ship, I had some reservations about the accuracy of that statement.

After launching, there is a long period of further construction, called "fitting out"—a holdover from traditions of the days of sail when "fitting out" amounted to installing masts and guns in a completed hull. It is not the launching, but the commissioning of a ship which signifies her acceptance for service. And, although launched on the nineteenth of August, 1958, *Triton* did not go to sea on trials until September, 1959. She was commissioned into the Naval Service on the tenth of November, 1959.

This period between launching and commissioning is critically important, for this is when the bulk of the crew is assembled and organized into a cohesive ship's company. In forming a crew, nuclear ships have a special advantage, thanks to Admiral Rickover's foresight. All our engineering personnel came directly from the *Triton*'s prototype at West Milton, New York, where they had been put through a rigorous training schedule on the dry-land reactor and engine room the Atomic Energy Commission had built there at the Admiral's behest. These men were already thoroughly trained and qualified in their primary functions. Nuclear ships are unique—and among the special aspects was that our engineering department, in effect, was handed to us ready-made. Its personnel could not have been better prepared for their duties. Proper preparation to take the ship to sea would have been impossible otherwise.

Some of the men came from other submarines, but most of them were in no way connected with the propulsion plant. One, Chester Raymond Fitzjarrald, a Chief Torpedoman's Mate with some eighteen years service, had last been in my old ship, *Trigger* II, where he had held the position of Chief of the Boat. (In submarines, the "Chief of the Boat" is the key enlisted man, direct assistant to the Executive Officer.) Fitzjarrald was a natural for this post, and was so assigned in *Triton*. In deference to her size, we promoted him a notch and made him "Chief of the Ship."

Another old shipmate who had been Chief Fire Controlman

in *Trigger* II, Loyd L. Garlock, was given a similar job in *Triton*. A third, William E. Constantine, had been in the *Amberjack* in 1948 and '49.

It was heartening to have these old friends serving with me, but it was not any of my doing; the Navy cannot operate with favoritism and personal interest. The submarine force is so small (it represents only three percent of the entire US Navy—approximately the same size as the WAVES) that after a few years, one may have served with almost everyone in the force at one time or another.

I did assert myself in one case, however: Lawrence W. Beckhaus, the Gunner's Mate who had dived from *Salamonie*'s deck into fifty-foot waves to rescue a man swept overboard from another ship, had since become a submariner. He also reported aboard.

Triton's crew had begun standing watches on our ship before she was launched; and as our personnel increased, we set up additional watches, not to make more work for ourselves, but because they were necessary. There were two officers on duty at all times, one for engineering and one for the rest of the ship. There was a "below-decks" watch whose job was to patrol the interior of the unfinished ship to guard against unexpected hazards, such as flooding, fire, gas, or failing ventilation; and we set up a crew with regular watches, under the Engineering Officer, to carry out those parts of the nuclear test program which were our immediate concern. The watches went on twenty-four hours a day, seven days a week. They are going on still—and will—until *Triton* is decommissioned.

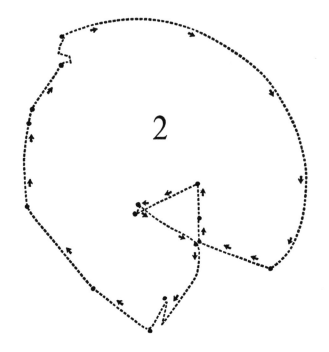

2

At 4:22 A.M. on the morning of October 1, 1958, we faced our first trial. The nuclear fuel had not been loaded in the ship, but many of the steam-generating components were installed and were being tested. Steam from an Electric Boat boiler was being led into number two reactor compartment to test a stand-by condenser. Lieutenant Commander Leslie B. Kelly, prospective Engineer Officer, was on board and supervising. Engineman First Class John R. Thomas was in immediate operational control, assisted by Engineman First Class James T. Lightner. As is common with ships under construction, the compartment was haphazardly strewn with heavy timbers and other working gear.

In the corner of the compartment, Ralph Harris, Engineman Second Class, Kelly's telephone talker, wore a telephone head-

12

set with earphones. In the center of the compartment stood one
or two civilian employees of the Electric Boat testing gang. At
this juncture, Thomas instructed Lightner to open one of the
valves to the stand-by condenser. After he had done so,
Lightner bent over to inspect the indicator at the side of the
valve to see whether it was fully open, thus, by great good fortune, removing himself from the direct line of the valve stem.
The very moment he did so, without any warning, stem and
valve wheel shot out of the valve body and hit the steel overhead of the compartment with such force that the steel valve
wheel was bent. Great vapor clouds whistled from what was
now a direct opening into the steam line, and within seconds
the compartment was full of scalding steam; visibility was zero.

Les Kelly immediately assumed charge of the situation.
"Secure the steam!" he bellowed, his voice rising above the
noise. The main valve was promptly shut, but high-pressure
steam continued to spew from the hole in the line until the
trapped vapor had been reduced to atmospheric pressure. Kelly
quickly ordered that necessary action be taken to safeguard the
plant and machinery. Then he directed the compartment to be
evacuated and the watertight doors shut. The two Electric Boat
workers dived out the forward hatch. Thomas, half-supporting
Lightner, who had been scalded about the face and hands,
came out aft. Kelly, quickly checking the compartment to see
that it was clear, also proceeded aft, and was the last man out
—or so he thought.

Calling a muster of all hands, checking by telephone with
the forward compartment to see who had left by that exit,
Kelly was dismayed to find one man not accounted for. Harris
was evidently still inside the steam-filled compartment. Without hesitation, Les dived back through the watertight doorway,
calling and groping for Harris in the blinding vapor. Feeling
his way back to the spot where he had last seen him, Kelly discovered Harris crawling on the floor, scalded and temporarily

blind, groping his way toward the exit. In a moment, the two men were back outside.

Both Harris and Lightner were hospitalized. Neither was seriously injured, fortunately, and both returned to duty within a few days. Les Kelly's dive into the steam-filled compartment was the act of a brave man. A few more minutes of steam inhalation would have seriously injured or killed Harris, and of course Les ran the same risk. It was a pleasure to recommend him for a life-saving medal.

As a result of an investigation to discover why the valve stem blew out under pressure, a new valve was designed to make this mishap impossible in the future; all submarines with similar installations made similar changes.

In April, we experienced an accident which might have had even more serious consequences. A fire broke out in the ship's galley from an improperly installed deep-fat fryer, and within minutes flames, sucked by fans, broke out in the ship's ventilation lines in the immediate vicinity. Most of the Electric Boat civilian personnel rushed out immediately to notify the fire department, but one man, A. B. Evans, remained behind, aiming smothering streams of carbon-dioxide from a fire extinguisher at the base of the flame. The men from *Triton*'s belowdeck watch, George W. McDaniel, Sonarman First Class, and D. R. Quick, Engineman Second, swung rapidly into action. The ship's Duty Officer, Lieutenant George A. Sawyer, Jr., had just completed his midnight inspection of the ship and had returned to our temporary headquarters on a barge moored nearby. Aroused by telephone, he mobilized all the temporarily off-watch people in the duty section and had them aboard *Triton* within a few minutes.

Lieutenant Tom Thamm, Engineering Duty Officer aft, ran forward to see what help he could give, calling up all the men he could spare from his test program. (It was impossible to leave this entirely untended.) Seizing fire axes, the *Triton* crew chopped away at the ventilation line, where the fire now was blazing furiously. Quick had stopped the ventilation fans, thus reducing the oxygen supply to the flames, and duty-section electricians cut off all electricity in the area, thus removing the basic source of the fire. Others set up temporary ventilation ducts to remove the acrid fumes and smoke from the space.

Firemen arrived within minutes, but the fire was already out. Estimated cost of the repair to the ruined galley was fifty thousand dollars. Had the fire been allowed to rage unchecked even five minutes longer, the loss might have been nearer a million dollars.

These two incidents, the faulty steam valve and the galley fire, illustrated the kind of thing that can happen to a ship going into commission. In each case, had our ship's company not been present, the damage would have been much more severe; serious injury or even loss of life could have resulted.

But naval ships, building or already built, are not supposed to have fires. Proper checking of the deep fat fryer before the test should have turned up the faulty wiring. For two days I worried over the barbs I could expect from the "Kindly Old Gentleman," Admiral Rickover. But when he finally telephoned, he was friendly and understanding, asking whether there would be any delay in our testing program or in meeting our date for sea trials. When I assured him there would be no delay, he enjoined me only to investigate the causes of the accident and be sure they were eliminated. I told him this was already being done, and he hung up the phone.

Some time in February our first reactor received its load of precious nuclear fuel. As "Officer-in-Charge," I signed the inspection report and somewhat nervously acknowledged responsibility for a reactor core worth several million dollars. As soon as it was received, the uranium fuel was stored beneath a headplate weighing twenty tons, and, though it has been partially used up, I am very sure it is still there.

Every man in the ship was anxious to be free of the building yard when the construction work and test program were finally finished. *Triton*'s hatches were then shut, the gangways connecting our ship to the docks were removed, and we warped her bodily out into the slip between our dock and the next. In this position we spent the next four days, secured tightly by seven heavy cables to the docks on either side, yet to all intents and purposes at sea.

We called this long drill period a "fast cruise," and it deserved its name in more ways than one. We were fast to the dock, but the series of drills that were performed during those ninety-six hours were also fast—and very serious. Our day started at about 6:00 A.M. and ended roughly at 0200 the following morning. We stood watches around the clock as though actually under way—and an inherent submarine advantage immediately became apparent. The only time we consciously realized that we were still alongside the dock was when we held periscope drill.

I planned one of these drills to coincide with the moment the *Patrick Henry*, second of our Polaris-type submarines, slid down the ways into the Thames River. Her skipper, Commander (now Captain) H. E. Shear, USN, had been executive officer in *Trigger* II years ago, and this moment, when his great new ship was launched, was one I wanted to share with him. *Patrick Henry* hit the water two hundred yards forward of our bow, and I watched it all through the periscope.

The "fast cruise" over, a day to catch our breath and to load a few provisions aboard, and then the day of *Triton*'s first under-way test, scheduled for Sunday, the twenty-sixth of September, 1959, was at hand.

Both Electric Boat Division and the Office of the Chief of Information, Navy Department, were anxious to get photographs. Someone, somewhere, had apparently decided that a blimp might be a better platform for photographs than the helicopters and airplanes usually used. I paid no attention; this was someone else's affair. My job was to run the ship, and if proper authority wanted a blimp to join *Triton* at sea and photograph

us as we put our ship through her paces, that was all right with
me. But it was at this point and over this issue, at about eleven
o'clock the night before we were to get under way, that it
seemed for a time the trials would be delayed.

It had been a long, hard day, starting about 0500 when
I had been called from my bunk in *Triton*. We had attempted
to cover so much territory with our drills during the "fast
cruise" that no one had had adequate sleep. Completing the
"cruise" and making preparation for the next day's excursion,
we had been fighting our way through detail on detail. Hundreds of problems, apparently, still remained to be taken care
of. I finally got home about 10:00 P.M., and was slowly un-
winding before getting a restful sleep in anticipation of the
morrow's crucial trials. We were scheduled to get under way at
0630, which meant no more than six hours sleep; so my reaction to the telephone call that night was not a happy one.

On the other end of the wire an instantly recognized, irate
voice demanded to know why I was having a blimp join Sunday's operation. Vainly I protested that I knew nothing about
the blimp, that my only interest was in carrying out the tests
successfully. Admiral Rickover held that the blimp might crash
at sea and that in this case we would waste valuable time fishing half-drowned sailors out of the water instead of carrying
out the necessary trials. My arguments, that the safety record
of the Navy's lighter-than-air arm was better than that of aircraft, got nowhere. Although I wasn't even sure who had
ordered it, the discussion, if such it might be called, ended with
my promise to cancel operations for the blimp—somehow.

Several phone calls later, this was successfully accomplished; no one seemed upset at the sudden change, except me
—and possibly the people who had already journeyed to Lake-
hurst to board the airship. But the tension of the days and
weeks just past suddenly gripped me. The last-minute "flap"
over, I tossed and turned in my bed for hours, unable to sleep,
unable to quiet my whirling brain, thinking out every detail,

previewing every move I was to make with *Triton* in the morning.

A few months later, the very blimp that had been assigned to photograph us crashed at sea while searching for a lost sailboat, losing seventeen out of a crew of twenty.

Sunday morning, shortly before six, I arrived at the dock where *Triton* lay moored, bow pointing to sea. Dawn was showing to the east and a dull haze hung over the Electric Boat docks.

The special observers going to sea with us on this first day were already coming aboard. All was in readiness; I directed that lines to the dock be singled up and that a crane be hooked on to the remaining gangway to lift it off as soon as the last passengers were aboard. Finally, only Admiral Rickover, due to arrive at 6:30 A.M., was missing.

At precisely 6:30 A.M., accompanied by Carl Shugg, General Manager of Electric Boat Division, and Captain A. C. Smith, USN, Supervisor of Shipbuilding, the Admiral appeared at the head of the dock and marched rapidly toward us. Rickover, per his usual custom, was in civilian clothes and hatless.

Saluting, I said, "We are ready to get under way, sir!" I followed him up the gangway, gave the signal to the crane, and mounted to the bridge.

The Officer of the Deck was Lieutenant Robert Brodie, a tall, slender carbon copy of the Admiral Brodie I had met a few weeks earlier. He saluted me and formally reported, "Captain, the ship is ready to get under way in all respects."

"Very well," I responded, "I'll take her. Stand by to relay orders for me."

I stood on the bridge step alongside the rail. From this vantage point, I could see the entire forecastle and part of our afterdeck. Two more steps up brought me to the upper level of the bridge, the so-called "flying bridge" from which the entire length of the ship could be seen. There was no protection on this upper level, and the morning fog clung to my heavy woolens as I took a long look forward and aft. All was in readiness.

"Stand by to answer bells," I called to Brodie on the bridge below me. He relayed the order via the bridge announcing system to the maneuvering room spaces. In a moment the bridge speaker squawked: "Bridge—maneuvering. Ready to answer all bells!"

I leaned forward. "Take in lines two, three, and four!" Then, "Slack one and five port, heave in one and five starboard."

Triton slowly and steadily moved away from her dock. Moored stern-to in the slip for torpedo-tube tests, she had only to go ahead and angle right to clear some pilings which were dead ahead.

The moment of decisive test was at hand. Rudder, engines, and propellers had been thoroughly tested. We knew the turbines would work; we knew that everything would work. Yet this was the first time we were to try it. I felt a thrill of anticipation as I gave the next few commands.

"Rudder amidships!" I ordered. "All ahead one-third!"

I turned aft. In a moment, I could see the disturbed water turned up by the two propellers as they rotated slowly in response to my order. Both were moving in the right direction. Water was being pushed aft.

"Take in all lines!"

This was the climactic command, intentionally given late in order, to retain our hold on the dock until the last possible moment. I heaved an involuntary sigh as our willing deck hands heaved the nylon cables swiftly aboard. *Triton* gathered way, moving slowly out of the slip where she had lain for so many months.

"Right ten degrees rudder!" I ordered. When you use rudder on a ship, you swing your stern away from the direction you wish to head. Too much rudder would send our port propeller crashing into the dock, but we had to come right because dead ahead were pilings indicating shallow water.

My initial estimate had been approximately right, I saw with pleasure, and the ship was answering her helm like the lady we hoped she was. As a matter of fact, she was coming around somewhat more rapidly than necessary.

"Ease the rudder to five right," I ordered.

Conning her carefully, we eased *Triton* out into the stream and pointed her fair down the Thames River. Once clear, I gave the order "all ahead two-thirds," and our great ship increased speed as she progressed down the river into Long Island Sound.

It was just after daybreak as we passed New London Light at the mouth of the river, and I beckoned to Floyd W. Honeysette, who had the quartermaster watch on the bridge. "Keep a sharp lookout to starboard on the first white house on the point," I told him. "Let me know if they flash a light or make a signal."

In a few moments, Honeysette reported that there was no light, but that someone leaning out of a second-story window was waving a red cloth. I directed him to return the compliment by flashing the ship's searchlight, and this is how Dr. and Mrs. Tage M. Nielsen of New London, friends of many years, became the first persons with whom *Triton* exchanged signals. Later, I learned the red fabric was a new nylon petticoat belonging to Claudia Nielsen, and that she had made a special reveille in our honor.

There is something about going to sea for the first time in a ship on which you have labored long and hard that is like no other experience. *Triton* was already quick with life, but when we got her past Race Rock and rang for flank speed for the first time, our spirits soared with her tremendous response.

Trigger had been a good ship, outstandingly effective in her business, and *Tirante* a ruthlessly efficient one, with spirit and stamina besides. *Piper*'s qualities had remained largely unknown because she had had no chance to win her spurs in combat, but *Amberjack* had originality and dash. *Trigger* II, the first of an entirely new class of submarines to enter service, had been a failure because of bad engines. Only recently, approximately eight years after construction and at last fitted with brand new engines, she was showing her mettle as one of the finest diesel submarines in the force. *Salamonie,* my previous ship, oldest of them all except the never-forgotten *Lea,* though still a "producer" was nearly worn out from years of strenuous operation.

But none of these, I knew instantly, had the heart and drive of *Triton.* The way she leaped ahead when the power was applied made my heart leap, too; we could actually feel the acceleration as we gave her the gun. Water streamed by us on both sides; spray pelted our faces on the bridge and more splashed against its forward edge into thousands of flying, multicolored droplets in the early morning sunshine.

We headed her southeast into Block Island Sound and toward Montauk Point, aiming her foaming bow directly toward the morning sun.

In an unbelievably short time we had roared past Cerberus Shoals. Shortly afterward, as we changed course to due south, Montauk Point came up to starboard, and soon we were free on the ocean where two years ago I had steamed with *Salamonie* and where fifteen years ago German submarines were on the prowl. I kept calling down below for reports of our speed, must have grinned like a small boy each time I heard the figures.

Once clear of the shoal water, I turned the deck over to Brodie and went below to see for myself how things were going. Everywhere about me was an air of relaxed, delighted intensity. *Triton* was handling almost unbelievably well. There were nothing but smiles in the control room, torpedo rooms, and galley. In the machinery spaces, men were doing their routine tasks with a light in their eyes and a lilt in their voices I had never seen before. One might have imagined we were an orchestra, playing on a new and greater instrument.

This air of confident optimism pervaded the ship, and as I listened to the reports coming and going, the watch reliefs turning over, the reports of log entries and the various other minutiae that go into operating a ship, I knew that we had a crew and a ship equal to the best anyone had ever had the good fortune to command. Except for a handful of "boot seamen," we were all veterans; our first hours under way had been going so smoothly one might have surmised our crew had been working together for years.

Even taciturn Admiral Rickover, who rarely expressed pleasure with anything (holding, I suspect that to do so might cause his underlings to relax when they should be working harder than ever), was forced to admit that he had never witnessed a more successful beginning to a set of trials. I caught a hint of a smile on his face as I sought him out in the forward engine room.

"Admiral, the water will be deep enough to dive very shortly, and with your permission we'll go ahead and take her down as originally scheduled."

Admiral Rickover nodded. While not exactly deafening, the roar of machinery was a high-pitched symphony composed of many different sounds from hundreds of pieces of machinery, all operating in a well-ordered cacophony of rhythm. To me, it was sheer music. Music it must have been to him, too, even though I could detect no visible sign.

I left the engine room and proceeded aft through the remaining engineering spaces, finally reaching the after torpedo room. There, all was calm except for the noise of two huge propellers whirling away just outside. I listened to them carefully. It was hard to realize that they were only a few feet from me, spinning with violent energy, driving water aft at an unprecedented speed and putting more horsepower into the ocean than any submarine had ever done. I could feel the induced vibration shaking the entire after structure of the ship. The noise of the propellers and the roar of the water as it raced past our hull were almost as loud as the machinery a few compartments forward.

"Do you think you could sleep through this, Rowlands?" I asked the husky First Class Torpedoman's Mate in charge of the after torpedo room.

Rowlands grinned. "You can sleep through anything if you're tired enough, sir, but it sure is noisy."

"She'll quiet down a lot when we dive," I pointed out.

Rowlands agreed. "But we'll have to go pretty deep, Captain, to quiet down them spinning wheels with all that power."

He was right. The deeper you go, the less noise your propellers make, but the bigger they are and the faster they spin, the more noise they make. *Triton*'s propellers, eleven feet in diameter, turning far faster than any other submarine's, could not avoid making noise at their present shallow depth. But, of course, no other submarine could go as fast on the surface as *Triton;* when we slowed down to comparable speeds or when we submerged, the chances were that our ship would be as quiet as the others—perhaps quieter.

It was nearly time to dive. I hurried forward. Lieutenant Tom Thamm, *Triton*'s Diving Officer, was already at his station with his number one diving crew. This entire group had trained together for several months at the submarine dive simulator at Electric Boat and at another, fancier, one in the Submarine Base; but, of course, this was the first opportunity for them actually to dive the ship.

They were, naturally, somewhat keyed up. The weights in a submarine must be so balanced that when she fills her main ballast tanks the ship will be in precisely neutral buoyancy. Otherwise, she would not be controllable. Naturally, as stores or torpedoes are put aboard, consumed, fired, or unloaded, there are changes in internal weights. These are compensated for by the bow and stern trimming tanks, and by two auxiliary tanks located amidships. These four tanks are known as "variable tanks," because the amount of water they contain may be varied. This can be done without danger of rupture due to internal or external pressure. The "ballast tanks," by contrast, are always open at the bottom, are empty for buoyancy when the ship is surfaced, and must be fully flooded to dive her. One of the trickiest problems in designing a submarine is to calculate the weights and the volumes so that, with all conceivable weights out of the ship, it is still possible to put enough water into the variable tanks to achieve neutral buoyancy. Conversely, she must be designed so that with maximum weight on board, enough water can be pumped *out* to restore her to neutral buoyancy. (Ballast tanks cannot be used for this, despite the misleading name, for they must always be fully flooded when submerged. Since they are never under any pressure differential, they are lightly constructed, unlike the extremely rugged variable tanks.)

As Diving Officer, Tom's job was to work out the compensation under the load condition that existed at any given time, and to calculate exactly how much water was required in each variable tank to insure that when *Triton*'s main ballast tanks were flooded, the ship would be both in neutral buoyancy and balanced fore and aft. When the right amounts of water are thus in her variable tanks, the ship, in submarine parlance, is in "diving trim" or "compensated."

"The ship is rigged for dive and compensated, Captain," Tom reported.

A submarine cannot submerge until it is "rigged for dive," by which is meant that all the proper equipment for diving is in correct position, either open or shut, in power or set for hand operation as designated, and that every compartment has been inspected, both by the crew members responsible for rigging it and by an officer detailed to check it. There have been cases when a submarine was lost, seriously damaged, or suffered loss of life because of an improper rig somewhere.

"How is your trim?" I asked.

"I've pumped it all in," Thamm said. He added, "I guess

we'll find out how good the trim is as soon as we pull the plug."

The indicator lights on the Ballast Control Panel showed that we were ready to dive, except that our main air inlet pipe and the bridge hatch were still open.

"Shut the induction, Tom," I said.

At Thamm's signaled order, Fitzjarrald, hovering over the Ballast Control Panel, moved the control toggle switch to the shut position.

I picked up the microphone controlling the speaker on the bridge, told Brodie to reduce speed and shift his watch to the conning tower. There was a "clink" of annunciators, a clatter of feet on ladder rungs, a thump as the bridge hatch slammed shut. The Ballast Control Panel indicated that the last important hull opening was now closed.

"All clear topside!" Brodie's voice came from the conning tower, where, according to plan, he would be manning the periscope.

"Bleed air, Tom," I said.

Thamm picked up a microphone in his turn. "Engine room, this is control. Bleed high-pressure air into the ship!"

For our first dive, we were using the so-called "safe-diving procedure." For the moment, we were driving along on the surface, entirely sealed, with no one topside. In the meantime, high-pressure air was being released from a connection in the engine room to increase the air pressure slightly within *Triton*'s hull. If air could not leak out of the ship, then presumably water could not leak in. At the Diving Control Panel was a barometer which would indicate the pressure inside the ship. If this pressure rose and did not drop back after the air valve was shut, the ship had to be airtight.

Thamm, Fitzjarrald, and I inspected the barometer closely. The needle rose a short distance, then stopped rising and remained rock steady.

Tom took a long minute to watch it carefully. Finally satisfied, he nodded to me. "The ship is tight, sir."

An interested group of observers had silently gathered in the control room. All experienced submariners, some of them tops in the field of submarine construction and design, every visitor aboard had a keen interest in *Triton*'s first dive. I gave Brodie the order to sound the diving alarm, and a raucous, automobilelike horn reverberated through the ship. Fitzjarrald, his hands on two of the control buttons on the Ballast Control Panel, was watching Thamm.

"Open the vents," Tom ordered.

Swiftly, the Chief ran his fingers down the panel of switches opening *Triton*'s main vents to the sea. The rush of water into the tanks could be heard through the thick steel plating of the ship's hull.

Thamm waited several seconds, then ordered, "Shut the vents."

This also was by prearrangement. Our purpose on this first dive was to ease *Triton* down into the depths easily and gently. Should something be radically wrong with the compensation, or should the controls somehow fail to function properly, we wanted to be able to regulate things immediately. Eight thousand tons of insensate steel running out of control could be a frightening, possibly disastrous experience.

Another long moment went by while Thamm checked all his instruments. Though lower in the water by several feet, *Triton* was not yet submerged. Again Tom ordered the vents reopened, and again he shut them. The third time he opened them still longer, and as we felt *Triton* angling down at the bow, he opened them all. It had taken us several minutes to dive, but we were all well satisfied; our ship had performed exactly as we had predicted. Later, of course, we would strive for a faster diving time.

The submerged trials started out simply, but rapidly increased in severity. Soon we were running the entire gamut of submerged operations, and our feeling of pride and confidence in our ship grew steadily. *Triton* behaved beautifully, like the queen she was designed to be. Despite her huge bulk, she could turn around so fast that her gyrocompass indicator would spin like a top in front of the helmsmen. When up or down plane angles were used, she responded immediately—and the smallest angle on the planes was sufficient to bend her to our wishes. When "flank speed" was ordered, we were surprised and delighted; surfaced she was by design faster than any submarine, faster than most surface ships, in fact. Speed under water had been a secondary consideration; yet, submerged, only her immediate predecessor, the football-shaped *Skipjack,* could equal her. There was absolutely no sensation of passage through the water, nor any water noise. Much of the noise created by a speeding ship is a result of the mixture of air and water at the surface. Thus the water noise is largely a boundary effect. But when the ship is deeply submerged, there is no such boundary, no opportunity for air to mix with water. Our superstructure and hull were firm and solid; there was no rattling or vibration here either; no noise of any kind except for *Triton's* propellers and internal machinery back aft.

Whenever I could absent myself from the control room, which was not very often on this first day under way, I took a turn through the machinery spaces. There, everyone was smiling. Assistant Engineer Don Fears, part of the time Engineering Officer of the Watch in number two engine room and later occupying himself by a continuous working check of all operating equipment, reflected joy and pride every time I saw him. So did Les Kelly, who, as *Triton's* Chief Engineer, had overall responsibility for the entire plant. Pat McDonald, our Reactor Control Officer, responsible for theory and practice insofar as the reactors were concerned, was positively ebullient.

"How's it going, Pat?" I asked him, cornering him in the reactor monitoring area which someone—Pat himself, I had always suspected—had nicknamed "Idiot's Alley."

"Just fine, Captain, just fine!" answered Pat. "She's humming away like a big watch. I wouldn't be afraid to take her clean across the Atlantic this very minute—just look at this!"

Pat pointed with his slide rule to one of the hundred or so "read-out" indicator dials which lined both sides of "Idiot's Alley." I looked. The Power Output dial was approaching the edge of the full power mark.

"We crept up on it slowly," said Pat, "but we've been running just below full power now for the past hour and a half. The Admiral sure believes in working out the machinery!"

"You can say that again," I told him. "When the *Nautilus* prototype out in Idaho was first fired up, he made them take it on a simulated voyage at full power all the way to Europe. Regular watches, course charted, daily positions, and all that. There weren't many who said it wouldn't work after that."

"Where does the standard Navy four-hour full-power trial come into this picture?" Pat asked.

"Sometime when we've got nothing else to do we'll run one off just to get it on the record," I said. "You don't suppose Admiral Rickover will let Les cut this initial run short of full power, do you—or that four measly hours will satisfy him? Any more than it would satisfy you, if you had to be on board this ship in combat?"

Pat grinned. Then, as we watched the Power Output dial, the needle slowly climbed until it was exactly centered on the full power mark.

"There's part of the answer, Pat," I said. "Excuse me, but this I want to see," and I started aft through the watertight door into the engine room, leaving a Reactor Control Officer staring with delight at the evidence his monitoring instruments were presenting.

In number one engine room, George Troffer had the EOOW watch. Les Kelly was standing right behind him, and Admiral Rickover was seated on a tool chest a few feet away, absorbed in a red-covered book which I took to be a power

plant testing manual of some sort. With a side glance at the
Admiral, who showed no sign that he had noticed my appearance, I addressed myself to Kelly. "Les, how much power
are you indicating back here?" I asked. I had to shout to be
heard above the powerful roar of the engine.

Kelly put his mouth to my ear and shouted back, "We've
just gone to a hundred percent power! She's running like a
million bucks! No trouble at all!"

I decided against asking why I had not been consulted before the speed change was made. No doubt a messenger was off
looking for me at that very minute. This was Vice-Admiral
Rickover's plant and his test. My duties, clearly stated for these
first trials, were to operate the ship in accordance with his
directives. Besides, I, too, wanted to find out what were the
actual limitations of our engines.

Les had something more to say, which he did with a broad
smile. "One more thing. That's no power plant manual the Old
Man's got his nose into. Take a good look at the name on the
cover, if you get a chance."

Casting a quick glance at Rickover, who appeared still engrossed in the book with the red cover, I decided to get a
better look at it soon, nodded my thanks to Kelly, and began a
tour of the remaining engineering spaces.

In number two plant, all was serene. The port engine and
reduction gears were spinning away with the greatest aplomb,
and every bearing was cool, every critical point reading well
within the specified limits.

Lieutenant Curtis Shellman, Machinery Division Officer and
presently in charge of the port engine-room watch, must have
been born with the sallow complexion and dark circles under
his eyes which made his normal everyday appearance that of
a man under severe strain; recently he had had every right to
look this way, for the main brunt of getting *Triton*'s engines
ready for her first engineering trials had fallen upon him. Practically all of the operating machinery of the ship was under his

surveillance, and the toll of many sleepless hours showed in the veritable death's head smile he gave me by way of salutation. But there was nothing beaten down or tired about the pure and happy sense of accomplishment which showed there too, as he called my attention to the pounds of steam flow per hour, the throttle setting, the steam pressure, and the effortless RPM of the port main shaft.

Not ordinarily given to use of the superlative, Curt essayed one this time. "She's just wonderful, Captain!" he yelled. "I've never seen an engine run as smoothly as this one. Why, we could take her anywhere, anytime!" His enthusiasm was contagious, and there were corroborating nods from Chief Electrician's Mates "L" "E" Poe (another old shipmate) and Walter O'Dell, members of the watch section.

It was not hard to believe. What *was* difficult to appreciate was that *Triton* at this moment was driving through the water at a speed which no member of her crew had ever experienced, which we would have dismissed as insane had anyone suggested it but a few years ago, which, had this ship but come a few years sooner, might have won the war in the Pacific for us in a matter of months, instead of the years it took.

During this time, Admiral Rickover seemed completely engrossed in his book. He rarely looked up, never changed his position, acknowledged with a brief nod Les Kelly's shouted reports of the progress of the various tests which were being run off.

One of the axioms of building a power plant is that all its components must be designed with a large safety factor, for one never knows just which component, or combination of components, will prove to be the weakest element in the chain, and thus limit the power. In the Navy, Admiral Rickover's nuclear plants were already famous for exceptional dependability. It was soon evident that the Admiral was of a mind to maintain that reputation insofar as *Triton*'s two-reactor plant was concerned. This was, at least, the only interpretation I could place upon his reaction to the trouble which shortly afterward developed in our starboard spring bearing.

Since *Triton*'s starboard propeller is driven by the forward engine, it follows that the starboard propeller shaft must be much the longer of the two. About midway in its length, its great weight had necessitated installation of a "spring bearing" —merely a line or support bearing to keep it turning true— and it was here, in the most ordinary of standard mechanisms, that the evil little god of misfortune had decreed that difficulty should develop. The first sign of trouble was a rise in the lubricating oil temperature.

Ordinarily, when in receipt of such a report, the immediate thing to do is slow down; but since the initial sea trials were being run by Admiral Rickover, I first sought him out to see what he desired. His red-bound book lay closed on the tool box by the de-aerating feed tank, and I found him down in the lower level of number two auxiliary machinery compartment, where the offending spring bearing was located high in the starboard after corner. When I arrived, the entire group of designers and engineers aboard for the trials were already present; and the gray-haired birdlike Admiral had climbed up into the corner for a close inspection, squeezing his wiry frame into the cramped space between the swiftly rotating propeller shaft and the curved hull of the ship, alongside the huge steel box containing the bearing.

"We're going to have to cut the power, Ned," said one of the bystanders, an Electric Boat supervisor. "It's too bad, but we can't take a chance on wiping this bearing."

This was the evaluation I sensed from everyone present. The decision, however, was Rickover's, as the officer responsible for the initial sea trials. He had evidently been listening to the bearing with a large screwdriver held against his head, and I got there just as Les Kelly handed up a stethoscope taken from one of our repair kits.

Long minutes passed while Rickover listened at various

spots on the bearing housing. There was a grim set to his jaw when he descended at last from his perch alongside the housing. "There's not a thing wrong with the bearing," he said shortly. "It's working exactly as designed, but it's not designed right."

"We've already proved the designed power of the ship, Admiral," said the Electric Boat representative who had spoken with me. "We'll get right on the bearing as soon as we get back to the Boat Division. I'm sure our designers can figure out what's wrong. . . ."

"The only thing wrong is that it needs more cooling. Any fool can see that," cut in Rickover. "Besides, we're not going back. Not yet—Kelly!" Abruptly he shifted his attention to *Triton*'s Chief Engineer. "Rig a hose. Get a constant spray of water going on the bearing housing. Set a special watch on the lube oil temperature!"

"But Admiral," protested the EB man, "there's no need to subject the bearing to additional stress. We've already satisfied the design specs, and there's no point to going further . . ."

Admiral Rickover's voice held a curiously flat, monotonous tone, which I had heard before. "We're here to find out if this ship is satisfactory for war. I'll not let this piece of lousy designing stop the trial, and I'll take the responsibility if it breaks down!" There was a singular lack of emphatic expression in the way Rickover spoke, effectively belied by the flinty look in his eyes.

Within minutes, Les Kelly had a squad of his men dragging a rubber hose to the vicinity, and a spray of salt water was played upon the steel box enclosing the defective bearing and its oil supply. A constant check of the oil temperature was set up, with results reported to Admiral Rickover and, upon my private instructions to Les, to me. In the meantime, *Triton* had not slowed her headlong dash through the water, and after a few more minutes, to our relief, the lube oil temperature from the starboard propeller shaft spring bearing stopped its steady rise.

We watched it carefully from this point on, and the design for a permanent "fix"—installation of the oil-cooling system which should have been there from the beginning—was complete in all essentials by the time *Triton* returned to the EB docks. Except for our natural concern that the temperatures continue to remain under control, the bearing gave us no further trouble, the all-out power test continued, and Admiral Rickover, with Les Kelly's stethoscope forgotten in his pocket, went back to his tool chest and his book.

Both Les and I were greatly heartened by the outcome of the apparent breakdown, for, like all officers attached to *Triton,* we wanted more than anything else to know her real ability to respond when the chips were down. Should an emergency occur, we might have need of that extra little response—perhaps sooner than any of us could then anticipate.

As the trials progressed, the thrill of watching a magnificent engineering plant out-perform the highest expectations worked its heady magic on even Admiral Rickover. We kept every critical bearing and every mechanism under special surveillance, and maintained power, running hundreds of miles south in the process. With the over-steam-demand alarms sounding their piercing, ringing, hornlike noise throughout the vast engineering spaces, every indicator on the reactor and electric control panels touching—but not exceeding—its maximum-allowed value, the great reduction gears and turbines shrilling their joyful song of superhuman strength and dependability, *Triton,* deeply submerged, roared through the water with the speed of an express train.

It is, unfortunately, not within the province of this narrative to state the speed actually achieved by our ship, nor any of the specific parameters of her power plant, but I don't suppose there can be any objection to revealing the title of the book Vice-Admiral Rickover was reading. I had snatched a glimpse of the name on the cover when it lay temporarily unguarded on the tool box. It was *The Memoirs of a Renaissance Pope.*

There are those who have claimed that the faster *Triton* went, the more slowly the Admiral read, and that toward the end he turned the pages very slowly indeed, if at all. As to this, I cannot testify, for I could not remain in the engine room; but my memory does record the impression, after the many hours and so very many miles, that the blank look he wore could only be a mask for his true delight.

The trials, an unqualified success in every way, became difficult only once, as a result of my own failure to appreciate fully the forces with which we were dealing. One of the tests required that the ship be operated submerged in the astern direction. I had done this before with *Piper, Amberjack,* and *Trigger* II, but I knew very well that it might be considerably more difficult with *Triton,* since she was much longer and bigger, and proportionately even more slender than they. She was also infinitely more powerful, a factor which I felt would tend to equalize the situation.

Some time after the completion of the main power trials, after a number of other evolutions had been successfully demonstrated, I directed Thamm, who was now OOD as well as Diving Officer of the Watch (the ship, deeply submerged, had no need for an officer at the periscope station in the conning tower), to reverse the engines and operate the ship astern.

"All stop," barked Thamm. "All back two-thirds."

We could feel the great bronze propellers swinging to a stop and picking up speed in the reverse direction. Our speed indicator began to slow rapidly, reached zero, where, unable to indicate reverse speeds, it stayed. Slowly we felt *Triton* gathering sternway, and Tom reversed the direction of action of his bow and stern planes in order to maintain correct depth. For a time all went very well, but then the ship began to oscillate with a great, slow seesaw motion, and at the same time she slowly increased depth. At first this was of no particular concern, but soon I realized that we were getting close to the ocean floor, and that a submarine of our great length could not be allowed to oscillate through very much of an angle before there might be danger of her striking bottom.

"Sounding!" I ordered.

The answer came back quickly. "Three hundred feet!"

Tom looked at me but said nothing. I knew what he was thinking.

"All stop!" I said. "All ahead two-thirds."

But still our speed indicator remained fixed on zero, and still our depth increased. Inexorably, we were approaching the bottom of the ocean.

Our speed was so low that touching bottom would hardly bother *Triton*'s strong hull, but there was always the danger of our hitting a rock with our vulnerable propellers or the delicate sonar equipment in the bow.

I ordered another sounding. The answer this time was two hundred feet.

"Tom," I said urgently, "blow all main ballast!"

All of us watched the Ballast Control Panel, and it seemed as if everyone in the control room was also watching me. Fitzjarrald opened the blow valves on the Diving Control Panel, blew the main ballast tanks for a long minute, then stopped on Thamm's order.

"Blow them again," I ordered.

But the depth gauges continued to revolve, though more slowly. *Triton* had not yet reached an even keel and was now down some ten degrees by the bow. If we gathered headway in this attitude, she might ram her nose against the ocean floor.

"All stop!" I snapped a second time, "Sounding!" And for the third time, "Blow main ballast tanks! Again!"

"Forty feet," called the sailor at the fathometer.

Triton's angle of inclination reduced, approached zero, and the depth gauge showed that the ship was rising.

"All ahead two-thirds," I ordered again, and heaved a sigh of relief.

It had been a thrilling moment, one which had come upon us by surprise and which could have done damage to our new ship. Mentally, I kicked myself for not having recognized the signs earlier; we should not have allowed the ship to back for so long or the oscillations to become so severe. But all that really mattered was that damage had been averted, and as we were proceeding back to port on completion of the trials, Admiral Rickover announced to the crew that our tests were among the most successful under-way trials of a nuclear ship yet carried out.

Altogether, there were about five days of initial sea trials before the Bureau of Ships and the Navy Department expressed themselves as satisfied. As always, a number of minor deficiencies were discovered, none of them serious. We went to sea several times more to check out one item or another until, finally, on the thirtieth of October, came what is called the Preliminary Acceptance Trials (PAT). On such occasions, a regularly constituted board of officers comes from Washington, D.C., to see whether the ship conforms to the operational standards specified when the contract was signed. The report of the trial board would decide whether General Dynamics would receive its entire fee for construction, whether any deductions for nonfulfilment of the contract were to be invoked, and whether *Triton* would be accepted for "unlimited service" or under some temporary restriction.

Naturally, these trials were of considerable concern to Electric Boat, for although it was hardly likely that a ship for which all this labor and expense had been incurred would not be accepted for service, it was quite possible that some inadequacy in its construction might cost the company a great deal to correct or result in a reduction in fee.

The PAT provided us with a welcome opportunity. *Triton*'s only major fault was that under certain sea conditions, in running on the surface at top speed, she took a perverse delight in driving her bow under. After a great deal of thought and careful perusal of photographs, I was sure I knew what her trouble was. Her extremely slim bow had most of its buoyant volume well aft, at precisely the point where the maximum hollow of her bow wave occurred at high speed. Thus, she lacked buoyancy exactly where needed. This was a serious deficiency, we argued. If we could add a little more buoyancy to the bow, especially in the forward part, we could greatly improve this condition. All we had to do was convince the officers from Washington that the modification was necessary.

The trial board happened to be headed by the tallest Admiral in the Navy, known to his contemporaries and close friends as "Tiny" McCorkle. When I mentioned the problem to him, he agreed that if the situation was as I represented, something indeed should be done. I promised an adequate demonstration.

Several hours later, with *Triton* making full speed through long seas sweeping from the Atlantic Ocean, I asked Admiral McCorkle if he would care to step up to the bridge. For good measure, I also invited Van Leonard, the highly competent young EB design boss who—in my estimate—could use a practical lesson in how ships behave at sea.

Up to the bridge we went, the six-foot, six-inch Admiral awkwardly ducking his head and hunching his shoulders as he maneuvered between pipes and fittings.

Once there, I told Dick Harris, Officer of the Deck, of my intentions. Both he and the lookouts were already heavily clothed in foul-weather gear—by design I suspect, for Dick, at least, knew what was up—and I noticed that the Quartermaster of the Watch quickly finished his business topside and headed below.

I nodded to Dick. He reached for the bridge microphone and gave the order. "Maneuvering—bridge! Make all available speed!"

Already at "full" speed—about half-power—*Triton* was riding with her bow still a foot or two out of water. Occasionally, a roll would break over the deck and sweep aft, bursting in a cascade of spray against the bottom of the sail. With the increased power, we would soon be taking considerably more water than before, and it suddenly struck me that perhaps I had not fully briefed Admiral McCorkle on what to expect. Harris and both lookouts were tightening up their parkas as I turned to him.

"Admiral, when she drives under we're liable to get pretty wet up here."

McCorkle laughed genially. "You can't scare me, Ned," he said. "I had my fanny wet long before you even got in the Navy."

The Admiral's belt line was in the approximate vicinity of my chest, and it would have to be a pretty big wave to reach that high, but I resolved that if he could take it, I could, too. The increased drive of the engines began to be noticeable, and in a moment the first really big sea hit us. The bow spray spouted above our heads. Water dashed high over the bridge, pelting down on top of the lookouts and completely inundating Dick Harris, who stood just behind us.

The forward part of *Triton's* bridge was fitted with a transparent plastic bubble, and under this Leonard, Admiral McCorkle and I huddled for protection. There was no room for a fourth person, and the Admiral grinned at Dick's discomfort, as he stood only a foot away. I grinned, too. There was more to come.

The spray increased; soon there was a steady stream of white water squirting high above our heads. Then, with a swoosh, green water swelled up over the sides of the bridge coaming, rising in its bathtublike confines to envelop Admiral McCorkle's fanny and higher parts of my anatomy. Simultaneously, solid water poured over the top of the bubble like Niagara Falls. I was relieved that Dick had stationed a man

to protect the bridge hatch; he now ordered it shut. The lookouts had given up, turning their backs, while Harris gasped
for breath, cupping his hands over his eyes in an effort to maintain a lookout ahead. Sputtering, Admiral McCorkle shouted
something which I interpreted as indicating that he was satisfied, that the demonstration had been successful, and Dick
gratefully relayed the order to slow down. The spouting water
ceased, *Triton*'s bow came up once more, and the world became drier for six thoroughly wet people on the bridge.

About this time I began to feel some trepidation that my
august guest's sense of humor might have been strained farther than the occasion demanded. But the Admiral was game.

"Beach," he shouted, mopping the salt out of his eyes, "that
was one hell of a demonstration!"

I started to apologize for getting the Admiral's fanny wet,
but he would have none of it.

"Sorry, hell!" he roared. "You've been planning to wet me
down for a week! Anyway, you can't hurt me; I've been
dunked in salt water for years!"

As McCorkle bellowed his laughter, Van Leonard, his
civilian suit bagging with salt water, could only shrug helplessly.

Needless to say, the repair work was done on *Triton*'s bow,
but poor Van was later heard to grumble that he had already
conceded the point and had ordered the work, that no "demonstration" had actually been required, but that *Triton*'s sadistic
skipper, having laid on the "demonstration," was not to be
deprived of his fun.

The next event on *Triton*'s program was the commissioning,
scheduled for the tenth of November. This ceremony is full
of meaning for all naval vessels. From this moment, *Triton*
would bear the initials "USS" before her name, become a part
of the fleet, and be ready for any kind of service required of
her.

The commissioning address was delivered by Vice-Admiral Bernard L. (Count) Austin, and Mrs. Louise Will presented us with a water color painted by the President of the American Water Color Society, Mr. Hans Walleen of New York. It shows a full-length silhouette of the ship, submerged at speed, and superimposed is a lithe, idealized Greek Triton holding in one hand a long trumpet made of a triton shell and in the other the trident of sea power.

When it came time to hoist the national colors on *Triton*, we used the biggest set we could borrow, and the whole crew together sang the national anthem, as our flag rose to the peak of *Triton*'s highest periscope.

In keeping with a tradition started at the end of World War II our ship had been named in honor of an older *Triton* long-buried beneath the waters of the South Pacific, a victim of Japanese depth charges after an outstandingly successful career. But before she experienced that ultimate misfortune, her ship's bell had been removed. Her first skipper had laid claim to it and had kept it for years after the war. Now he, too, was gone; and so it was that Mrs. W. A. Lent, his widow, was present at the commissioning ceremony to bequeath the first *Triton*'s old bell to the namesake of that valiant ship.

Following commissioning, we made a trip to Newport, Rhode Island, for torpedo trials and to Norfolk, Virginia, for certain special tests. Early in December, we returned to our birthplace at Electric Boat. The Navy Department wished to put some new communications equipment aboard.

The layover was most welcome, for it was Christmas and we might have been at sea as many other ships were, but when January came and we were still tied to the dock at Electric Boat, we grew restless. We were scheduled to get under way on February sixteenth for a shakedown cruise to northern European waters, in company with the flagship of the Second Fleet, USS *Northampton*. Time was passing, the sixteenth of February was approaching rapidly, and our impatience mounted.

When the new equipment was finally installed, late in January, we got under way immediately, vowing to work twenty-four hours a day, if necessary, to make up for lost time. Tests scheduled to take three weeks or longer were telescoped to twelve days. Late in the evening of the first of February, we returned to New London, all tests and evaluation complete, hoping there would be nothing further asked of us and that our projected cruise with *Northampton* was still on the docket.

On my desk, as I came down from the bridge after *Triton* had been safely moored, was a soiled envelope addressed to me, slightly crumpled as though it might have been carried some distance by hand.

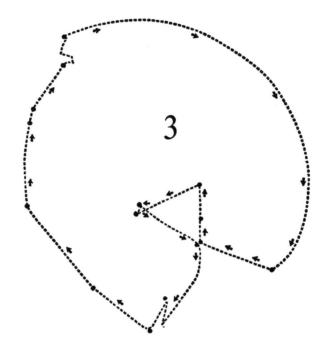

3

One of the curses of the modern Navy is paperwork. Early in their careers, therefore, all officers develop the technique of determining in the shortest possible time which papers require immediate attention and which can be postponed. Consequently, I had no difficulty recognizing that the handwritten note which somehow appeared upon my desk that day was more important than the sacks of carefully mimeographed official mail our "Mail Petty Officer" had laboriously dragged from the dock a few moments before.

The note simply said, "CSL wants to know if you can be in Washington on 4 Feb. Please phone ASAP."

CSL stood for ComSubLant, the operational boss of all Atlantic Fleet submarines, and ASAP was good old Navy jargon for "as soon as possible."

Next day, the second of February, I met with Rear Admiral L. R. Daspit, ComSubLant, in his office at the Submarine base. He revealed nothing about the purpose of my trip to Washington, but hinted that it probably involved the shakedown cruise we had been planning for so long, and that there could be some questions relating to how long a cruise we might be able to make.

The following day and a half were full of suspense. Early on the morning of the fourth, I appeared, as directed, in the office of the Deputy Chief of Naval Operations for Fleet Operations. I was wearing a civilian suit, as requested, and was ushered immediately into an inner office.

Conferences with a Deputy Chief of Naval Operations are hardly ever ordinary; but this one, I immediately realized, would be absolutely extraordinary. Maps were spread out on a large table, and besides Admiral Wallace M. Beakley, the Deputy Chief, there were two other admirals and a number of captains and commanders whom I recognized, plus a few whom I did not. Seated at the center of the table, Admiral Beakley was studying one of the charts. He looked up, waiting until the door had closed behind me.

"Beach," he said, as soon as the door had swung to, "what kind of shape is your ship in?"

I assured him that *Triton* was in excellent condition and ready to carry out any mission she might be given. The Admiral nodded as though it was what he had expected.

"Sit down," he said, indicating a chair at the table opposite him. "Beach," he said again, "you're about due to start your shakedown cruise. Can *Triton* go around the world—submerged—instead?"

The room swayed. Since my talk with Admiral Daspit I had tried to imagine the reason for this Washington conference, and I must truthfully admit that the possibility that *Triton* might be asked to try a round-the-world mission had crossed my mind. I had even considered several full-of-confidence responses with which to answer such a request. But the actual situation hardly seemed appropriate to any of the replies I had thought of, and after a sudden, nervous cough, I said, "Yes, Sir!" That was all I could say.

"When can you get under way?"

Admiral Taussig's famous response, when asked a similar question in World War I: "We will be ready when fueled," flashed across my mind, but of course *Triton*'s dual reactors would not need fuel for two or more years. Mindful that work already in progress was scheduled to be completed on the sixteenth of February, and aware that any change in schedule, even to prepare for a longer trip, would be upsetting, I answered, "We are scheduled to get under way for shakedown on the sixteenth of February, and we will still meet that date!"

The next thing we discussed, as I recall, was the matter of a nonclassified name for the expedition. I was told that henceforth the *Triton*'s voyage would be called "Operation Sandblast."

The code name was a logical choice. Our trip was in the nature of a tour de force and would "take a lot of sand" on our part. Hence, "Sandblast." Hence, also, my own personal code name: Sand, instead of Beach. Most beaches were full of sand, I was informed.

By this time I didn't care what anyone wanted to call me. Our long and diligently prepared trip to the North Atlantic was being replaced by one infinitely more exciting. But I did have a twinge of regret. The Navy's need for crews to man still-newer ships had already claimed members of the wonderful crew which first took *Triton* to sea. Her Chief Engineer, Les Kelly, had received detachment orders which were ultimately to lead him to his own nuclear command. Several other of the ship's stalwarts—some of them sporting newly won commissions—were about to leave her or had already left. Having given so much to bring *Triton* this far, what wouldn't they give to go along on this trip, I thought. But, of course, they could not even be informed of it.

There were other things to think about. One purpose of our trip was to collect oceanographic and gravitational data in one continuous circuit around the world, bringing all our original instrumentation and recorded data back to the starting point and thus establishing a base line. A submerged submarine was the most satisfactory platform for such a survey, and it turned out the Navy Hydrographer, Captain Hank Munson, a submariner of great reputation, had been looking for just such an opportunity.

It was apparent that we would almost automatically follow the track of Magellan's famous circumnavigation of 1519, but passing through the Strait of Magellan, which we studied carefully on the charts, did not appear feasible. This was not so much a navigational problem as one of security. To pass through the Strait of Magellan, we would need permission from the Republic of Chile. And though our relations with Chile were such that we would undoubtedly be granted this favor, the request itself would violate the Top Secret classification of our cruise. Time was too short to allow the more complicated negotiations which might possibly have been undertaken; so it was decided to side-step the issue by going around Cape Horn.

Considerable discussion arose regarding the site in the Philippines where Magellan met his death, and I advocated *Triton* should visit it, if only to photograph the area. It was apparent that the length of the voyage would create a morale problem which could be partially solved by adding elements of interest. Psychologically, we needed some halfway objective during the cruise, much as visits to foreign ports are permitted to crews of ordinary ships during long voyages. Since we were to be permitted no visits to any ports, a pilgrimage to the place where Magellan died, I argued, would provide a welcome break to monotony. Permission was finally granted.

Several hours later, as I was leaving the Pentagon, my head was buzzing with the thousands of details. But most of all, churning over and over in my brain was an almost off-hand remark made just as the conference broke up. "There's a lot more riding on this than what you've heard today, Ned. We're depending on you to get back on the tenth of May!" The speaker's remarks continued to puzzle me. Apparently there was much more to this voyage than even I was to know.

Questions and problems were tumbling through my mind like an avalanche, and try as I might to concentrate on the important details of the planning, the most prominent thought in my mind, the one I could not cast aside, was "what in the world will I tell my wife?" Ingrid was not even in New London, having been called suddenly to California, where her father was again seriously ill. How, in fact, could I even ask her to come home without revealing that something special was going on?

At the conference it had been decided that the voyage would be classified; nothing was to be made known about it until its completion. If we failed for any reason, considerable thought would have to be given to precisely what sort of announcement would be released, if any. Obviously, in this event, our location and the circumstances would influence the decision. As everyone was quite aware, if we were to have an embarrassing failure, the effect would be a serious disservice to our national interests and to the prestige of the Navy. Again I could hear those portentous words: "We're depending on you!"

"We'll not fail!" I had told them determinedly. "We will get under way on the sixteenth of February, and return on the tenth of May, as scheduled." No one volunteered an explanation as to why the timing—and secrecy—were so vital, and I did not ask.

Yet there was so much that my wife—and the other *Triton* wives—would have to be prepared for, and so little time.

Every man in our crew would have his problems, too, without the consolation of knowing what I knew. Their personal lives, thus, became my responsibility. How could I inform them before departure that we would be away much longer than expected, that no mail could be sent or received during the entire cruise, that they would have to make personal preparations for an unusually long absence, attending to income tax, automobile-license tags, insurance policies, payment of rent, arrangement for financial support—a thousand details?

It was more than a matter of crew morale; all but about forty of our crew were married, and all the officers but one. I had additionally been informed that about half-a-dozen civilian scientists with various specialties would be placed aboard to help us accumulate the desired data. None of them was to be informed of the basic purpose of the cruise or its duration. This was to be left to me, after we had gotten under way. Providing for these men (whom I didn't know and hadn't met, and would not meet until the day before we left) and their families was to be my responsibility also.

As the train rattled north toward New York and New London, I mentally discarded one scheme after another. With some misgiving, I finally resolved to announce that an unknown bureaucrat in Washington had so fouled up our shakedown cruise schedule that we would have to proceed directly from the North Atlantic into the Caribbean for special tests requested by the Bureau of Ships. "Unknown bureaucrats" for years have been blamed for things that have gone wrong, especially when the complaining parties do not care to be too specific about placing the blame. For years I had seen this happen and had defended the unknown bureaucrat whenever I had an opportunity. Now, I was about to add to the ridicule heaped on the Washington civil servant, despite the fact that he works harder and gets less thanks than perhaps anyone else in the country.

As a result of this nameless bureaucrat's inefficiency, we

would not be able to send or receive mail at any time, I would tell my people, and hence (here was the kicker) a list of "things to do" (which included all preparations for a long voyage) would be given to all hands. In the name of efficiency, each man would be required to return a signed copy of the list, attesting to his having carried out all the various instructions.

This was, of course, far from my only problem. The idea of diverting slightly from our cruise to visit the place where Magellan died had met with approval, and someone had proposed, in addition, that as *Triton* passed near Spain she should pause momentarily to render homage to that famous and unfortunate navigator. This, too, had met with favor, as did the idea of a commemorative gift to Spain in his honor.

The Navy, however, has no budget for such commemorations, but I had told the conference that *Triton* herself would somehow design and finance the casting of an appropriate plaque. It had to be big, as befits a gift from one nation to another, but small enough to fit through our hatches; it had to be memorial in nature, in keeping with the intent; and it had to be something that both Spaniards and Americans could henceforth look at with pride.

Another problem was to obtain adequate charts, in secrecy, and to lay out our course in meticulous detail in advance, so that the Navy would always know precisely where we were. Our track was to be some thirty-four thousand nautical miles, in itself a fantastic plotting job, and this, too, had to be done surreptitiously!

As for the necessary provisions, submarines have had years of experience in preparing for long cruises, though never for one so long as this. *Triton* had been designed to carry food supplies for seventy-five days, and we knew her huge hull could easily carry more. Arbitrarily, I resolved to increase this by at least a half, and directed that the ship be provisioned for one hundred and twenty days. If worst came to worst, and a long extended cruise became necessary, we could go on half-rations and stretch the voyage to six months.

There was the scientific equipment to get ready, also. Most of it would be sent to us by the Navy, but it was up to *Triton* to decide where it was to be stowed and to make special arrangements for the installation of whatever foundations, telemetering circuits, and remote controls were needed. A whole package had to be prepared without spilling the beans to anyone.

At 5:45 A.M., when I finally stepped off the train in New London, with sheets of notes in my hand, I realized fully that there were but twelve days left in which to get ready.

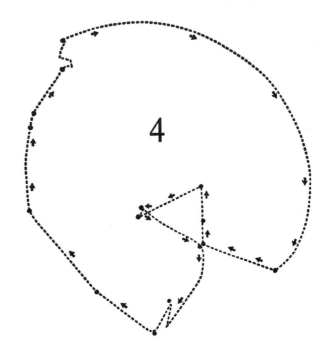

4

By the fifteenth of February, most of the problems had been solved, and we were nearly ready to begin the voyage. The last eleven days had been crammed with work. Les Kelly, our inspired engineer who had put the ship through her trials, had made his envious good-byes. Commander Will Adams and Lieutenant Commander Bob Bulmer, Executive Officer and Operations Officer respectively, had spent most of their time in ComSubLant's locked chart room plotting our course. With them was the only enlisted man to be informed of the real nature of our trip, Chief Quartermaster William J. Marshall, Adams' navigational assistant.

The secret of our voyage was not, in the end, kept from *Triton*'s officers. After much thought, I got them together and told them, holding back only the indicated super-importance of

50

getting back on time. There was simply too much to be done for them to be kept in the dark; we had to spread our work in too many different directions at once. Except for Marshall, neither *Triton*'s crew nor the passengers who came aboard a day or so before our departure could be told anything. An announcement had been made that we would be under way for a much longer time than originally scheduled, using my bureaucrat as an excuse. All hands had been advised that our Squadron office—the headquarters of Submarine Squadron 10, to which *Triton* belonged—would be glad to assist in all personal emergencies, and men expecting additions to their families were especially told to notify the Squadron. A broad hint was given out that strictly personal information pertaining to family increases might find its way into official radio traffic, as it had during the war.

All hands were advised to lay in a private supply of tobacco, chewing gum, toothpaste, soap, and other personal necessities, for submarines carry no ship's store where these items may be purchased. (Quartermaster First Class Curtis Beacham was, as a result, observed trying to stow eighteen boxes of cigars, which he figured would just about last him the trip.)

There was one other person, I realized in a few days, who apparently knew of the real nature of our projected voyage. About midway during our period of preparation, a telephone call came for me. I took it on the private line which had been connected to my stateroom.

A female voice said, "Captain Beach? Admiral Rickover calling." I recognized Dixie Davis, the Admiral's secretary for many years.

"Beach here," I said.

"Beach"—this, after a moment and without preamble, was Rickover's soft tone—"I'm sending you some changes in your power-plant settings. You may need them. Have them put in immediately. Will you do this?"

"Yes, sir."

"They will increase the safety and dependability of your plant. We're doing this ahead of time because I want to do everything I can to help you. Do you understand what I'm saying?"

I did, indeed. "Yes, sir," I said again.

"Leighton is putting them in the mail this afternoon. Let me know personally if there is anything else we can do. I'll be watching your progress. Good luck!"

I started to say, "Thank you," but the receiver clicked before I was able to say a word.

Next day, as promised, a thick special-delivery envelope arrived for me. Its contents were confidential and must remain so, but perusing them before passing them on to Don Fears, who had taken over Les Kelly's duties as Engineer, I recognized them as following a pattern already established in earlier nuclear plants. After a period of running in, certain changes, essentially a relaxation of initial operating plant conditions, had been made in both *Nautilus* and *Skate*. Dennis Wilkinson and Jim Calvert had had, as a consequence, greater flexibility and a higher safety factor during their subsequent operations, and Bill Anderson, when he took over *Nautilus* from Wilkinson, had similarly profited. I could imagine the special work it must have taken to get a similar change ready on such short notice for us, and I wondered whether Dave Leighton had had any knowledge of why the extra labor had been so suddenly demanded. I doubted it.

Triton's supply officer, Lieutenant Commander Bob Fisher, Supply Corps, USN, was an especially busy man. In response to the order to load the ship for 120 days, he crammed aboard 16,487 pounds of frozen food, 6,631 pounds of canned meat, and 12,130 pounds of canned vegetables. With interest, I noted that he had taken more coffee (1,300 pounds) than potatoes (1,285 pounds). He also stowed as much fresh stuff as he dared, considering spoilage. In all, we carried 77,613 pounds of food.

In addition, Bob secretly laid in a large store of candy. His reason for this, when I asked him what in thunder he was thinking about, was that he had noted, among the tests planned for the cruise, a period of several days when smoking would be prohibited throughout the ship. In his experience, an extra supply of candy in such cases always proved of value. It was something I hadn't thought of; I wondered what Beacham would say when he found out.

There were, indeed, several tests to be carried out during this abstinence-from-smoking period, in addition to those planned for the cruise as a whole. Among them was a test to determine the psychological effects of the smoking ban, and a purely mechanical test to discover the percentage of contaminated aerosols which the smoking ban might remove from the atmosphere inside the ship. With these tests, the Navy's Medical Research Laboratory hoped to learn whether smoking should be restricted in nuclear submarines during long-submerged cruises, whether the crews of such ships should comprise only nonsmokers, or whether special equipment should be devised and installed to remove the aerosols to allow smoking.

Fisher exercised great ingenuity in placing his supplies. Submariners have always taken pride in their ability to do this in these cramped vessels, and Bob proved himself adept despite the fact that, before *Triton,* he had never been to sea in a submarine. Our wartime submarines, designed for crews of sixty-five men, sometimes went to sea with as many as eighty-five and still maintained their sixty-days-provisions capability. *Triton,* designed for a crew of 171 and endurance of seventy-five days, was to make the world cruise with 183 persons; but we loaded her for 120 days nonetheless.

Our crew stowed away the increased amounts of foodstuffs, even when the stacks of supplies threatened to usurp their bunk spaces. Since the increased supplies were compatible with our cover story of a lengthened cruise, we did not concern ourselves about crew reactions, but I did worry considerably about Electric Boat workers, many of them experienced, though retired, submarine Chief Petty Officers, who might draw conclusions pretty close to the truth we were so carefully concealing.

Adequate sleeping space for our expanded complement was also a problem. True, submariners have for years been accustomed to "hot-bunking"—the term used to describe the system in which three men, one in each of the three watch sections, occupy only two bunks in rotation. For a cruise as long as ours, however, I thought individual bunks should be provided for all. But even *Triton's* huge size could not comfortably accommodate all of the men. We crammed extra bunks into every conceivable spot, including the atticlike space above the false ceiling in the wardroom and the yeoman's office, but we were still short.

I was for a time very pleased with the eventual solution: *Triton,* the world's most modern and marvelous ship, would also be the only undersea craft in our Navy to be fitted with the traditional oldtime sailorman's joy and comfort, the hammock! We installed two of them; one in the forward torpedo room, the other in the after torpedo room. There were some difficulties, however. No one aboard except myself, apparently, had ever slept in a hammock. No one had ever rigged one—no one knew, for instance, that for sleeping it must be stretched just as tightly as possible, or that a short wooden batten is generally desirable near the sleeper's head to keep the heavy canvas from curling over his face. No one, in fact, had ever seen a hammock of the kind I was describing. Or at least, so they would have had me believe. I delved deep into my own hammock-sleeping experience during midshipman cruise days in the old battleship *Arkansas,* designed the hammocks myself, supervised their installation, and personally checked out the men when they used them the first time.

I was sure that once it was known how comfortable a hammock could be, the lucky occupants would everlastingly bless my thoughtful kindness—and our berthing problems would be over.

It was not until later that I realized the hammocks were not getting the use I had expected. For a while, someone, anyone, climbed into them when the grapevine announced my approach, but even that custom gradually fell into disuse, and the swaying nests hung empty. Horatio Nelson and Horatio Hornblower both slept in hammocks, and so did John Paul Jones. But times have changed.

One of our more perplexing tasks was to prepare a suitable memorial to be delivered at Cadiz, the point from which Magellan departed on his successful but, for him, ill-fated circumnavigation. Having optimistically stated that *Triton* would herself design and procure a suitable plaque, I now found myself in the foundry business, all highly classified, of course, wishing mightily that I had been more reserved. Fortunately, in Tom Thamm *Triton* had an excellent and imaginative artist, and at the Submarine Base there was a superb woodcarver who, we hoped, could be prevailed upon to make the necessary wooden mold.

The second design Tom turned out was a beauty. Twenty-three inches in diameter, it depicted a globe in relief, upon which a wreath of olive branches was superimposed. Forming the bottom of the wreath was the US Submarine Force twin-dolphin insignia, and in its center a representation of Magellan's flagship, the 120-ton *Trinidad*. Beneath the ship we placed the dates 1519-1960, representing the dates of Magellan's trip and our own, and inside the circumference of the globe the Latin motto, *"Ave Nobilis Dux Iterum Sactum Est."* Freely translated, this means "Hail, Noble Captain, It Is Done Again."

I questioned Tom closely about his Latin. He had gathered it by stratagem from an acquaintance, a Latin instructor at neighboring "Conn College"—Connecticut College for Women. Tom had told the teacher he needed the correct wording and spelling of a number of Latin phrases to settle an argument in the wardroom, and she suspected nothing. Still, in looking at the inscription, I could not shake off a feeling that something was wrong. A mental warning bell tinkled, but I ignored it.

Carving of the wooden form was entrusted to Chief Electrician's Mate Ernest L. Benson of the Submarine Base. He had a fine reputation in New London for his carefully executed woodcarvings and already had far more orders for them than he could comfortably fill. Benson finally agreed to give our order priority without asking questions, though we could see he was burning with curiosity.

Our foray into the business of casting plaques taught us, however, that artisans cannot be hurried. Thamm, working in his spare time, took several days, the woodcarver required several more, and casting the metal was practically a trial-and-error operation. Twelve days were simply not enough, and the job was not finished when it came time for us to depart. This, therefore, became one of the items we had to leave to others for execution. The tiny Mystic Foundry was entrusted with the mold of our plaque and Captain Tom Henry, the much admired "Commodore" of Squadron 10, agreed to supervise its completion. He also promised to send it to meet us off Cadiz.

Every man and officer naturally had his own difficulties to resolve, in addition to his duties on board *Triton*. Having listed each individual's chores, I had also prepared a private check-off sheet for myself—but being deeply involved in preparations for the cruise, the daily work which could not be neglected, and a tremendous amount of official correspondence, it usually was not until midnight that I was free to deal with my personal problems. At least twice I saw the first light of morning; and I will long remember how I cursed the income tax and Form 1040, which I was rushing to complete.

On the fifteenth of February everything had been done, and

it seemed as though our last day could be spent in relaxation. But caution, compounded by years of service and the concern that our carefully laid plans might run afoul of some unpredicted problem, dictated a sea trial. It was not a popular decision on board or in the Admiral's office; and it must be admitted that Ingrid, just returned from California, was less than enthusiastic when she learned that I had asked to go to sea for a single day and night to test equipment, just before shoving off for so long a time.

After some argument, Admiral Daspit granted permission, and on Monday morning, the fifteenth of February, *Triton* bade a regretful farewell to Clyde Eidson, our efficient Chief Yeoman, who was scheduled for OCS and commissioned rank in the near future, and headed to sea. This trial run was a good thing, even though it did us out of a holiday. A number of small malfunctions turned up in some of the hastily installed gear, and on Tuesday morning, preceded by radioed emergency repair requests, we were back alongside the dock at Electric Boat. A swarm of specialists descended upon us to set things right.

Not everything could be put back in order, unfortunately; one piece of equipment out of commission was a special wave-motion sensor which had not been made properly watertight and had flooded as soon as we dived. When external electric equipment in a submarine floods with submergence pressure, it means a long repair. Invariably, the cable connected to it also floods, like a garden hose, all the way to its terminal inside the ship, necessitating *its* replacement as well. We could not delay for repairs to the wave-motion sensor, important though it was. All else was back in commission by 2:00 P.M.

I went ashore for a couple of last-minute errands, grabbed a phone, luckily caught Ingrid just as the course she was auditing in Shakespeare at Connecticut College ended for the day.

"Come down and wish us bon voyage," I told her.

Unfortunately, Captain Henry, whose steady support had

been invaluable, was ill in the naval base hospital and had to
send apologies for not being able to bid us good-bye in person.
Thus Commander James M. Calvert, recently skipper of the
famous submarine *Skate,* Carl Shugg, General Manager of
Electric Boat, and my wife were the only people to see us off.

Commander Joseph Baylor Roberts, assigned to us by the
Chief of Naval Information, a Naval Reserve officer and a
friend of many years, was on the dock with his camera, and
insisted on photographing Ingrid's good-bye kiss. Though we
both felt that we were entitled to some privacy on the occasion,
we dutifully posed for him.

Partings are sad when one is young and in love, and they
are no less sad when one is older and still in love. But Ingrid
is a courageous Navy wife. "Good-bye, sweetheart," she said,
as she kissed me. "Take good care of the *Triton!*"

It was sixteen minutes after 2:00 P.M., EST when *Triton*'s
last line was taken in and we backed her gently away from
the dock.

She was on her way at last!

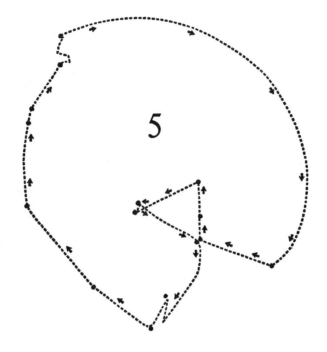

5

Tracing its origin to the glacial period during which our country's outlines were formed, the Thames River in New London flows southward through a cleft between massive piles of time-worn New England granite. For tens of thousands of years the river has worn its way through the channel left by the receding ice, smoothing the rough edges of the stone and carving its channel deep amid the silt and debris which has ineffectually tried to choke it. Sometimes the river between the rocky headlands is roiled by a storm sweeping to the south, and at these times it takes on the gray colorless hue of a lowering overcast; at more quiet moments the river is blue with the reflection of the sky, as it courses past the massive stone-and-brick lighthouse at the entrance to the buoyed ship-channel.

On the sixteenth of February, *Triton* stood out in a channel whipped by a cold north wind. Low in the water, extraordinarily slender in proportions, sinisterly beautiful as only a submarine can be, her huge size dwarfed the bald domes of granite on either side. On deck, a few men busied themselves housing the capstans, stowing away mooring lines and other equipment. Upon the forward part of the long, clean silhouette jutted the angular outline of the ship's "sail"—some twenty feet high by seventy-five feet long—which provided the support structure for periscopes, radar masts, radio antenna, and other retractable submarine gear. A number of men clustered on the forward part of the sail, which served as *Triton*'s bridge.

We were beginning the voyage submariners had been dreaming of ever since nuclear energy had made it possible. Gently, the ship clove the sea-blue water, as though loath to leave yet eager to be on her way. My pulse, had I permitted anyone to take it, might have belied the calm demeanor with which I outwardly surveyed the conning of the ship.

From my exposed position on our "flying bridge"—on the very top of the sail and unprotected by bulwarks—I had a clear view in all directions. In the wrong kind of weather this could be an unpleasant watch-keeping station, but today, with the north wind at our backs, I was not uncomfortable by the standards to which seamen are accustomed. Little, if any thought, however, was being wasted by anyone on personal comfort or discomfort. Taking a ship to sea, even through a familiar and uncomplicated channel, requires unremitting attention. I was the only person on the bridge who could be said to have any free time at all, and between checks on our navigation in the channel, I focused my binoculars on a prominent boulder at the eastern mouth of the river.

There she stood as she had said she would, alone on a granite ledge where the Thames River meets Long Island Sound. The chill February wind whipped the red scarf about her head. Feet thrust into wool-lined galoshes, one hand holding her coat tightly around her, she waved a mittened hand at me. Well I knew that the distance was too great for Ingrid to distinguish me with the naked eye. But I waved my white uniform cap in answer.

This was the same blue-eyed girl who had married me during the flaming years of World War II, when both of us feared so desperately that life would pass us by. Many times during the war, and many more times since, she had watched my ship dip below the horizon. For sixteen years she had minded the home and the children when I was at sea, and whenever there was a mail bag from home, a letter from her was always there.

As I waved at that rapidly receding figure—she had now taken off the scarf and was holding it as a banner, the better to be seen—it suddenly came to me: "She knows! She *must* know!" After nearly sixteen years facing the unpredictable vicissitudes of Navy life together, sixteen years during which our mutual dependence had steadily deepened, the more I thought the more certain I became. I had also learned to appreciate the strength of character and depth of loyalty my Ingrid had inherited from her Swedish forebears, and I knew that if she had indeed guessed, the Navy need have no fear of her speaking out of turn.

I couldn't wave my cap continuously, for there were many demanding duties. Every time I turned my binoculars back toward the point of land, however, the red scarf was still streaming. Several more times I waved my cap through a wide arc, in hopes she could still see it. Finally a point of land came between us, the spot of red drew out of sight, and my last tie with land was broken. In a few hours, as soon as the water was deep enough to dive *Triton*'s huge bulk, we would submerge for almost three long months.

Despite all the arguments in favor of doing it earlier, there were sound technical reasons why a submerged circumnavigation of the world was not attempted until *Triton* was built, and the most important of these, stated simply, was the factor of dependability. Our two main power plants were completely separate and independent. No conceivable casualty in one could affect the other. Thus, while the dependability record of *Triton*'s single-reactor predecessors was unsurpassed in our Navy, a ship with two reactors would be able to complete the voyage safely even if one of them were to break down.

Another factor was adequate provisions for a long voyage. *Triton*'s size gave her a tremendous amount of room for storage. And, of course, it was her great carrying capacity which made our ship the ideal vehicle for the scientific aspects of our mission.

As we passed New London Ledge Light—a square, solid structure marking the mouth of the Thames River—we increased to standard speed, about fifteen knots, and angled our course slightly to the left to head for Race Rock, the wave-lashed lighthouse at the western tip of Fishers Island which marks the division point between Long Island Sound and Block Island Sound.

In a few minutes, *Triton* described a large curving sweep around it, as we squared her away on a nearly easterly course for the run down Block Island Sound toward the open sea. Once set on the new course, we increased speed to "full," clipping our way through the small chop in Block Island Sound in a manner more akin to a destroyer than a submarine. *Triton* rode easily, with hardly a quiver in her big hull—the well-ordered activity below decks barely evident from the small noises by which well-attuned persons keep informed of what is going on.

Doubtless, I felt, some of the crew were experiencing the emotions which were also crowding upon me. Approximately one-third of them were on watch and therefore occupied, but others were preparing themselves for a lengthy cruise, settling into the routine which would be ours until we returned to port. With the exception of the officers and Chief Quartermaster

Marshall, no one knew where we were really going, but I wondered whether some of the men, observing the unusual activity in getting ready and the secrecy with which Will Adams and Marshall had gone about their plotting chores, might not have surmised that something special was in the offing. They were to find out soon enough, I thought to myself, but I could not tell them until we were well on our way.

According to our log, it was at 1543, approximately an hour and a half after our departure, when *Triton* swept across the bar at Montauk Point, turned due south, and, free of the shore, increased speed to flank.

Lieutenant James Hay came on the bridge to relieve Brodie as Officer of the Deck about fifteen minutes before the hour, in accordance with custom. At the same time, Quartermaster First Class Beacham would be taking over the watch from Quartermaster Second Class Honeysette in the conning tower; one after the other, the oncoming lookouts bawled for permission to come on the bridge to relieve their opposite numbers. With the extra people, it was becoming a little crowded.

"Bob," I said to Brodie, "I'm going below for a while. The course is south. I'll let you know when it's time to dive."

Bob interrupted his turnover to Hay, nodded gravely at me. "Aye, aye," he said, a surprisingly deep voice booming out of his slender physique. Bob was the tallest officer on board and ate like a horse, but it seemed to have done little to fill him out. Perhaps a few more years of service would put enough pounds on him to go with that voice.

Triton was beginning to feel the sea. There was a longer period to her impatient motion as she pierced the ocean rollers, a slight tremor from the increased power as she drove through them. She rolled gently from side to side, but the whistle of wind coming over the bridge cockpit, the spume of angry spray flung back from her razor-sharp prow, and the white foam racing down her dark sides testified to the power and urgency with which she drove southward. Astern and to starboard the looming mass of Long Island reflected the rays of the southwesterly sun. Montauk Point Lighthouse and the nearby radar towers jutted prominently into the sky. At their foot, extending for some distance to the west and at right angles to the frothing wake we were leaving straight behind, could be seen a white, almost steady line where the small Atlantic surf met the white sand beaches of the land.

Ahead was the sea, the horizon, and the cold blue sky. I swung onto the ladder leading below, climbed down to the lower bridge level and through the watertight hatch into the conning tower.

"—that's about it, Beach," I heard Honeysette saying. Beacham and Honeysette looked just the slightest bit startled as I appeared.

"Quartermaster of the watch properly relieved, Captain," Honeysette quickly said. "Beacham has the watch."

"Aye," I acknowledged, and then mocked severity: "How many times do I have to tell you that while I'm captain of this ship, Beacham's nickname is abolished!"

Both men grinned self-consciously. Honeysette strove to retrieve the situation.

"Sorry, Captain, I didn't see you come down, and it just slipped out by accident."

Beacham has probably been known as "Beach" to his cronies ever since he enlisted in the Navy some twelve years ago. But, claiming prior rights in the circumstances, I had decreed that so long as he and I were both in the same ship something was going to have to give, and that it was going to be Beacham. I frowned. "It's a court-martial offense, you know."

Beacham took a well-chewed cigar out of his mouth. "I'm doing my best to teach all these guys, Captain," he said, "but some of them don't seem to want to learn."

"Humph!" was all I could think to say, as I stepped on the rungs of the ladder and started below into the control room.

Honeysette's intelligent face was framed above the circular hatchway as I passed through. "If we have a court martial, Captain, we'll have to go back!"

"Humph!" was all I could say again. Honeysette had got the best of this interchange. It was also obvious that he had guessed that this cruise might be more than it purported to be.

Directly beneath the conning tower is the control room. Its bulkheads and overhead are painted a soft green, but the color scheme as a whole, with all the instruments, is predominantly instrument gray like the conning tower above. In this area *Triton* is three decks high—and the control room, occupying the highest compartment, has the basic shape of the attic of a Quonset hut. The curved cylindrical pressure hull of the ship, insulated with an inch of smooth cork glued directly to the steel, sweeps in an unbroken arc from starboard to port.

Covering the entire port half of the forward bulkhead is the diving panel: a large gray metal affair in which a great number of instruments are mounted. Here are depth gauges, gyrocompass repeater, speed indicator, engine-order telegraphs (frequently called "annunciators") a "combined instrument panel" for the bow planesman and another for the stern planesman, and controls for our automatic depth-keeping equipment. Two armchairs, upholstered in red plastic, face the diving panel. Directly before each of them is a control column that would make a bomber pilot feel right at home.

Submerged, the control room is one of the most important nerve centers of the ship, but while a submarine is on the surface there is very little going on. The seats in front of the diving stand were at the moment unoccupied; on diving, the two lookouts on the bridge would come down below and take over the two stations. The Officer of the Deck is the last man down; he personally shuts the bridge hatch and then swings below to take his station as Diving Officer. Up to now this would have been Bob Brodie, but as he was being relieved, Jim Hay would be the "Diving Officer of the Watch." I saw with approval, however, that Tom Thamm, the ship's official Diving Officer, was still on hand, sitting on the cushioned top of a tool box located just in front of the ship's fathometer. Apparently, he had finished his compensation calculations, for the circular slide rule he had devised for this purpose was nowhere to be seen.

Thamm rose to his feet, "Afternoon, Captain," he said. "How is it on the bridge?"

"Cold and windy."

"How soon do you think we'll be diving?" he asked.

"A couple of hours," I said. "It's a pretty long run out here you know—have you got your trim in yet?"

Tom shook his head. "It's still going in, sir. We'll have it in about fifteen minutes more. It takes a while to compensate this big boat."

"Ship."

"Sorry, sir. 'This ship,' I mean." Tom grinned at me.

Submarines have been called boats ever since 1900 when our Navy's first submarine, USS *Holland,* was indeed a "boat" —only fifty-four feet long, twenty-feet shorter than *Triton's* sail. Since then, the term has been affectionately perpetuated, despite great changes in the craft themselves. Even before World War II, however, submarines were for various purposes officially designated as "major war vessels," and since that time their significance and importance have increased still further. *Triton,* with the size and horsepower of a cruiser, with unmatched operational versatility, speed, and endurance, is far more than a boat. With bigger craft sliding down the ways, Rear Admiral Warder, the "Fearless Freddie" of World War II renown and Admiral Daspit's predecessor as ComSubLant, had directed submariners henceforth to refer to their boats as ships. But old habits die hard, and no one in the *Triton* was so constant an offender as I. This was the reason for Tom's grin.

"If we're not going to dive for two hours, Captain, I'd like to secure here as soon as we get the compensation in. I'll be back about"— Tom looked at his wrist watch—"1700."

"That will be plenty of time, Tom," I said. "Will wants to dive at about thirty-five fathom curve, and even at this speed we won't be there until some time after five o'clock."

The continental shelf on the eastern seaboard runs for many miles out to sea. The water is actually much deeper in parts of Long Island and Block Island sounds. We had arbitrarily picked thirty-five fathoms as the depth we wanted under us before diving; here, in the open sea, there would be a long surface run before the continental shelf dropped off to that extent.

Triton's control room is really two spaces. Her periscopes and some of her radar masts are so long that when retracted they project into the hull of the ship nearly to the keel. Consequently, the control room is bisected in the middle by the periscope and radar mast wells. The Diving Station takes over most of the port side; the fire control gear and sonar compartment are located to starboard, where there is also room for passage fore and aft. Gray boxes containing a great amount of complex equipment are mounted on the center structure, thus making it a solid mass several feet thick.

Flush against the port side of the ship, but with a bulk that leaves barely enough room between its face and the periscope well structure for a crew member to man it, is the Ballast Control Panel, looking rather like a large electronic instrument console, which is exactly what it is. The face of this BCP is covered with dials and gauges; and a line of switches, contrived so that each knob has a different shape, borders its face. One of the requirements of the Chief Petty Officer in charge of the control room, whose post is a built-in swivel chair facing the BCP, is that he be able to distinguish all the operating switches blindfolded.

A prominent section of the Ballast Control Panel is devoted to the Hull Opening Indicator system, by which the condition of the crucial valves and hatches in the ship, whether open or closed, can be told at a glance. In the old days, this was done with red and green lights and the Chief's customary report on diving was "Green Board." In the war it was found, however, that wearing red goggles to preserve night vision made it impossible to distinguish between red and green. In the new system, all the lights are red; a circle represents open and a straight bar means closed. And "Green Board" is now reported as "Straight Board."

Located on the BCP are the controls for diving and surfacing, blowing tanks, closing or opening vents. Variable tanks and trim pump are regulated, as are the hydraulic systems and the high-pressure air systems. The post is the charge of the senior enlisted man on watch in the control room, the Chief Petty Officer of the Watch, and it is located so that he can control the dive and give instructions to the planesmen should the OOD be slow in arriving from the bridge.

Lining either side of the narrow and cluttered passageway aft of the Ballast Control Panel are interior communication switchboards and various electric panels. Still farther aft, occupying the entire port after corner of the control room and protected by a soundproofed bulkhead and door is the chart room, ample in its original design but, like all other space in the ship, now crammed with assorted equipment mostly relating to radar.

Immediately forward of where I now stood in the control room, beyond a pressure-proof bulkhead and its watertight door, is a big compartment devoted entirely to crew's berthing, accommodating a total of ninety-five men on two deck levels. Each man has a locker, an aluminum bunk, a foam-rubber mattress, individual ventilation controllable by a louver near his head, and an overhead fluorescent light for reading. Lest the provision for reading in bed seem unwarranted luxury, it must be realized that it is hardly possible—in fact undesirable—for all hands in a submarine to be up and about at the same time, except for certain general duties such as battle stations or emergency drills. The more people in their bunks at other times, the more room for those who must be up.

Still farther forward, the foremost compartment in the ship, is the forward torpedo room, containing four standard-size torpedo tubes, considerable high-powered sonar equipment, and, as always, berthing for as many persons as can be accommodated.

I still had on the blues and bridge coat I had worn as we got underway; so now my immediate destination was in the other direction, aft to the officer's berthing compartment where I had my tiny stateroom. I glanced swiftly at the Rigged for Dive Panel, which showed that all compartments in the ship had been rigged and checked in the condition of "readiness for diving," and at the Hull Opening Indicators, which showed that the only hull openings not closed were the bridge hatch and the main air intake valve, and stepped aft.

Triton's cruiser size did not extend to the Commanding Officer's quarters. My stateroom in *Triton* was about a five-foot capital "T," with a pull-down bunk filling the entire crossbar of the letter. By stretching out one arm and pivoting, I could touch all four walls. But I couldn't complain very loudly. Thamm's room, for example, was the same size as mine, but he shared it with two others. Will Adams' room was also the same size. He had one roommate and the mechanism of one of the ship's main vent valves, which took as much space as a man. Normally, these days, the Executive Officer is so besotted with paper work that whenever possible he has no roommate, so that the vacant bunk can be used as an adjunct to his tiny fold-down desk. But there were no spare bunks anywhere in *Triton* on this cruise, and the extra bunk in Will's room was assigned to Joe Roberts.

I drew the curtain on my stateroom, in which I was to spend a good part of my time for the next three months. Electric Boat had hopefully painted it a so-called "beach sand" color, thus, perhaps, attempting to apologize for its lack of size. It contained a standard fold-down desk, several drawers for linen and personal belongings, a large safe which Bob Brodie had appropriated for his classified publications, a folding wash stand, a medicine cabinet, a one-foot-wide clothes closet, a convertible bunk—cushioned on the bottom to form an uncomfortable settee when raised—and a single straight-backed chair. Under the folding wash stand, at my request—since I needed a place to have at least one other person in for a conference—had been built a small circular folding stool about eight inches in diameter (dubbed the "hot seat" by irreverent members of the ship's company). And in every conceivable nook, not occupied by some other equipment, there were lockers.

At the foot of my bunk were depth gauge, speed indicator, and gyro repeater, and when I counted them I discovered that the room contained five telephones and two loudspeaking attachments with which, after learning which buttons to press and which dials to turn, I could talk to anyone in the ship.

In a few moments, having shifted to the sea-going khaki that would be my standard garb until May, I drew back my door curtain and walked aft. On either side of the narrow formica-lined hallway were curtained doorways similar to mine, marking the entrances to the wardroom and the six staterooms *Triton* had for the seventeen officers assigned. At the extreme after end of the compartment was the yeoman's office, fortunately rather roomy as submarine offices go.

The watertight door in the pressure bulkhead at the end of the passageway was latched shut. I pulled the latch handle, stepped high over the coaming, ducked my head, and slipped through, carefully latching the door behind me. We were now more than three miles from the nearest land and by regulations could leave the door open, but as a matter of common consent it was habitually kept shut in order to make a sharper division between number one reactor compartment on its after side and the living quarters forward of it.

A few steps aft and I was standing directly over the reactor, on a slightly raised platform surrounded by a heavy pipe-guard rail, and surveying the area with satisfaction.

Triton's twin reactors hummed softly as they generated the steam for her two huge engine rooms, but in their watertight compartments there was not a moving thing to be seen. Only the muffled whine of the vital circulating pumps and the whirr of the ventilation blowers could be heard. The general quietness and good order hardly conveyed an adequate impression of the new-found source of power cooking away beneath my feet. A red deck, partly covered by green-shellacked rubber matting and surmounted by the ubiquitous gray boxes, formed a color scheme pleasing to the eye. The reactor spaces are seldom visited; with no watch stations to be manned, they are generally immaculate—Pat McDonald's twin pride and joy.

Pressed against the skin of the ship on either side of my platform stood two heavily insulated domes, from which large steam pipes rose and went aft. Control equipment of all kinds —valves, dials, gauges, special electrical machinery—lined the walls of the compartment. Yet it seemed extraordinarily spacious, clean, easy to get about in, and uncommonly quiet for a ship making full power.

A few feet below me, beneath the insulated deck, stood one of *Triton's* two huge steel pressure vessels, containing half of the precious uranium fuel for which I was official custodian. Through it raced distilled water at high pressure, extracting heat from the uranium and transmitting it to the steam generators. Over against a bulkhead and also concealed beneath the deck, an array of encased pumps drove the water around its simple circuit. The watertight door in the after bulkhead was latched open, and through it I glimpsed a repetition of the red, green, and gray color scheme in number two reactor compartment—a duplicate of the first.

I knew I had but to step aft another bulkhead or so to have this illusion of quiet thoroughly dispelled. There stood the ridiculously small starboard turbine and one of our two tremendous reduction gears, which at this speed would be filling the engine rooms with their roaring.

The ship lurched impatiently. Probably the sea was building up. I ducked quickly into number two reactor compartment, moved aft another two dozen steps, opened a second closed watertight door, and stepped through the bulkhead into number one engine room.

This was the largest compartment in the ship, in cubic volume not far from the entire displacement of a World War II submarine, and it contained all the massive components of the starboard main engine. A high-pitched roar of machinery reached my ears, and for all its racket it sounded wonderful.

Chief Engineman Hosie Washington, an ex-Navy steward who had changed his rate and was now our Chief Chemist, grinned happily at me. "She sure sounds nice, Captain!" he shouted, his eyes dancing in his handsome Negro face. I nodded my agreement as I passed him, and walked a few feet farther aft to the main control center of the engine room.

Lieutenant Commander Donald G. Fears, Les Kelly's assistant during the building period, had taken over as *Triton's* Engineer Officer. Fears, a slightly built man with an intense face which belied his relaxed leadership, had the forward engine room watch, and I could see that he, too, was exhilarated by the performance of the machinery under his charge. He stood at a small watch-stander's table before a low gaugeboard, displaying dials and switches. To one side, surveying two large consoles covered with a profusion of instruments, a Chief Petty Officer and a First Class Electronics Technician were perched on built-in stools, standing watch on the nerve center of the starboard reactor. Directly forward of Don, the starboard throttleman faced a similar console that recorded steam conditions.

This was "Maneuvering One," the control station for the starboard engine. The efficient way in which the men moved about their tasks no doubt filled Don with pride, for their actions were a result of his training and indoctrination.

The purposeful noise of the great reduction gear beat upon our ears. It was not a shriek of protest, but the powerful frequency of a finely meshed set of gears doing their job without fuss, so solidly constructed and so perfectly matched that they transmitted a minimum of vibration into the water even though some of them were spinning thousands of revolutions per minute. Could they continue to run this way, without stopping, for almost three months? This was one of the answers our voyage was to determine.

Bidding Fears a silent farewell I continued my journey aft. Number two engine room contained identical equipment to number one, although arranged somewhat differently because it drove the other propeller, and I passed through it rapidly with only a brief greeting to Lieutenant George Troffer, in charge. Satisfied that the same atmosphere of calm confidence was evident here, I opened the watertight door into the after torpedo room.

Triton has torpedo tubes at each end, and as the name implies, this compartment contains *Triton*'s stern set. In the after part, brightly lighted in contrast to the dimmed lights farther forward where forty-two men had their berths, I found Allen W. Steele, Torpedoman's Mate Third Class, on watch. A sandy-haired, serious-faced sailor, twenty-one years old, he had made a good try for the Naval Academy Preparatory School a few months ago, but with insufficient time to prepare, his marks in the competitive examination were not high enough. He had done his best, as we had for him. Steele rose from the tool box upon which he had been sitting and gave me a cheerfully respectful salute.

Here, I had no trouble appreciating the power of our two huge bronze propellers, which clearly could be heard spinning in the water just a few feet away. As during our initial trials, the drumming of the steel fabric of *Triton's* great pressure hull could be felt through the soles of our feet or through our fingertips resting against the solid structure of a torpedo-loading skid.

I grinned. "How is it going, Steele?"

"Fine, sir!" he answered soberly, "but I'll be glad when we dive and get rid of all this racket."

Only a couple of years in submarines, he already had the submariner's outlook. I found myself agreeing with him, as I made my way forward again.

On the bridge, the shrill wind sweeping over our exposed cockpit was cutting cold. I quickly became chilled through, despite the heavy coat, gloves, and old cap I had slipped on. *Triton's* course was still due south, and her throttles were open to allow full steam flow. It was now a little after five in the afternoon. The sun lay low in the southwest and dusk was gathering.

I turned to Lieutenant Hay. "What's the latest sounding, Jim?" I asked him.

"We just got thirty-three fathoms a few minutes ago, Captain," he said. "Do you want me to go ahead and dive at thirty-five fathoms?"

"Go ahead and get the bridge thoroughly secured, Jim," I told him. "By the time you are ready, we'll probably have reached the thirty-five-fathom line. I'll let you know when to dive."

As Hay busied himself with these last-minute preparations, I raised my glasses and scanned the sea to the horizon. There was a slight chop, with whitecaps coming from the south. Spray and spume closed *Triton's* foredeck, and occasionally the waves buried her sharp snout as our ship split them with her knife-blade stem. Our wake, a long, straight, broad furrow of white water, reached aft beyond the visible horizon. The lighthouse and radar towers of Montauk Point were long out of sight, and the coast of Long Island had receded from view.

The "21 MC" speaker on the bridge blared: "Bridge—Control! Sounding, three five fathoms!"

"That's it, Jim," I said. "When you are ready in all respects, take her down." I deliberately spoke loudly for the benefit of the lookouts who, I knew, were eagerly hoping to get an inkling of where our mysterious trip was to take us. They were to get no satisfaction from me, yet. But there would be nothing wrong with teasing them a little. I swung myself on the ladder to go below.

"Be sure you get everything tightly secured," I said. "We're going to be a mighty long time down before we come up, and we don't want any of this stuff shaking loose up here where we can't get at it!" I chuckled inwardly. In a few minutes that bit of information would be all over the ship.

As I passed down through the conning tower into the control room, everyone sensed that this time my appearance heralded the time to dive. In the control room, Chief Radioman Joe Walsh, in charge of *Triton*'s radio gang, was Chief of the Watch. When he saw me, he put down the cup of coffee he was holding. Slight, with blond hair and aquiline features, Walsh had been one of the first to check out on our Ballast Control Panel. It must have been Walsh who had been operating the fathometer. No one was near it at the present time. Tom Thamm stood unobtrusively in the background. To Walsh's left stood Bob Carter, Machinist Mate First Class, Auxiliaryman of the Watch. In build and size similar to Walsh, though darker and with jet black hair, Carter might have posed for illustrations of the lanky sailor so often characterized as the ideal man-o'-war's man. Career Navymen and submariners for years, Walsh and Carter both had thoroughly checked out *Triton*'s complicated equipment. We were in good hands.

Noting my attention, they self-consciously pretended unconcern. Inwardly, I smiled to myself. Diving was routine; *Triton* had already dived many times. But this was the start of our shakedown cruise, and they sensed that something out of the ordinary was planned. That this cruise was to be no ordinary cruise, this dive no ordinary dive, everyone on board must have realized.

I gripped the handrail of the ladder beneath the conning tower hatch through which I had just descended. Without even realizing they were doing it, Walsh and Carter ran their eyes over each of the individual controls before them, mentally checking them at the proper position and reviewing what they would do when the diving alarm sounded. For a moment or two nothing happened. Jim must be making a final check of the bridge, I thought. I hoped everything was tightly secured up there. Finally, I heard his voice through the bridge speaker system. "Clear the bridge. Clear the bridge!" Simultaneously, the diving alarm—an old-fashioned automobile horn—resounded through the ship.

Walsh's hands flew to the controls for the hydraulic plants, started the stand-by pump, then waited, with his right hand hovering near the switch to the air inlet valve. It was a similar valve which somehow failed to close in 1939, when USS *Squalus* sank near the Isle of Shoals off Maine, losing nearly half her crew. In *Squalus*, this valve had been much larger than our own, for it supplied air to four great diesel engines in the engine room, whereas in our case it only provided ventilation below decks. But it was still important that it be closed when we dived.

The horn stopped; then came a second blast. I stepped clear of the hatch, and moments later a pair of legs clattered down the ladder, followed closely by another pair. Tom Schwartz, Torpedoman's Mate Third—known variously as "the nose," "the face," or "the profile"—scrambled off the ladder and threw himself into one of the seats at the diving stand. William

A. McKamey, Seaman, practically on Schwartz's heels, settled himself at the other seat.

Jim Hay, as Officer of the Deck, would be the last man off the bridge. His next duty was to see that the watertight hatch leading to the bridge was properly shut. He would be up there right now checking it.

With the second blast of the alarm, Walsh snapped the switch to shut *Triton*'s main air valve. Then, playing upon the Ballast Control Panel as though it were an organ console, while intently eying the board of indicator lights glowing before him, he swept his hand swiftly and precisely across the face of the panel to open the twenty-two main ballast tank vents with which *Triton* was fitted. That done, he remained poised, one hand on the master switch which would shut at least half of the ballast tank vents, the other on the main air blow valve control. The bridge hatch still indicated open on his panel—as it should until completely closed. This is one of the crucial operations in diving; no skipper can completely divest himself of the urgent need to know that the bridge hatch has been properly shut. As soon as McKamey had passed me. I stepped back to the ladder and looked up into the conning tower. The ordered bustle there reassured me, as it always did, and as I looked up, Beacham's voice sang out to Hay, "Hatch secured, sir!"

I cast my eyes quickly back to Walsh. He had relaxed ever so slightly. The red circle, indicating that the conning tower hatch was open, had been replaced by a single short bar.

McKamey and Schwartz, each pulling the steel pin which had locked their control columns in the neutral position, pushed the bow and stern planes forward, positioning them to a dive angle. Approximately fifteen seconds had passed since the end of the second blast of the diving alarm, and *Triton*'s surface motion had already changed. Our wide open main ballast tanks had taken aboard nearly all of the two thousand tons of water they could hold—and our six-thousand-ton

Triton, cruising powerfully on the surface of the sea, had become an eight-thousand-ton submarine. Her bow began to incline; Jim Hay slipped around me and took his station behind the two planesmen. The depth gauges were showing that our keel was forty feet below the surface and going deeper.

"Depth, Captain?" asked Jim, his eyes on the depth gauges.

"One hundred and fifty feet, Jim," I told him. "Keep the fathometer going and don't get any closer than seventy-five feet from the bottom."

This area had been well swept by many years of submarine operations south of Montauk Point. All wrecked ships or rock outcroppings, which might present a hazard to a submarine operating close to the bottom, had been discovered and plotted. Nevertheless, and particularly at the speed we were going, it was desirable to be more than careful.

A thirty-five-fathom sounding from *Triton's* fathometers indicated an actual depth of water, counting our own draft, of nearer to forty fathoms, or two hundred and forty feet. A keel depth of one hundred and fifty feet, therefore, should leave us ninety feet of water between our keel and the bottom of the sea. At this depth our periscopes could not extend to the surface, but our speed would have rendered them useless anyway. On the other hand, even if the biggest ship in the world were to pass directly overhead—though we'd probably be startled at the noise she'd be making—there would be no danger of collision. The only thing we needed to worry about at all was the possibility of encountering another submerged submarine, and this had been taken care of administratively, so far as our own subs were concerned, by assigning *Triton* a sea lane from which all other submarines had been excluded. There was, of course, a chance that a submarine belonging to another country might have chosen this precise moment to be submerged in this very area. But it was a remote possibility, barely worth consideration.

"Jim," I said, "the bottom drops away very gradually on the

continental shelf until it reaches the hundred-fathom curve. From there on out, it drops much more rapidly into the deep ocean. Stay at this depth until the fathometer indicates a hundred and fifty feet of water under us; then follow the bottom on down until you get to our running depth."

"Aye, aye, Captain!" said Jim, and looked up at me expectantly. I knew what was in his mind. He was thinking, "Are you going to announce where we're going, now that we've dived?"

I shook my head slightly, hoping he could read the answer.

Taking a gentle inclination by the bow, *Triton* effortlessly descended to her assigned depth. With our tremendous speed and the shallow water, an easy angle was indicated. With practiced ease, though I knew they were watching their controls carefully, Schwartz and McKamey drove her down and leveled her off, coached occasionally by a few words from Jim. Directly behind Hay, Walsh had a number of additional duties on the Ballast Control Panel, which he carried out automatically and without command, occasionally checking with Jim or vice versa.

Carter, in the meantime, and Bruce Gaudet, the IC Electrician stationed on his far side, had a number of operations to carry out, consisting mainly of securing topside electrical connections, speaker talk-back circuits, and the like. Thamm, apparently satisfied, quietly departed.

It was considerably warmer in the control room than on the bridge, and I felt it. Jim was struggling out of his bridge gear, while he kept close attention on the diving station in front of him, and in a few minutes, when the bustle of diving had pretty well died away, Seaman Jim Smith, evidently the off lookout—he must have been hiding somewhere for I had failed to see him earlier—came forward in a light dungaree shirt and trousers and offered to relieve McKamey.

With the ship steady at one hundred fifty feet, the depth

gauges no longer moving, Jim gave the permission. Smith squatted alongside McKamey, and in a low voice McKamey passed over the instructions he had received.

"OK," said Smith in a moment, grasping the control stick. "I've got it." In a long-practiced motion, with his left hand he swept up the right arm of the seat in which McKamey was seated—it had been built with a hinge at the back for precisely this purpose—and at the same moment, McKamey, releasing the control column to Smith, flipped up the arm on the far side of the seat, shifted his feet, rose, and stepped back. Effortlessly, Smith slid into his place, and as McKamey passed behind him, he pushed back both arm rests. *Triton* was already settled into her normal submerged routine.

I nodded to Hay. "You have the deck and the Conn, Jim," I said. "I'm going aft now. Keep the fathometer going and maintain a careful sonar watch. Call me if you hear anything."

"Aye, aye, Captain," said Jim. "Course 180, speed full, depth 150 feet, stay 75 feet above the bottom, when we reach 150 feet sounding, follow it on down to running depth. I understand, sir!"

I nodded again and left him.

McKamey was seated on a tool box in the passageway, pulling off his sou'westers.

"Nice job of diving, McKamey," I said.

His boyish face glowed with pleasure. McKamey had very recently reported aboard from submarine school and had already showed himself to have the makings of a fine sailor. He couldn't be long out of high school, I thought, forgetting that I had left home permanently at probably an even younger age.

A few feet farther aft, crammed into a corner among a plotting table, some air-conditioning monitoring equipment, a large stack of radar components, and some fire-control equipment, was a tiny compartment labeled "sonar room." Here was the nerve center of *Triton's* underwater listening equipment. Lieutenant Dick Harris, known as "Silent Dick," was there, along with two of our Sonarmen, rangy "Dutch" Beckhaus, once of the *Salamonie,* and Kenneth Remillard, the shortest man aboard and, by dint of his size, probably the most comfortable. Dick was no doubt checking the cruising organization and laying out initial sonar watches, and none of the three saw me. A few feet farther aft I stepped through a watertight hatch, and in a few more feet entered my tiny stateroom.

William Green, our Chief Steward, for some reason known to most of the crew as "Joe," was standing in the passageway outside my door. Gratefully, I peeled off the uncomfortable heavy garments and passed them to him.

"Dry them out well, Green, and then put them away," I said. "I won't be needing them for a while."

Chief Green, a heavy-set Negro, could upon occasion assume an artless manner calculated to elicit information. It had more than once worked pretty well, but this time I was ready for him.

"It might be cold on the bridge up there in the North Sea, Captain," he said. "Maybe I'd better just fold these up and keep them where you can get at them."

Almost, but not quite, his face assumed the expression of solicitous concern he wanted to convey.

"Get out of here, Green," I said with feigned severity, "and take that gear with you."

"Aren't we going up north, sir?" Green's carefully contrived expression—his big round eyes and innocently questioning face—were too much to hold, and he broke into a broad, white-toothed grin. "Are we going to keep heading down into the warm water, Captain?"

"Green," I said, lowering my voice to a confidential tone, "I'll tell you right where you can go in about five seconds. You're not about to get around me this time!"

Not a whit abashed, Green exited with his arms loaded, chuckling loudly. I sat at my desk and pulled a fresh sheet of paper toward me. A rather comprehensive report of our trip was going to be required of us and we might as well start.

"Dived," I wrote on the paper. "We shall not surface until May."

But then, with this bit of incriminating information in black and white before me, I carefully hid the sheet for the time being among the ever-present pile in the basket marked "incoming."

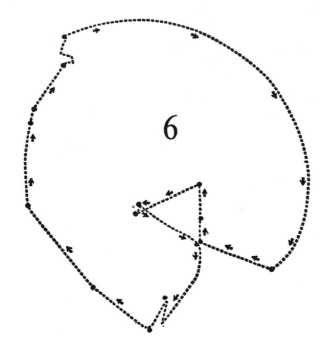

6

About 2240, traveling deep at high speed, *Triton* crossed the south boundary of the submarine operating area off Montauk Point. The last statutory restriction on our movements had been satisfied. But instead of changing course from south to east, which would have been in order had we intended only to clear Nantucket before heading into the North Atlantic, we changed half as much, to southeast. Some time would pass before the crew recognized the difference, I felt. It was logical to get well clear of the coast before squaring away on our run to the north. But the big secret could not keep very much longer, for submarine sailors are traditionally alert to their ships' movements.

We had actually started the first leg of our voyage, a 3,250-

mile run to a seldom-visited islet several hundred miles off
the Brazilian coast and nearly on the equator.

We had plotted our course to travel the length of the Atlantic Ocean twice: first, on a southerly track; and second,
on the return leg, on a northerly course. The shortest route
brought us close to South America on our way to Cape Horn;
and our return put us on a course for the bulge of Africa after
rounding the Cape of Good Hope. From there, we could head
for Spain. But following this course had a great disadvantage:
though we would two times have traveled the length of the
Atlantic, the earth would not be girdled until we closed the
gap between our nearly parallel north-south tracks—until
arrival home, in other words. Yet by a relatively slight diver-
sion, we could intersect our original track somewhere near the
equator. Completing our circumnavigation at the equator
made sense, for if our radioed instructions from Washington
for the ceremony off Spain called for us to surface the ship,
we might be forced to break our submergence record.

Operationally, there was no legitimate reason for a diver-
sion; but morale is most important in ships on long, lonely
voyages like ours. It would take us a few extra days—three as
I recall—and after urgent argument in Washington it had
been agreed that the circumnavigational part of our trip should
be completed before any ceremonies, and should have a starting and ending point which could be photographed. A suitable
spot was a tiny islet in the mid-Atlantic some fifty miles north
of the equator, marked on the chart as "St. Peter and St.
Paul's Rocks." And it was there, we decided, we would close
our loop around the earth. After that, we could surface if
necessary without giving ammunition to some technically-
minded heckler. But we hoped to go the entire route submerged anyway, as a submarine should, and we had made
preparations to photograph the "Rocks" through the periscope,
while submerged.

Before dawn on the morning of the seventeenth of February, we brought *Triton* to periscope depth for morning star sights and for ventilation. The necessity of doing this was a far greater restriction on our progress than might at first appear, for with periscopes raised the ship had to proceed at slow speed. If *Triton* were to make all the speed of which she is capable, an extended periscope would be seriously damaged, or possibly snapped off at the base, by the force of driving through the water. In addition, before coming to periscope depth, one must first listen cautiously at slow speed for surface ships in the vicinity. The entire process—slowing down, changing course to listen on various bearings and at various depths, coming up and then remaining at slow speed for a variety of purposes while at periscope depth—takes considerable time. Naturally, the time is programmed for the maximum possible use. Not much can be done with the time spent coming up, but while at periscope depth, in addition to making celestial observations, we can raise our air-induction mast and pump in a good fresh supply of air (thus preserving our precious oxygen supply); we try to pick up a news broadcast on our tape recorder for later rerun; and, since there is less resistance from pressure of the sea at shallow depths, it is easier to eject our garbage and to blow out our refuse from the sanitary tanks.

But every minute spent at reduced speed requires many times that minute to recover the distance lost. Every hour was precious, because the high "speed of advance" (SOA) required to complete the trip within the allotted time did not give even *Triton*'s fabulous power plant much leeway. One of our objectives was to determine the limiting factors of sustained high speed, and there was little doubt that the test would be pretty conclusive.

A recently developed device was being tried out this morning. One of our periscopes featured a new development of the Kollmorgen Optical Company by which the altitude of celestial bodies could be observed as accurately through a periscope as with the trusted sextant. Until recent years, submarines were navigated in the same manner as any other ship, and to get their sights they had to be on the surface. Since nonnuclear subs have to be on the surface every day for long periods anyway, either to charge their batteries or to run at the high speeds which they can't make while submerged, taking a sight presented no special problem—although I can recall several times during the war when I had to lash myself to a heaving, wet bridge and protect my sextant between sights with a sou'wester hat. The snorkel did not completely release the submarine from the surface, since air was still needed for the diesel engines, but it enabled the engines to be run at periscope depth, and this in turn focused attention upon the need for a new way of shooting stars. With the nuclear submarine's greatly increased radius of action, taking sights through a periscope became a necessity. Many special periscopes have been built for the purpose, mainly by the Kollmorgen Optical Company, and perhaps a certain Lieutenant Fred Kollmorgen's tour in the USS *Skate* has had something to do with this.

Two of the latest devices under development we did not yet have in full measure: a really effective way of generating oxygen from the sea, and a dependable means of determining position by gyroscopic instrumentation without celestial observations. Intensive effort had gone into the research and design necessary for a workable and safe oxygen generator for submarine use, and pilot models destined for the Polaris submarines were already being produced. All nuclear submarines carry stored oxygen, compressed in huge steel bottles. Having been completed too soon to have an oxygen generator, *Triton* also carried an extra supply of large "oxygen candles," similar to those used by miners in some of our country's deep pits. When ignited, these compounds of sodium, barium, and iron give off intense heat, some smoke, and lots of oxygen over and above that needed to support their own combustion. Appropriately, they must be set off in an "oxygen furnace," and lest anyone see in them an answer to some personal or industrial need for oxygen, let him be warned that they are tricky and difficult to handle safely.

As for the gyroscopic navigation system, we had a pilot model for evaluation. Called "ship inertial navigation system," or SINS, it was designed to measure earth rotation and other normally undetectable forces by means of extra-precise gyroscopes. Automatically it calculates latitude and longitude, and the results appear on dials on the face of a black box. Many a navigator, plagued by fog and bad weather, has thought of inventing such a gadget. As a midshipman at the Naval Academy, I had designed one, too, and, theoretically speaking, it might have worked. Now, many years later, similar computers are used in our ballistic missiles and two of them, "robbed" from missiles, had been placed aboard *Nautilus* and *Skate* for their polar explorations. One of our missions on this cruise was to give our SINS a thorough checkout, continually comparing its computed positions to our own best-determined fixes. When SINS is perfected, the only use a navigator will have for the stars will be for an occasional check—and to preserve one of the ancient and romantic arts of the seaman. This device will someday spell the end of that respected professional, the navigator of the open sea.

After exactly an hour of ventilating the ship, we pulled down the periscopes, shut the induction valves, and went deep again. In *Triton,* the "inboard hull ventilation valve"—our back-up in case the hydraulically operated outboard valve fails —is right outside the Captain's stateroom, and is shut on diving by the duty wardroom steward. But despite Chief Steward William ("Joe") Green's extreme brawn, he could not shut the inboard hull ventilation valve. When I came aft from the conning tower, I found him grunting and heaving, tugging with bulging muscles at the long-handled operating mechanism. Before going deep, the ship had been checked tight with hydraulic and electric outboard valves both properly shut; thus, there was never any danger of flooding, but this critically important valve could not be closed no matter how hard we tried.

Submarines always have a "backup" for everything, so that a single casualty should not, of itself, spell catastrophe; but one of the reasons why the *Squalus* sank was that when her hydraulic air valve failed to shut, two hand-operated valves in the same tremendous air pipe also could not be shut. About a third of her crew drowned in the flooded after compartments and the rest were rescued through a newly developed diving rescue chamber. *Squalus* herself remained on the bottom for months until she could be raised and salvaged. It is perhaps appropriate to note that within a few weeks of the *Squalus* incident, the British and Japanese navies suffered similar submarine disasters, and in neither of those cases were any personnel rescued.

Triton's design featured, among other things, a large, heavy steel plate in the overhead of the "officer's country"—also right outside my room—which could be removed for inspection of the induction piping. The job took several hours, and the men working on the plate were so cramped for space that they could barely swing a wrench. But the plate finally came off and we found a smashed and rusted flashlight which had lodged in the induction valve seat, its crushed case testifying to the strength in "Joe" Green's arms. Some careless workman had probably left it there months ago.

Who knows but what some other careless workman, or perhaps a survivor of *Squalus'* crew, may even today carry in his soul the secret knowledge of why a similar valve could not be shut—or unaccountably swung open again—on that dreadful day?

Shortly before noon, Will Adams sought me out, carefully closing the door behind my stateroom curtain before speaking.

"Captain, when do you plan to make the announcement about our trip?" he asked.

"Sometime tomorrow," I told him. "What's the hurry?"

"The whole crew is on edge, sir," Will said. "They know we're well clear of Nantucket. We should have headed northeast long ago, if we're really going up north. Continuing on down this way is a giveaway that something is up." Will paused. "Is there any special reason for not passing the word out now?"

"The only reason left," I said, "is that if anything were to go wrong we might still have to turn back; and I wouldn't want to come into port and have the word get out about this operation."

Will nodded. "Yes, sir," he said, "but that could happen and wreck the trip any time. The crew knows that something is up and are making up all sorts of rumors."

"There's more, too," I said. "For the time being, if we did have to go back, there would still be a chance to fix whatever is wrong and, by speeding up a little, make the trip on schedule anyway."

Will nodded, not entirely convinced that staying on schedule was a matter of so much importance. He was my right-hand man, but I couldn't tell him the one thing which I knew would change his mind.

There was a strain among all the officers, too. I felt it the moment Will and I joined them for lunch. In the wardroom, we resolutely kept the conversation away from this subject, but as the afternoon wore on I realized that regard for the feelings of our men required that they be informed earlier than I had originally intended. This being our first complete day at sea, after an extremely strenuous period of preparation, Will had scheduled no drills. Perhaps this was a mistake; it gave everyone more leisure to think about our prospects. In the meantime, our glorious ship was throwing the miles astern in joyous abandon. Shakedown cruise or no, she was on her way, and every mile made me all the more certain that here, at last, was a ship which would repay with interest all the heartbreak and unfulfilled promise of *Trigger* II.

It was about four o'clock in the afternoon, I believe, when I finally decided there was nothing to be gained by delaying the announcement any longer. It was easily done, using the ship's general announcing microphone in the control room.

Everything seemed to stop when I said, sententiously "Now hear this!"

I could sense conversation stopping, people settling themselves to listen, some of them perhaps adjusting the volume of the speakers in their compartments the better to hear. Even the muted clamor of our pumps and blowers, the whirring hundreds of small motors whose continued performance was essential to *Triton's* survival, seemed to hush—and yet they grew more distinct as surrounding noises subsided even more.

"Men," I said, "I know you've all been waiting to learn what this cruise is about and why we're still headed southeast. A number of you may have guessed before this that something special is taking place. The amount of provisions we have loaded aboard and the special preparations we've had to make have been a tip-off. I know also that you can guess why we have had to keep the real objectives of this cruise concealed until we were well on our way. Now, at last, I can tell you that we are going on the voyage which all submariners have dreamed of ever since they possessed the means of doing so. We have the ship and we have the crew. We are going to go around the world, nonstop. And we're going to do it entirely submerged!"

If someone had dropped a wrench at that moment it would have sounded like a depth charge. There was absolute silence throughout the ship. My thumb, holding down the microphone button, was aching. I shifted hands, put the microphone to my lips again.

"I know you all realize what a test this is going to be of our new ship, and of ourselves," I said. "No ship in the world, so far as I know, has ever made a voyage of such magnitude at the speed of advance which we shall have to maintain. There are many missions to accomplish. We have a regular schedule to meet. There are a lot of experiments to perform, a lot of readings to make, a lot of recordings and data to take. When we get back to the United States, we will be expected to turn in the most complete set of scientific data ever taken by a submarine." I paused again, wondered why my hands were paining me so, shifted them for the second time, and went on.

"I know I don't have to remind you of the importance that every man do his duty properly and exactly as required. I know you'll all do that, for you all realize that upon each and every one of us depends the success of this cruise. I know that no one aboard would like to be the cause of our failure.

"But the cruise goes even farther than that," I said. "For in a sense it will never end. We, in our ship, are here and now endeavoring to accomplish something of importance for the glory of our country and our Navy. From now on we will be bound together by a shared experience which will be with us the rest of our lives. Little though anyone hearing these words may appreciate it now, if we can make this cruise successfully we will carry from now on the knowledge of having recorded one of history's great voyages. Regardless of what fate has lined up for us after this, we must remain worthy. For whatever we do, now or hereafter, will reflect upon what we are here starting to do today."

I paused again, still wondering why the microphone button was so hard to hold down. Both hands were now gripping the mike, thumbs superposed upon each other and squeezing the button as though they could better convey by sheer force the sense of urgency which possessed me. My fingers were trembling slightly and I realized I was perspiring.

It seemed as though there should have been a lot more to say, but somehow this covered it. I made a couple of false starts, finally put the microphone to my lips again.

"God bless you all," I said. "My deep thanks for the work you have already done and for the additional work which I know will be performed by everyone on board. That's all."

The silence lasted nearly a minute. I could sense everyone drawing himself up, furtively eying the men nearby to see whether any of them revealed the emotions he felt. The unofficial code of the sailor requires that he remain outwardly unaffected by words of praise or blame, condemnation or exhortation. Yet I knew, deep inside, the thrill of the adventure must be stirring in their chests as it was in mine, along with fervent determination to see it through.

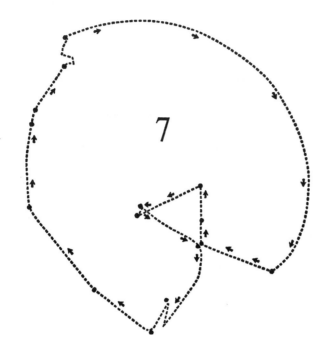

7

It was only a few hours later that my hopes for an uneventful voyage were dashed and my warning premonition of trouble fulfilled. Don Fears, face taut, brought the bad news. "I'm afraid we'll have to shut down the port engine, Captain. We have a bad leak in one of the condenser circulating pumps—"

"How much water are we making, Don?" I asked anxiously, after he had given me the details of the problem. "How long will the engine be out of commission?"

"Can't tell yet," said Don. "The leak is on a main condenser circulating water pump, and there are no valves between it and the sea except the main sea valves themselves. To fix it, we have to take sea pressure off. To do that, we have to close the main sea valves, and that shuts down the condenser. That's why we have to stop the engine."

I went back with Don to take a look. It was exactly as he had stated. Although the work was started immediately, the leak was in a very difficult place to reach; several failures were experienced, and it was early morning of the next day before we finally got a patch to hold.

In the meantime, I had become acutely aware of the great versatility of *Triton*'s dual-reactor power plant. With the port engine stopped and locked fast, we were dragging our immobile port propeller through the water like a great bronze parachute. But the starboard engine, unaffected by anything that happened to its mate, was driving away with great ease. Although the leaking pipe caused our port engine to be stopped for over five hours, when the job was done, we had virtually maintained our required speed of advance—losing only a few miles which would be easy to regain.

One of the safety features designed into nuclear ships is a warning siren which sounds piercingly in the engineering spaces when certain important electrical circuits connected with the reactors malfunction. Hardly had the leak been fixed—I seemed to have been asleep less than a minute, though it actually was a couple of hours—when I heard the siren shrieking. Within seconds the engineering messenger had sought me out—as though I needed a special call after *that* alarm! It could signify only one thing; something was wrong with one of the reactors.

"What could be the matter?" I worried. The tremendous effort in design and training which had gone into our nuclear ships had produced a record of dependability unparalleled in the history of any Navy. It was unthinkable that the very heart of one of our power plants—the reactor—should have suffered a casualty, and at the very outset of our cruise. Yet this was the significance of the alarm.

Our casualty control organization was already in action when I arrived. The procedures laid down in the instruction book were meticulously followed. The entire circuitry of the plant was rigorously checked, and we soon found the source of our trouble: a bad electrical connection in the warning circuit itself. Our precautionary moves had been well taken, but the record of reliability of our machinery plant was so far unblemished.

As we sat down for breakfast, neither Don Fears, nor I, nor any of his engineers wished to go through many nights like the previous one. And yet, with some eighty-one more days to go on our cruise, it was inevitable that this one would not be the last.

According to *Triton*'s Log, shortly after completion of the general drills on that same day a message from New London informed us that Richard W. Steeley, Engineman Third Class, had become the father of a baby girl. The message, in duplicate, was brought directly to me from the radio room, but instead of sending immediately for Steeley, I sent instead for Jim Smith, Seaman First Class. Almost every ship has a cartoonist or artist of some kind. Smith was ours. By the time Steeley arrived to get the good news, Smith was gone. One dispatch form, labeled "Mother's Copy," was duly decorated with cupids and hearts and flowers. The carbon copy, marked "Father's," had two ugly pot-bellied old men.

Steeley had evidently been on watch in the engineering spaces when the summons for him arrived, but the self-conscious grin of happy relief on his face more than made up for the smudges and perspiration which were also there. Mother and daughter, the message stated, were fine—baby's name: Bonnie Lynne.

One of the advantages of our new Kollmorgen celestial navigation periscope was the elimination of the need for a horizon. The periscope computes its own horizon; thus observations of sun, stars, or the moon can be made at any time the celestial bodies can be seen. Just after midnight, on the morning of the nineteenth of February, we had *Triton* back at periscope depth for a fix and ventilation. This fix, when computed, showed us to be short of our **PIM** (position of intended movement). In preparation for the voyage, a detailed track chart with our exact routing and the times we were supposed to pass through each point had been left with ComSubLant, so he would always know our exact position. Loss of time getting the feel of our ship, learning the techniques of getting some of the observations expected of us, and the somewhat reduced speed necessary for recent repairs had caused us to fall behind schedule. But for *Triton,* this was no serious problem. With a slight increase in power, our submarine cruiser began to tear through the water at a speed few ships could match, even on the surface. And but for the roar of steam passing through her turbines, there was no sensation of speed at all.

On this day, also, we released our first hydrographic bottle, a procedure we would carry out twice a day throughout the remainder of the trip. The United States Hydrographic Office has a standard form, available to all US merchant and naval vessels, which requests that at appropriate times the form be filled out, sealed in a bottle, and dropped over the side. The so called "bottle paper," printed in several languages, simply asks the finder to note the time and place it was found, in the blanks provided, and to forward the paper to the nearest US government authority. We could not, of course, surface to put the bottles into the water, but this turned out to be a very easy problem to solve. A standard medical bottle easily fitted into our submerged signal ejector (we had previously tested one to full submergence pressure with no apparent bad effects), and to release it we had only to shut the inner cap, equalize to sea pressure by opening a valve in an equalizer line, then open the outer cap. The bottle floated out on its own buoyancy and within a short time reached the surface.

Concern over possible premature discovery of one of these bottles, however, had prompted a certain amount of circumspection in Washington. We had been directed not to fill out the bottle papers completely and under no circumstances to put the name, *Triton,* anywhere on them. They were, as a consequence, filled out in a simple code. To assure authenticity, each was written in duplicate, with the carbon copy preserved for later transmittal to the Hydrographic Office.

Another important event of this portion of our cruise was recorded when the *Triton Eagle* began publication with a four-page issue of fifteen copies. The stated objectives of this daily newspaper were to publish news (received by the editor on our radio and transcribed directly by typewriter to the master copy), editorials (conceived by the editor and typed then and there on the master copy), jokes (thought up by the editor or possibly handed in by someone else and transcribed directly on the master copy), humorous happenings on board (related to the editor and likewise taken down verbatim), and cartoons (drawn by the originator directly on the master copy). In an attempt to be useful to all hands, the first issue contained the following sample letter home, recommended to everyone as a start:

LETTER HOME

We dove to a depth of (*classified*) and turned the ship toward (*classified*). We rang up speed for (*classified*) while the pressure on the hull was (*classified*). I went aft to check our (*classified*) and passed a civilian from (*classified*) who was riding us to check on (*classified*). About this time Dr. (*classified*) from (*classified*) asked me to step into the (*classified*) to fill out a form concerning (*classified*). Hope to see you in about (*classified*) days.

Love to you and the kids,
(*Classified*)

As in most naval ships, for fairly obvious reasons, the editor of the newspaper was a radioman; in our case, Radioman First Class Harold J. Marley, Jr. His assistant and general factotum was Audley R. Wilson, Radarman First. A third member of the staff occasionally contributed a column and rendered assistance in certain important ways, such as selection of periscope depth periods to coincide with the best news broadcasts, but refused the honor of being listed as a contributor because of his official position as Commanding Officer.

We had only been at sea a few days when a serious deficiency in the ship's ventilation system came to light. Our SINS had been installed in a compartment which used to be a provisions storeroom, and unfortunately the addition of a considerable amount of high-powered electrical equipment had not been accompanied by enough air-conditioning. As a consequence of the slowly increasing warmth of the sea on our way south, the ex-storeroom had kept creeping up in temperature. George Troffer, who as Electrical Officer had responsibility for the SINS, became increasingly concerned as the temperature increased, rose in rebellion when it reached 105° F. Something had to be done, he said, to protect the precious equipment. Specifically, some auxiliary ventilation had to be provided quickly. It wasn't the discomfort of the Electrician's Mates keeping watch on the SINS that bothered us, for our men could stand that with never a complaint. The problem was that the tubes and circuitry of the equipment were not built to withstand continual high temperatures.

Several alternative ideas were discussed, and then *Triton*'s submarine jury-riggers turned to with a will. After several hours of cutting and bending sheet metal and squeezing a collapsible duct into a confined space alongside one of our radar masts, a cool air supply was channeled into the compartment, reducing the ambient temperature in the vicinity of the SINS to 90° F.

The problem was by no means a new one to submarines, nor was the solution; and I was in the end glad it happened. Nothing is better for the crew of a ship, particularly a new ship, than to have a difficult problem to solve, and to solve it efficiently.

A day or two later, as *Triton's* mighty engines drove her deep under the ever-warming sea, trouble of another kind arose. This time it was a jammed outer door on our garbage ejector. During the war, it was customary to bag the garbage in weighted sacks and carry it to the bridge right after surfacing every night (one submarine early in 1942 did not do this, instead kept all of it on board during an entire patrol—and raised an unholy stink in Pearl Harbor when the hatches were opened upon her return). The problem created by the continuous submergence of our new submarines had been solved by a small-diameter torpedo tube, mounted vertically, with a watertight and pressure-proof closure or "door" at each end. All garbage and trash was packed into the ejection tube through the open breech door, while an interlock system made it theoretically impossible to open the outer door until the inner one was properly locked shut, and then the positions of the doors were reversed for flushing.

The garbage ejector is a large potential hazard to submarines because of the frequency with which it must be used and the fact that the men handling trash and garbage are generally the least experienced on board. It is so vitally important that at least one ejector door be kept closed at all times that these mechanisms may only be operated by a fully qualified auxiliaryman. Maloperation could result in uncontrolled flooding of the ship.

Despite our careful handling of the garbage ejection system, a problem arose; after the garbage was flushed out, the outer door could not be closed. Full sea pressure, consequently, was riding against the breech door of the ejector—a door built to close *against* sea pressure instead of *with* it. The situation was highly undesirable. No one knew how much pressure the hinge of the inner door could stand.

Fortunately, my worries were short-lived. About an hour's work by Chief Engineman Edwin Rauch, Machinist's Mate First Class Bob Carter, and Engineman Third Class John

Boreczky restored the door to normal operation. Tom Thamm, whose responsibility this was, looked a little sheepish when I asked him what had caused the trouble. This day happened to be the day the garbage ejector was supposed to be greased; so much grease had been rammed into its operating mechanism, and under such force, that a pressure lock was created and the gears had jammed.

During this portion of our trip, we began our weekly divine services. These were held every Sunday in the crew's mess hall, the only suitable compartment in the ship (where forty-six persons could be accommodated at a single sitting). The first turnout was disappointing; possibly the fact that there was no ordained minister of any faith on board reduced the appeal of the service, but we resolved, nevertheless, to keep up the practice whenever *Triton* happened to be at sea on a Sunday. Will Adams and I discussed the matter at some length, and finally decided that we should not attempt in any way to pressure our shipmates to attend. Despite our own feelings, attendance, we decided, should always remain entirely voluntary.

On any map where the contour of the bottom of the Atlantic Ocean is shown, an elongated shallow area passing through the Azores can be seen; it curves approximately in the center of the ocean as it crosses the equator and heads into the South Atlantic, where it finally disappears. This area is known to oceanographers as the Mid-Atlantic Ridge. The Azores are mountain peaks, where the Mid-Atlantic Ridge projects above the surface of the water, as are St. Peter and St. Paul's Rocks.

The Mid-Atlantic Ridge, a pressure ridge created as the earth's mass cooled millions of years ago, has never presented a hazard to mariners. Only the Azores themselves, or certain other islands, are surrounded by water shallow enough to be of any concern. Much of the Ridge, therefore is not even well charted. Deep traveling submarines are not at all like other ships, however, for they require much more depth. This was another reason for our voyage, to make a world-girdling recording of the bottom contour. One of the special devices with which *Triton* had been fitted during the hectic two weeks before she sailed was for this purpose. Outfitted with many miles of expensive, sensitized paper, the device operated from our fathometer, taking many soundings per minute and recording them graphically so as to show a virtual photograph of the shape of the bottom of the ocean over which we had just passed. It was with justice officially called the "Precision Depth Recorder (PDR)."

As is well known, the ocean is full of mountains, just as is the land, but very few of the ocean's mountains have ever been mapped. As *Triton* approached the vicinity of St. Peter and St. Paul's Rocks, we expected to notice a gradual shoaling of water, and the PDR was carefully watched.

Civil Engineer Gordon E. Wilkes was aboard to monitor the equipment. In addition, in order to obtain immediate value from anything the PDR might detect, a special watch was detailed to observe it. During the early morning of the twenty-third of February, more than twenty-four hours before we should reach St. Peter and St. Paul's Rocks, sudden and very rapid shoaling was recorded on the PDR. This was immediately brought to the attention of the Officer of the Deck by Jerry Saunders, Radarman Second Class, who at the moment was on PDR watch. We were still quite some distance from where we expected to find the Mid-Atlantic Ridge, and soundings recorded but a few moments earlier indicated a depth of roughly two thousand fathoms.

This "seamount" must have been of extremely solid structure, for it towered over the relatively flat sea bottom to a height of nearly nine thousand feet. Its sides were precipitous and its craggy form, profiled on the PDR, resembled the spires of a medieval cathedral. We slowed to creeping speed as we came up on the mount, for we had to be able to avoid it should it extend to our depth level. Slowly, we crept over the area, recording a minimum sounding of nine hundred and thirty fathoms, and then reversed course and ran over the same track. Criss-crossing, we pinpointed the peak's location and traced an outline of it from all sides.

It must be admitted that coming as it did without warning, the abrupt decrease in soundings startled me. We could not see ahead, of course, except by sonar, and until we actually had passed over it and determined the minimum distance between the top of the seamount and the surface, there was no way to guess how high the peak might actually reach. Had it reached higher, had we been traveling much deeper than we were, and had we not been keeping the careful watch that we *were* keeping, we might have struck it in the manner of an aircraft striking a mountain. The results would have been equally calamitous.

As I left the control room, with the peak safely astern and its location carefully logged, I noticed that this particular submerged mountain had already received a name.

Conforming to the tradition that the discoverer of prominent geographical features has the right to name them, Jerry Saunders had neatly inscribed "Saunders Peak" opposite its location on our track chart.

Saunders Peak will present no hazard to submarines until they travel much deeper than they are yet able to do. But, nevertheless, it had not been marked on any chart before this. We had made a new discovery.

The twenty-fourth of February was the day we expected to sight St. Peter and St. Paul's Rocks. According to navigator Will Adams, we should see the islet dead ahead on the horizon at about noon. Prior to this time we had studied every bit of lore we had on board about the Rocks, but there was very little to be learned. *Sailing Directions* described it as bare and useless, a one-time guano collecting spot, noting that there had once been a small dock, long since washed away, and that the highest rock had an abandoned lighthouse surmounting it.

We had been totally submerged for over a week, and as bad luck would have it, for the last thirty-six hours the sky had been overcast. It was consequently impossible for Will to get any sights through our new-fangled periscope. At 4:00 A.M. there was not a star in the sky, and at 0830 we went to periscope depth again in hopes of shooting the morning sun. At this time, as we rose through a temperature layer in the water, the sound of foreign propeller beats suddenly came in loud and clear. It was a striking example of how a temperature or salinity difference in the water will block the sonar return of a ship at relatively close range.

Carefully, we conned *Triton* through the evolutions necessary to come safely to periscope depth, and finally got the fragile periscope tube out of water. Our contact was a motor ship of eight thousand or ten thousand tons, with a white hull, buff stack, nice-looking clipper bow, a large deckhouse, many king posts, and apparently considerable deck machinery. She must also have been fitted to carry passengers—an easy deduction from the size of her deckhouse and the number of portholes evident. But we were much too far away to make out her nationality.

In the meantime, we had been looking for the sun in hopes of getting an observation. No luck. If there were an unexpected current or, during the last thirty-six hours, a slight error in our dead-reckoning position, it would be more than easy to skid right by this tiny island a few miles either way and never see it. My good friend Fred Janney, navigating the *Whale* during the war, once missed Midway Island in exactly this manner, and had to spend half a day, with his grumbling crew, groping about looking for the tiny atoll. (I have never let him forget the episode, and he will not be happy to read about it here.)

At 1156, Adams announced St. Peter and St. Paul's Rocks should be eleven miles dead ahead. Again we brought *Triton* to periscope depth, and at 1206 I saw a tiny white spot on the horizon bearing exactly two degrees to the left of dead ahead.

For the Rocks to show up so precisely on schedule, from dead-reckoning navigation alone, was an indication of Will's great ability.

As we approached the islet, it presented varying shapes. The white spot looked at first like the sail of a ship, then like a sun-kissed minaret, finally like a huge birdcage. At last I recognized it as the structure of the abandoned lighthouse. The upper parts of the rocks were pure white from bird droppings, and the lower levels, as we approached, were a sort of brownish-black, ceaselessly washed by the waves. The sea was relatively smooth, yet there was considerable surf breaking in and among the rocks, foaming madly like a miniature waterfall one minute, stopping abruptly the next and reversing itself. As we came closer, we could distinguish a great number of granitelike outcroppings scattered about everywhere, and there were large numbers of sea birds.

The whole scene reminded me of a photograph published after the Battle of Midway, which had shown a Japanese cruiser, the *Mikuma,* after she had received a tremendous drubbing from our carrier-based aircraft. By squinting a little and using a bit of imagination, St. Peter and St. Paul's Rocks in profile looked exactly like His Imperial Japanese Majesty's ship, *Mikuma.*

We certainly had to agree to one thing: the *Sailing Directions* description of this place was exactly right. As a matter of fact, its barrenness had been one of the arguments in favor of selecting it for the official terminus of the circumnavigation. German submarines had been in the habit of stopping at the Rocks, during World War II, to exchange mail, supplies, and munitions. For them, as for us, the Rocks were a convenient navigational reference point and also, no doubt, a concealing backdrop should a strange ship unexpectedly appear on the horizon.

We took a lot of photographs and went through a complete photographic reconnaissance drill. For three-and-a-half hours we cruised slowly about at various ranges, conforming to the bottom topography and carefully avoiding shallow spots. Everyone who wanted to do so was permitted to come to the conning tower for a look, and many crew members availed themselves of this opportunity.

Not a single engineer came forward, however, for Don Fears had taken advantage of our time at reduced speed to make some minor repairs and some low-power checks on various machinery. Mindful of our experience with the condenser, and not one to neglect a chance of this sort anyway, he used every available hand.

At a few minutes after 1600, we turned *Triton* south and headed for Cape Horn. The equator was only fifty miles away.

For the last two or three days, there had been a steady effort by the Shellbacks to exaggerate the various tortures that would be inflicted on the lowly pollywogs when we crossed the equator. Among our pollywogs, who composed most of the crew, were some apparently made of fairly stern stuff. One obnoxious character, calling himself the Little Gray Fox, attempted to foment a rebellion. He posted signs reading "Pollywogs arise" and "shellbacks take heed and surrender while you may." And King Neptune's crown, the equipment for the Royal Barbers, and the painstakingly made shillelaghs for the chastisement of the guilty pollywogs mysteriously vanished. A thorough investigation by the Shellbacks uncovered the information that their paraphernalia had disappeared permanently through the garbage ejector.

I remembered vaguely having given permission to flush the garbage disposer while we were cruising about the Rocks, and I suppose I had been an unwitting accomplice to a foul deed.

At a few minutes after eight in the evening, we hit the equator. There was a grinding jolt from somewhere forward (which sounded suspiciously like a torpedo tube full of water being fired, which, of course, I knew it was, having given the required permission to shoot it). A confused report, broken off unfinished, came over the ship's announcing system, and shortly after, I received a note that King Neptune and his Royal Court had arrived on board and desired my presence in the crew's mess hall.

Buckling on my sword and putting on my cap for the occasion, since undue informality would, of course, have been unseemly—and possibly would have resulted in even sterner measures being visited upon the unworthy pollywogs, for whom I felt the deepest sympathy indeed—I headed for the appointed place.

Neptune, when I met him, looked suspiciously like Loyd Garlock, who had crossed the line with me in the *Trigger* eight years before. The Royal Queen, half a head taller than he, with brilliant red lips, long stringy curly hair (which was not surprising since it came from a floor mop), and smoking at all times a long black cigar, might have been Torpedoman Second Class Wilmot A. Jones.

The Queen's bosom (which some of her friends seemed to think ought to be pronounced "buzzoom") looked to me like a pair of strategically slung grapefruit, but of course my imagination was probably working overtime and I knew I should resolutely put aside such unworthy thoughts. Someone considerately handed me a piece of paper containing a typed and smudged script, with the assistance of which, and with a little ad-libbing, the following colloquy ensued:

MYSELF: Unless I miss my guess, sir, you and I have had the good fortune of meeting before.

KING NEPTUNE: Many pass through my kingdom, Captain, and I never forget a face, but I'll be surfaced if I recall yours. Davy Jones, check the records on Captain Beach here to see if he really is one of my own.

DAVY JONES: Your Majesty, the records show that if you're a Shellback then so is he. [That Davy Jones is a good man, but this was a low blow on the part of Neptune.]

NEPTUNE: Ah, quite so, Davy. And now that you mention it, I recall he crossed the equator as if it were yesterday. My, he's gained a little weight here and there, hasn't he!

MYSELF: Speak for yourself, your subnormal Majesty! And now, may I have your Majesty's permission to introduce you and your royal retinue to those of my crew who have never had the displeasure?

NEPTUNE: Permission granted, Captain. And by the way, sir, would you mind standing just a bit straighter, and use a little more reverence in my grandiloquent presence?

MYSELF: A thousand pardons, your Horrific Magnificence. Men, once again it becomes my great privilege to introduce the ruler of the Mangy Mane, I mean Raging Main, Neptunus rex and the members of his Royal Family, including Her Majesty, the Queen, the Royal Babe, the Royal Scribe, the Royal Concubine, the Royal Prosecutor, the Royal Sea Lawyer, the Royal Barbers, Dentist, Baker, High Sheriffs, and their mighty company.

NEPTUNE: Thank you, Captain. It's a pleasure to be aboard your ship and see so many familiar faces again. And Captain, before I forget it, would you do what you can about those blasted propellers of yours? Kept the mermaids up all night last night.

MYSELF: I shall direct my engineer to attend to it at once, Your Majesty. I know it is hardly an excuse, but we are going pretty fast, and my engineer is a pollywog.

NEPTUNE: You can be sure that he's in my book for extraordinary torture. Now, Captain, down to business, if you please. My Royal Prosecutor reports that great crimes and incredible wickednesses have been committed by the vast majority of your crew. You know very well that we cannot tolerate such tomfoolery in this domain. Besides, my Prosecutor hasn't had a case in days and he's getting a little rusty. As you know, he's never lost a case.

MYSELF: Your Majesty, I've done my best with the trusty Shellbacks in my command, but these pollywogs are the worst of the lot, and once a pollywog, always a pollywog, until initiated into the mysteries of the deep.

NEPTUNE: Precisely why we are here, Captain. Now, as is customary, I call upon the assistance of yourself and your honorable Shellbacks in doing the duty of the great waters.

MYSELF: We are at your command, sir. But before we begin, I feel I must ask mercy for those of my crew who, unworthy characters though they be, have worked hard to make *Triton* a great ship and, through no fault of their own, come to your domain without credentials and in fear and trembling.

NEPTUNE: A standard request, Captain, and my answer is as always: "Nonsense!" In my domain, they can always be assured of a fair trial before being convicted. And now, sir, I assume command of this ship and direct that the first guilty pollywog show his unworthy carcass before my Court.

The little play here recounted did not go quite so smoothly as it might have, since no one had thought to provide extra copies of the script. King Neptune and I had to hand the solitary script back and forth so that each could read his lines.

Neptunus and his Queen then seated themselves at a long table. The clean-cut, well-combed, blindfolded accused had to kneel before them and present his plea as to the charges. He was legally assisted in his defense by the Royal Sea Lawyer, who unfortunately never won a case. Occasionally, during the trials, the Queen punctuated the learned discourse by drawing a water pistol from her ample bosom and squirting the accused in the face. This always discomfited the unhappy pollywog and caused him to assume a guilty look. The impartial dispensing of justice was thus made easier.

To the right of the Queen sat the hefty Royal Baby, whose real name was Harry Olsen. Babbling playfully between puffs on a large black cigar which he had bummed from his mother, the baby sat on a stool, with his large round belly completely bare except for a heavy coating of black, sticky grease. All pollywogs received a fair trial, were impartially convicted, and all received the maximum sentence. They were first required, in acknowledgment of their fealty, to kiss the Royal Baby's greasy belly. Then, in penance for his many crimes, each one got a haircut at the hands of the Royal Barbers, before proceeding through the initiation line. For some reason, more than one seemed reluctant to kiss Olsen's tummy and had to be assisted by a gentle shove from the Sheriff or sometimes from the Royal Defender and once or twice, it must be admitted, from their skipper.

The Royal Barbers looked an awful lot like Lieutenant Tom Thamm and Chief Engineman Alfred Abel, and the artistic jobs they did were beyond compare (since Thamm, the head Barber, was normally in charge of *Triton*'s auxiliary division, all pollywogs belonging to his own outfit came away with a large "A" cut in their heads). But aside from certain special cuts of this nature, ingenuity and esthetics were the order of the day, and many artfully sculptured pates ensued. Once in a while, to be sure, a bald pollywog came by, but this presented no particular problem. In such cases, the most effective way to improve a pollywog's appearance was to add hair instead of removing what little there was. The Barbers found this easy to do, with plenty of extra hair lying about and black grease to paste it on with.

In the next compartment, the Royal Dentist squirted unmentionable substances into the shorn pollywog's ears and awful-tasting concoctions into his mouth, accompanied all the while by an insane giggling as though the person administering the treatment were actually enjoying it instead of being engrossed in a most serious and important duty. The next stop was up a deck to the officer's wardroom, where a lusty gang of Shellbacks with brand new shillelaghs speeded the pollywogs' passage. Then, they painfully shambled aft to the Royal Bathroom, a canvas-enclosed space beneath a deck hatch, where a bucket of cold salt water cascaded down on each man in turn and ceremoniously removed the last vestiges of his erstwhile status as a pollywog.

It took some time to initiate all the new men, since there were so many of them. After a while, leaving Neptune and his Royal Party to dispense justice by themselves, I proceeded aft to see how things were faring.

The ship was a mess, all right. In some dismay, I realized it would take days to repair the mess which the fun-loving Shellbacks and pollywogs had made of our clean decks and immaculate bulkheads. But it was a price worth paying. Chief Electrician's Mate Herbert Hardman, covered with grease, minus half his hair, dripping water, expressed it. "I've waited thirteen years for this," said he. "Nobody is a real sailor until he's been across the line!"

By this standard, the luckiest man on board was John Moulton, Fireman Apprentice, only seventeen years old, who became a Shellback three months after graduation from boot camp.

During the entire initiation ceremony, the identity of the Little Gray Fox remained a secret, despite occasional attempts by the Shellbacks to elicit information by judiciously applied torture. None, however, would give him away, but I have always personally believed that it was Lieutenant George Sawyer, *Triton*'s First Lieutenant and the youngest officer on board. He also happened to be an ex-Yale crew man, who looked capable of taking care of himself in almost any kind of situation.

I missed seeing Sawyer tried, but was later informed by eyewitnesses that when asked whether he pled guilty or not guilty to the charges, he shouted, "Banzai!" at the top of his voice, drew a water pistol of his own, and before anyone could stop him, shot the King, the Queen, and the Royal Prosecutor. He was finally overwhelmed by the Prosecutor, the Attorney for the Defense, and a number of other Shellbacks, who, with a right good will, hurled themselves upon his struggling grease-plastered body.

The shillelagh-swinging Shellbacks prepared for a tough

battle when Sawyer appeared, but he scuttled between them so fast that they did more damage to themselves and the surrounding furniture than they managed to do to the thoroughly guilty Sawyer.

Finally, with all pollywogs properly initiated, King Neptune and his Royal Party announced they were cheered by the high caliber of our crew and that they had all been inducted and accepted into the august society of Trusty and Loyal Shellbacks. Promising at all times to be ready to assist his Loyal Shellbacks of the deep against pollywogs of the shallow coastal waters and especially pollywogs found on other ships, Neptune bade *Triton* farewell and returned to his watery realm.

Nowhere does it appear on the record, but the day before the ceremony, King Neptune had made a personal advance call on me to ask whether haircuts would be permitted. In 1952, when *Trigger* II crossed the line, I would not allow hair to be cut because within a few days we would be going ashore in Rio de Janeiro on liberty, and I didn't want any of *Trigger*'s sailors wandering around town with zany-looking haircuts.

But this case, I now told Garlock, was different. There would be plenty of time for the hair to grow back.

There were, indeed, some dismayed looks, as the new Shellbacks regarded themselves in a mirror after the ceremonies, but all were assured that their hair would regrow by the time we got back to port. And, as a matter of fact, hard though it was to believe at the time, that is what happened.

It was a mighty funny ship's company that carried *Triton* down the eastern coast of South America toward Cape Horn. Some men cut all their hair off; to give it all an even start, as one ex-pollywog expressed it. Others tried by one stratagem or another to make their heads look halfway decent, or at least symmetrical, but most simply didn't bother, letting them stay the way they'd been trimmed by the Royal Barbers.

One noticeable thing was that the two Barbers cut each other's hair some time during the ceremony, apparently to forestall any possible attempt by pollywogs to seek revenge; and at least one Shellback took to wearing a sou'wester cap, strings tied snugly under his chin, whenever he went to sleep. His theory, he explained, was that while awake he was pretty sure he could defend himself; and before anyone could get the sou'wester off his head, he would be pretty sure of being awake.

Shortly after midnight of this day I turned in; the first leg of our trip was completed and the second one fairly started. We had had our share of ups and downs during these first days, and I wondered what the next leg would bring. Our course was now to the southwest, and in another week we would be at Cape Horn.

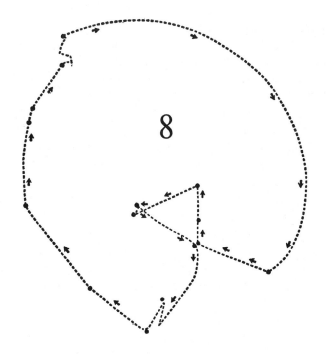

8

We had calculated that it would take us about seven days to make the long run down the east coast of South America to Cape Horn. It was technically the first leg of our circumnavigation, and I was glad that our first landfall and the horseplay at the equator were behind us. Now we could settle down and organize the ship for the long run. If all went as we hoped, we would see St. Peter and St. Paul's Rocks again on the twenty-fifth of April.

Various projects were already under way. Dr. Ben Weybrew, a psychologist from the Navy Medical Research Laboratory in New London, had issued a series of questionnaires to various volunteers from the crew. They were to mark them at different times during each day and turn them in daily. The Doctor's project was to record such prosaic things as sleeping hours; smoking and coffee-drinking habits; general feelings and moods, such as laziness or energy, depression or euphoria; how much food a man consumed and whether his eating habits changed during the cruise; his reading habits; how often he thought of his family; and other related matters. His questions seemed a bit strange to a number of us and when I asked about them, he explained that they were, in fact, derived from diaries kept by the men on *Nautilus* and *Seawolf*, who had carried out similar investigations during their long trips. Our data would add to the information thus amassed regarding the psychological effects of long cruises. The basic information would be valuable not only for future submarine operations, but for space travel as well.

My off-hand comment that there would be plenty of time for the hair to grow back had apparently reached a large audience. The short bristles standing on stark white skin where there had been a handsome head of hair were a constant reminder that we still had a long way to go.

One thing was already very evident: all hands were just beginning to realize how long a trip ours was to be. The crossing-the-line ceremony and the abandon with which hair had been cut brought our isolation home to all of us.

For a while, I was worried by the conduct of our high jinks the day before. Three of our pollywogs had refused to participate in the ceremonies. Even our technical and scientific personnel had accepted the full treatment, including Joe Roberts, who had been across the equator four times but never "officially," as he put it.

In hopes the three holdouts would change their minds, I had refused to allow them to be dragged into the initiation. Later on, it was evident that I had missed my chance, if there had ever been one, to avert bad feeling—something we could not tolerate with a long cruise still before us.

For several days the matter preyed upon my mind, for it became apparent that some animosity was growing. Could this be the beginning of a breakdown in the spirit of togetherness, which as a crew we must have for maximum efficiency, if not for an harmonious life aboard ship? Had I acted wisely in permitting our three holdouts to get away with their defiance? Might it not have been wiser to have haled them forth at the first sign of rebellion and have it over with, hopefully as a big joke—or would other things gradually occupy us and the whole affair blow over?

The matter was discussed privately with Ben Weybrew and Will Adams. There was considerable resentment of the three among the rest of the crew, Shellbacks all. If we were to give the holdouts credit for crossing the line, which they certainly had done even though not officially received by King Neptune and his Court, there would undoubtedly be even more resentment. If we held a special ceremony for them the next time we crossed the line—during the voyage there would be three more crossings—the best I could hope for was to minimize any possible outburst of vindictiveness by instant repression; active rancor was almost a sure bet, and during this sort of situation there is always a measurable loss of control.

Perhaps I felt the risk of trouble more than was necessary, but at any rate, all moves to give the three a special initiation were vetoed. In the end, we merely placed an official entry, carefully worded, in the records of everyone else, stating that they had crossed the line on such and such a date and had been received by Neptunus, rex, and his Court. Pollywogs were converted officially into Shellbacks, and Shellbacks were re-affirmed as such. No entry of any kind was made for the three holdouts. They would have to find another ship going across the line should they change their minds at a later date. Though we were to cross the equator thrice more, I decreed, there would be no further visits from King Neptune.

Along with everything else, this was the *Triton*'s shakedown cruise, and so a daily schedule of drills and exercises was laid out. In addition, a number of extracurricular activities blossomed. The ship's newspaper had become one of our primary sources of daily interest. Once a week we held our religious services. Courses in Spanish, mathematics, history, and civics were begun, with instructors, textbooks, and scheduled classes. The *"Triton* Lecture Association" was formed, created by Lieutenant R. P. (Pat) McDonald with the provident thought that after we returned from our cruise, there might be numerous requests for members of the ship's company to lecture before various audiences. A little practice in advance, Pat suggested, would be useful.

There were indeed many separate and diverse activities going on. Some of us brought along books we had been planning to read or correspondence courses which, in many cases, were a prerequisite to advancement in rank, or rating. I found room in my cabin for the entire six-volume *Story of Civilization* by Will Durant, Samuel Eliot Morison's biographies of Columbus and John Paul Jones, Admiral Mahan's *The Life of Nelson* in two old volumes and Dr. Charles McKew Parr's carefully researched life of Ferdinand Magellan, *So Noble a Captain.*

All in all, there was plenty to occupy everybody as we proceeded on the first leg of our "official" circumnavigation.

As it happened, the run down the coast of South America started out smoothly enough, but it didn't end that way. On the first of March, 1960, Jim Stark, a Commander in the Medical Corps, USN, and our ship's doctor, sought me out.

"Captain," he said rather abruptly, looking serious, "I'm afraid we have a pretty sick man aboard."

This, of all things, was what I had been dreading most. "Who is it?" I asked. "What's the matter with him?"

"It's Poole," said Jim, "Chief Radarman. I'm afraid he might have a kidney stone."

My tone of voice must have indicated relief that it wasn't something highly contagious like smallpox or meningitis. "Oh," I said. "He's not really sick then, is he?"

Stark grinned wryly. "It's not infectious, Captain, if that's what you mean, but he's a pretty sick boy, all right. The trouble is there's nothing I can do about it."

"You mean you can't treat him on board?" I asked, feeling the glimmerings of worry again.

Jim nodded. "He's not sick in the sense of having a germ or a bug of some kind, but if you take a look at him, you'll agree that if he doesn't improve, we do have a problem. You need special tools for this, and we don't have any of them. This is a job for a hospital."

Stark produced a thick medical book with photographs and drawings to illustrate Poole's problem. A stone had formed in one of Poole's kidneys, had been dislodged, and was now in a ureter tube where it was damming the normal flow. The specified treatment was rather similar to what one might do with a clogged drain line on board ship, but as Jim patiently explained the techniques of doing it and described the delicate equipment which we did not have—which included an X-ray outfit—I began to understand his concern.

"Suppose the kidney stone remains stuck in the tube," I said. "What happens then?"

"Well," replied Jim, "in the first place, it's terribly painful —and that's what's happening to Poole now. That's why I've had to give him sedation. If there's no relief—in extreme cases —there can be mild or serious damage of the kidney, which could result in a permanent injury. In an extreme case," he said soberly, "if unrelieved, a person could die."

"You mean he's in danger?"

Jim hastened to assure me that this was not so. The treatment Poole was receiving at his hands was the standard treatment in the early stages of a kidney stone ailment. In most cases, the trouble cleared up more or less spontaneously, with the stone passing the rest of the way down the tube and out of the body in the urine. Poole was already using a specimen bottle, he explained, and his urine would be carefully examined.

"I'm giving him morphine to ease the pain," Jim said, as he rose to leave. "All we can do is wait."

I sat pondering. Prior to leaving New London, I had been briefed on the general locations of all US naval units in the areas near which we might be passing, and I knew that the *Macon*, a cruiser built at the end of the war, was somewhere in these waters. Maybe we could effect a rendezvous with her. But even if we were to do so, how could we transfer Poole without surfacing—and if we were to surface, would this not ruin our submerged record? Suppose we were to surface, transfer Poole to the *Macon*, and keep it a secret. Would our submerged record still be valid? Suppose the press discovered it; suppose—after the cruise was announced publicly—the newspapers of the Soviet bloc were to get hold of the item? Would it not be terribly embarrassing to our country? What about the special purpose of our mission? Would this not, in fact, utterly destroy it?

To this last question, at least, I knew the answer as soon as I formulated it. As for the rest, going around the world submerged was naturally tremendously important to us as a morale factor. No doubt it held real value for our Navy and our country, particularly in view of the Russian successes with their Sputniks. But so far as the fundamental purposes of our voyage were concerned—the research to be made, the data to be collected—surfacing for an hour or so would make no difference at all. But we could not under any circumstances pretend to an accomplishment we had not done.

And I knew, or sensed, another thing, which was simply that either Poole passed the kidney stone and recovered, or we would have to get help for him somehow, somewhere. Were this war, were our mission one of life or death, were the ship to be endangered with the possibility of more lives lost if we exposed ourselves in order to help Poole, then there might conceivably be some excuse for gritting our teeth and making him grit his. But not under the circumstances that existed.

Jim Stark, however, had made it clear that the situation was not yet desperate. We could hang on a while longer and await developments.

I had just about reached this point in my reasoning when there came a rap on my door, and Dick Harris pulled aside the curtain. He, like Stark, wore a troubled look.

"What's on your mind, Dick?" I asked. "Have you a kidney stone in your sonar?"

Dick's face twisted. "Something like that perhaps, Captain," he said. "It's the fathometer."

Constitutionally, I needed much less background information to become excited about a sick fathometer than about a sick kidney, and I was intensely concerned. "What's the trouble, Dick?" I asked.

As he answered, Dick characteristically chose his words carefully. "We've been slowly losing sensitivity with the fathometer," he said, "and I've started checking into it. The strength of the echo is becoming noticeably weaker. I worked on it for a couple of hours last night, but it is still weaker than it should be, even though we seemed to have been able to make some improvement in it. We're getting only a faint echo, and it could go completely out of commission at any time."

"Where do you think the trouble is?" I asked. "Is it in the transmitter head, do you think, or the transmitting or receiving section of the set itself?"

"Dunno yet, Captain," he said. "As far as we can tell, the outgoing signal is about the same strength as ever, but the return signal seems to be weaker. Maybe we'll find something wrong with the receiver section, and if we can get the right parts, we should have it back in commission soon."

"Keep me advised, Dick," I said. "The fathometer is a

mighty important instrument for this cruise, especially since we are passing over waters that are basically uncharted."

Dick tried another twisted half-grin. "I know that, sir," he said. " 'Whitey' Rubb is in there helping us with his electronic technicians. Maybe that will speed up the process of figuring out what's wrong with it."

After Dick left, I sat for a long moment. Now there were two problems to ponder. Shallow water areas near most of the big land masses of the world are well charted these days, and a surface ship has generally little difficulty picking its way along an unfamiliar coast as long as it has the right chart. But nobody had ever gone to much trouble to make accurate charts of deep waters, the so-called "off-soundings" areas, which comprise ninety-nine percent of the oceans. Our unsuspected discovery of a new and previously uncharted mountain peak as we neared St. Peter and St. Paul's Rocks a few days ago was a case in point. The chart of the South American coast showed a number of very shallow spots—just dots on the charts—where evidently some submerged mountain peaks had been discovered more or less by accident as ships passed overhead. Surface vessels had been passing over these peaks in perfect safety for centuries, their existence entirely unsuspected. But our situation in *Triton* was very much different, for we were traveling many hundreds of feet deeper than a surface ship. At the speed we had to go, our ship would be heavily damaged by even a glancing contact with the bottom, and I didn't even want to think of the result of striking the vertical face of a cliff like the one we had found a week ago. Traveling in uncharted waters, the fathometer was absolutely vital to us.

Fortunately, an immediate decision on this, too, could be postponed for a little while. At the moment, *Triton* was proceeding over a particularly deep section of the South Atlantic, and for some hours the fathometer had been showing a relatively flat, level bottom. There would be small chance of sudden peaks, since the topography of the bottom indicated that the granite substructure required for such peaks was most likely not present. In a couple of days, however, we would pass into more shallow areas. There, the structure of the earth could very likely be composed of stone outcroppings of one sort or another, and we would need that fathometer desperately.

In the control room, Chief Sonarman George McDaniel, assisted by Sonarmen First Class Beckhaus and Kenneth ("Shorty") Remillard, had already removed the cover from the fathometer console, and they were taking electrical measurements of the electronic equipment inside. The space where they had to work also happened to be the Diving Officer's watch station. And Lieutenant George Sawyer, whose watch this was, appeared to be having a little difficulty staying out of their way.

One deck below and one compartment aft, in the air-control center, where the data supplied by *Triton*'s radars is plotted and evaluated, Electronics Technicians Gordon Simpson and Martin Docker were huddled with their division officer, Lieutenant Milton R. ("Whitey") Rubb, over the manufacturer's instruction book for the fathometer.

It was apparent that all these men, at least, fully shared my appreciation that our fathometer needed to be put back in commission quickly.

In the crew's berthing compartment, just forward of the control room, I came upon Poole. In spite of Jim Stark's warning, I was unprepared for what I saw, and was instantly shocked into concern.

Eyes half-closed, face swollen, Poole had risen to his forearms and knees and was quivering with obviously excruciating pains.

It so happened that he had one of the higher bunks in the ship, normally reached by a portable aluminum ladder. The ladder had been placed against the side of his bunk, and

First Class Hospitalman Richard Fickel stood upon it in such a manner that if Poole, in one of his uncontrolled movements, were to fall out of his bunk, Fickel would be in a position to catch him or at least restrain him and break his fall.

One or two off-watch personnel, who occupied the same bunking area as Poole, looked uncomfortably at me. The message in their eyes was unmistakable, though they knew that everything possible was being done for him. "Can't we do *something* to make it easier for him?" they appeared to ask. One thing I did know—though this did not seem the appropriate time to mention it—Jim Stark had explained that despite his painful writhings and muffled groans, Poole was in fact not fully conscious. Later on, he would remember nothing at all about his sufferings. The morphine would take care of that.

Abruptly, I turned about and went back to the wardroom. There, ignoring the troubled gaze of two or three of the ship's officers, I silently drew a cup of black coffee and retired to my stateroom. There were a number of things I needed to think out.

Taking the easier one first—casualties to fathometers were rare. I had never heard of one going out of commission before. Fathometers are, after all, not extremely complicated pieces of equipment, and the Navy has been using them for many years. By this time, surely, they should have been perfected, made proof against all the ordinary hazards of shipboard service. Perhaps there was something about ours that was improperly hooked up, perhaps some part in this particular fathometer was a little extra fragile—just enough to cause the trouble. In that case, we'd find it. But the worrisome thing was Dick's report that the fathometer head was slowly losing sensitivity. Was anything actually happening in the fathometer head? If this were so, there would be nothing we could do about it.

The fathometer lay up in the bows of the ship, adjacent to the keel; the only way it could be reached was by dry-docking the entire ship. In earlier submarines, perhaps with this very casualty in mind, the fathometer had been located in the forward trim tank, where it was accessible. Would that this were true in *Triton!* Without a fathometer, the hazards of our trip would be infinitely increased. What to do if it proved impossible to repair?

One thing seemed to be clear. The importance of our voyage, the responsibility which the Navy had placed on us to complete it—for its stated and unstated purposes—justified every reasonable effort to continue. Serious though the loss of the fathometer might be, if this were our only debility, we could and would keep on. Will Adams, I knew, could be depended on to take all reasonable and possible precautions to compensate for the lack of this vitally important navigation aid.

Poole's problem was considerably more difficult, and I had much less experience to guide me. Jim Stark's medical book detailed the treatment for a kidney stone, which involves an extremely complicated operation, and I found myself reading the book quite carefully in order to understand the problem. I read and reread the description of what would happen in the event proper treatment could not be given. As Stark had already said, there would be a backing up of the normal flow; swelling of the tiny ureter tubes; dreadful pain, less and less controllable by opiates; serious illness, possibly involving both kidneys; ultimately, permanent injury to the kidneys; possibly death.

Unlike most complaints, however, kidney stones can suddenly and dramatically cease to be troublesome. If Poole passed the stone, and there were no others, he might well make a complete recovery in a few hours. This, Jim had assured me, was the normal experience. Or, should the stone not pass, it might not create a complete blockage. If this were the case, Poole might become a sort of arrested case which could be "held"—Jim's expression—under careful surveillance until our return home.

A third possibility was that there was not one but a number of stones, any one of which could hang up in an already irritated and inflamed urinary passage. A "remission" could occur, after which Poole might well experience more attacks. There was no possible way, short of X-raying him, to find this out.

Fourth was the possibility that a complete and permanent blockage had already occurred; that Poole was fated to become progressively worse until he received proper medical attention.

With a sigh, I recognized that this problem was entirely out of our hands. It was a question of whether Poole got better or worse.

But suppose Poole recovered for a day or two, or even for weeks, and then had another attack? Suppose by then we were well out into the Pacific? What would we do then? Where could we take him, how get him the medical help he needed? On the other side of South America there was Chile, with its lovely port city of Valparaiso, where surely there was competent medical care to be found. Farther along our route— many thousands of miles farther—lay Pearl Harbor in the Hawaiian Islands. Here, we would be among friends and be able to get all the assistance necessary.

But either Valparaiso or Pearl Harbor would be well out of our way, far enough to cost us many days of travel.

In the meantime, we were passing two of the largest cities in South America, Montevideo and Buenos Aires, both bordering on that enormous Rio de la Plata which Magellan had first joyously assumed to be the long-sought south passage to the Pacific. Entering Montevideo, Buenos Aires, or Valparaiso would all be about one and the same, so far as the effect on our intended submerged circumnavigation. But the USS *Macon* was scheduled to visit Montevideo in a few days. This was an important consideration. On this side of South America, help from the US Navy could best be received from the *Macon*. On the far side, we would have to wait to reach Pearl Harbor, a matter of about three weeks.

It would be unfortunate to be forced to surface and wreck our submerged record, but doing so to enter a foreign port was not to be thought of, unless there were no other alternative. Here was a dilemma!

Fortunately for my peace of mind at that moment, *Macon* was not due to arrive at Montevideo for a few more days. Besides, Jim Stark had impressed upon me that Poole's condition, although serious, was still promising. The stone or stones might clear up at any time. We could afford to let events move along at their own speed for a little while longer.

Feeling depressed, I decided that the first of March was certainly not "our day," and that troubles came in twos. The only cheery note was that both of our problems had a common quality: we could allow them to develop a little farther.

This was a far from satisfactory way to handle either, but it did have the virtue of postponing the real decision.

I think it was about seven o'clock that same night when Jim Stark and Don Fears came to see me together. I immediately sensed that something else was wrong.

Stark spoke first. "You'll be glad to know that Poole has been asymptomatic for some time now, sir. The morphine is wearing off and he's up and around. Apparently, he's in no pain."

"Good," I said. "Have you found the stone?"

"No, but that's not surprising. Sometimes these things are very hard to find." Jim's report came in a rush, as though he were anxious to get it over with.

"Well," I said, unable to shake off the foreboding in my subconscious, "that's good. What's the new problem?"

Don deliberately shut the metal door behind the curtained entrance to my room, then, very quietly, informed me that something might be seriously wrong with one of our reac-

tors. So far as *Triton* and the first of March were concerned, it seemed that troubles were not to be confined to
pairs. On that day we were to have them in threes.

Naval reactors, let it be understood, are constructed and
inspected with the most extraordinary care. Very precise operating instructions are prepared before anyone is permitted to
use them, and the most careful training is given all hands. The
remarkable record of dependability which Admiral Rickover's
fantastic new machinery has established is only one of that
gentleman's great gifts to the Navy and our country.

Among the operating instructions are a carefully calculated
set of allowed operating parameters. Should any of these
parameters be exceeded, there are in addition precise instructions as to what is to be done next. In some cases, all that is
necessary is to change certain operating criteria. In others,
we are required to shut the reactor down to find out what is
wrong and are not permitted to start it again until the difficulty is resolved. In still other situations, there are automatic
safety circuits which, when triggered, instantaneously shut
the reactor down without further action by any person. This
is called a "scram." It is accompanied by a deafening siren and
all sorts of whirring, grinding, and pumping of automatic machinery.

The trouble in our case came under the second heading.
Les Kelly had instituted a system to log all the readings on
the instruments in the machinery spaces periodically, and then
the readings were carefully compared to detect changes. Several of the ship's officers willingly participated in this check,
and it so happened that Jim Stark, in poring over the batch
of forms consigned to him, had noticed a slow but steady
change in certain entries.

"So, what do you think it is?" I asked.

Jim and Don both started to talk at once.

"Don," I said.

"Well, I can't be sure, Captain," said Don. "But here's

what the book says about it." He showed me one of the manuals, his finger marking the place.

I read the paragraph carefully. It applied specifically to our situation, described what we were then experiencing, and stated in clear language the several possible causes. Two of the possibilities we could immediately dismiss. Two others, after some discussion, we were satisfied did not apply. But one, very clearly, applied only too well.

My stateroom was barely big enough for the three of us, and our impromptu conference became a rather packed affair when Pat McDonald unceremoniously opened the door and entered. I slid over on the padded bench beneath my folded-up bunk and motioned Stark to sit beside me.

Pat had a slip of paper in his hand. "Here's a new set of readings, Don," he said.

I reached for the paper and held it for both Fears and Stark to see. The new figures were not encouraging.

"Well, Pat," I said. "It's your reactor. What do you think?"

"We're still in limits, Captain," Pat replied, "but I don't like the way this is moving. Of course, it could be . . ." Here Pat described an innocuous possible explanation which had occurred to all of us—"but all we can do is keep on checking."

"Who's checking?" I inquired. "You're all in here with me."

"We're all into it, Captain," Don said. "All our reactor technicians, all the officers. Everybody."

"What do you think?"

"Well," Don answered reluctantly, "we either have a problem or we don't. If we do, it's a lulu. We'll know for sure in another couple of hours. We're checking everything, naturally, and I should be able to tell you more pretty soon."

"All right," I said, trying to show an assurance I did not feel, "get with it. I don't want to alarm the troops about this and take their morale down any further, unless we can't help it. Anyway, it's not as though there were any danger to personnel. I'll not come back with you right now, but I'll join you about the time you have another set of data readings."

"Right, Captain," Fears said, as he and Pat rose to leave. "If we go over limits, shall I shut down?"

"Of course. And when you do, say a blessing for Admiral Rickover and the few farsighted officers in the Pentagon who insisted on the development of a multiple reactor plant."

Jim Stark made a move to follow the two engineers.

"Don't, Jim," I said. "One of your duties is radiological safety, you know, and having you be the one who spotted this in the first place is bad enough. If you continue to show interest, the men will think there's a radiation hazard of some kind. We've got enough problems."

Stark nodded. "You're right," he said. "Anyway, I've got Poole to worry about. Should check him right now, as a matter of fact."

It took real will power not to go back into the engineering spaces myself right then, and I knew I shouldn't be able to wait it out very much longer. Kidney stones, a fathometer that wouldn't work, and now this—all in a single day! If anything could force us to give up our voyage, this latest difficulty would come closest.

The trouble was, so far, localized in the mechanism of a single reactor, and there was no reason to expect it to appear in the other. Catalogued as an improbable possibility by our manual, this had never happened before in any naval reactor. Could there have been a design error, a weakness undetected in all the testing, something which had at last slipped by Admiral Rickover's vigilant group? Ergo, might we expect the same problem in the other reactor?

Triton was fortunate in having two. Indeed, it was precisely for this kind of contingency that Rickover had insisted on building her. The Admiral also wanted to amass the practical experience of operating such power plants, which might be installed in future surface ships and later-model submarines.

The casualty facing us would have immobilized any other submarine, forced her to surface and radio for help. In our case, it only threatened to slow us down. We could still keep on with our mission, unless, by sad mischance, the investigation now going on would show both reactors to be involved.

But time spent in fruitless worry could do no good. Restlessly, I began to wander about the ship.

Almost the first person I ran into was Poole, up and fully dressed, his head buried in the innards of one of the radar receiving sets in *Triton*'s air-control center.

"How are you feeling?" I asked.

"Fine, Captain," he replied, "I feel swell. I think it's all over now."

I didn't recall Poole as being a particularly placid individual, and something about his bearing, perhaps his half-shut, sleepy eyes, seemed not exactly normal. I found Jim Stark in the ship's pharmacy and put the question to him.

"What you're seeing, Captain, is the after-effects of the dope he's been given during the last twenty-four hours," said Jim.

"You mean he's still hopped up? He looked just the opposite," I said.

"No, what I mean is that the effects of the medication haven't worn off yet. That's why he seemed a bit strange. He's not himself at all. But he feels fine, and maybe he'll be free of the kidney stone attacks from now on. We can only wait and see."

"Then what's he doing up and working?" I said.

Jim grinned. "Well, Captain, I'm not very far away from him, and don't plan to be." Jim indicated a little tray containing a hypodermic needle and several small bottles. "All this stuff here is Poole's."

"Good man, Jim," I nodded approvingly. "But why is he working? We don't need him that badly, do we? Is it because

all the other radar technicians are out working on the fathometer?"

"Nobody has put Poole to work, but he wants to. As long
as he wants to be up and working and doesn't overdo it, it's
the best thing for him. That's why I'm sticking around."

I nodded again. "I get it."

As I left the pharmacy, I glanced into the air-control center
once more. All I could see of Poole was a rear view. His head
and forearms were deep inside the radar console in quest of
some stray electron or grid voltage somewhere.

In the control room, I found that what had been the passageway was now a blueprint reading room. A long, blue-
printed diagram of the sonar equipment had been laid out on
the passageway deck, and grouped around it on their hands
and knees were Lieutenants Rubb and Harris and Electronics
Technicians Docker and Simpson. Had the blueprint been a
green-felt cloth, I might almost have expected to hear the
rattling of dice and low-voiced incantations soliciting the
favor of Dame Fortune.

Despite their ridiculous posture, however, these four gentle-
men were in dead earnest. Both ends of the compartment were
marked, "No Passageway—Men Working." Crew members
needing to go from one end of the ship to the other were
required to drop down a deck and pass through the crew's mess
hall immediately beneath the control room.

Jim Hay now had the dive, and he had crowded as close
as possible to the planesmen in order to leave room for Beckhaus and McDaniel, who were apparently taking readings on
the fathometer cabinet itself.

One of the unwritten rules in the submarine service is that
men engaged in important work do not throw down their tools
and snap to attention merely because the Commanding Officer
happens around. Only Dick Harris rose to greet me.

"We've found out a couple of things, Captain," he said,

"and there may be more than one thing wrong with the fathometer."

I nodded. This was about what I had expected.

"One thing is that the gear is running too hot. There's a ventilation motor in it which is supposed to be running at all times, but it was hooked up wrong and apparently hasn't been working. So there's a transformer burned out and at least one, maybe two, crystals are gone. But I still can't explain the reduced sensitivity in the fathometer head itself. That's what has me worried."

This was, of course, disturbing news; but compared to what was perhaps going on in the after part of the ship, where Don Fears and his engineers were wrestling with their problem, it was not the worst I had heard this day.

"Keep me informed, Dick," I said. "Maybe we can at least keep the sound head from getting any worse."

Dick nodded as I left, probably both relieved and surprised that I had not questioned him further. A glance at Jim Hay's diving crew and the instruments before them showed me that *Triton* was rock steady at the ordered depth and still at ordered speed. Here, at least, things were under control.

Of all the urgent things on my mind at this moment, the condition of the engineering plant was the most critical. I could stay away from it no longer.

I can recall a feeling of resolution as I walked swiftly toward the engineering spaces; this was what *Triton* was built for. Even though we had to shut down one plant—even though we might have to keep it shut down for the entire remainder of our cruise—there was no reason why the other should have the same bad luck. We could and would carry on. This was the traditional Navy way, and it was, I knew, what Admiral Rickover would have had us do, was in principle what he had himself directed when the prototype of USS *Nautilus,* out on the flats of Idaho, had made that famous full-power simulated run across the Atlantic Ocean.

When I joined the engineer group, I could see that the news was not good. Don handed me the sheet of paper on which the latest readings had been logged. They were similar to the ones I had seen earlier, but higher.

"We can't figure it out, Captain," he said. "This just doesn't add up, but here they are!"

"Were they taken by the same person?" I asked.

Don shook his head. "I thought of that, too," he said. "These are an independent set taken by another man."

Gloom deepened. Everyone fully understood the implications of the situation.

"What do you recommend, Don?" I said, knowing what it must be.

Don looked back squarely. "We've gone over every reading, every bit of the instructions, and all the prints. We're logging another set of readings right now with a third man taking them. I would have taken them myself, but I wanted to stay here to check over what we've already got. We'll just have to keep checking until we're sure, until we know exactly what's happened. We haven't hit the limit yet."

The whirring of the main turbine and the great throb of the reduction gears sounded as though nothing could ever disturb them. But this was not so. A minor dislocation somewhere else, in some important control circuit perhaps, down in the reactor space where we could not get to it, could still them at any time.

My face must have mirrored the gravity of my thoughts. A bell tingled. The telephone. Someone answered it, listened briefly, handed it to me.

"It's for you, sir."

The caller was Harris, with good news.

"We've found the trouble with the fathometer, Captain, and I think we have the right parts on board. We'll have her going again in a couple of hours."

This was, at least, a weight off my mind. We would be

approaching shoal water shortly, and would need this piece of equipment.

"Good, Dick," I said. "Tell your people that was a fine job, and I'm very much relieved and grateful."

"Will do, Captain," Dick said, sounding pleased.

I hung up. "Well," I said, "that's one problem solved. The fathometer's OK, anyway."

But our somber mood could not be lifted for long. *Triton*'s machinery was too well designed, her research engineers and builders too careful for anything to go wrong. And yet, the evidence could not be denied. Instinctively, I realized, we were all waiting for the check observations, even then in the process of being taken. But we all knew what the results must be.

The watertight door at the far end of the compartment opened and Pat McDonald entered. Immediately following him were Jack Judd and Harry Hampson, both Chief Electronics Technicians. Pat walked directly to Don Fears and handed him a slip of paper. "I took the readings myself this time, Don, just to be sure."

Don scrutinized the figures, pursed his lips, silently handed the paper to me.

The readings had reached the allowed limits.

"Shut her down, Don," I said. "As she cools off, get everybody back there and start making a thorough check as soon as you can get into the space. We have to get to the bottom of this immediately."

Fears excused himself. In a few moments, the mighty beat of *Triton*'s huge propellers slowed.

The atmosphere of quiet gloom could be felt, as it settled over the ship. I could sense it in everyone's attitude, in the subdued manner in which people went about their duties, in the care each man took that nothing he said or did would make matters worse.

Don came back in a moment, sober-faced. "Well, it's done, but I still can't believe it," he said. "Let's start over again at the beginning." He pulled a sheaf of papers toward him. "The first sign of anything was when Jim Stark started to notice a steady climb in certain readings . . ."

We all looked on as Don went through the entire episode.

"An hour later," he said, glancing at me, "we notified the Captain. "Then we went over everything again . . ."

Step by step, feeling our way, we reviewed the events of the past two hours. The strenuous training all of us had received during *Triton's* precommissioning period was never more valuable than now, as we tortuously reworked the data.

Finally, Don struck the paper lightly with his index finger. "Here's the crucial item, right here," he said.

"That's what it read, all right," said Pat.

"Something wrong here," Don muttered. "Your last reading is one-tenth of what they had the time before."

McDonald compared the two sheets of paper, side by side. "I know mine was the right reading," he said, "I read it off the dial myself. The decimal point is tricky, but this is correct."

Hope suddenly flooded through my mind. The matter was more complicated than a simple misplacement of a decimal point. The readings we were required to take and record were sometimes to the millionth or ten-millionth of a gram or an ampere. A mistake in conversion was understandable.

"If this is right, Don," I said, "we don't have any problem at all. Could the readings have changed that much in this short time?"

Don and Pat shook their heads.

"Judd, who took these first two sets of readings?" Fears suddenly asked.

Judd told him the names. "They're both good men, sir," he said. "They know what they're doing."

"Well, what about this one, then?"

Hampson shook his head. "We saw Mr. McDonald take these readings, sir," he said. "I know they're right!"

"Let's see the calculations again," said Don.

They were put before him in a moment. Silently, we watched while Don compared one set of log readings to another and checked the three sets of calculated results. Pat McDonald did the same, alongside him and sharing his slide rule. I scratched them out too, on a third piece of paper.

After long minutes, Don looked up. "It looks as though we made a mistake, Captain," he said. "The first two sets of readings were written down in a slightly different way from Pat's here, but they made a mistake in working them out. Look, here it is."

I guarded myself from being overeager to accept this sudden release. "This is too easy, Don," I said. "You mean, while I've been standing here, after we've gone through all this flap, now you say there never was any problem?"

Don nodded. "Let me go through this whole thing once more very carefully, Captain," he said. "It looks as though we have a couple of problems to straighten out, and I'll be up making a report to you within the hour."

"Very well," I said, not knowing whether to be angry or relieved. "Have a fourth set of readings taken—you and Pat had better do these yourselves—I need to know exactly where we stand."

Both nodded soberly.

"You may not have permission to start the reactor," I told them, "until you report to me that you're absolutely sure it's all right and always has been."

With a considerably lighter step, I made my way forward once more. We would be absolutely sure of the plant before starting it again, for the instructions were explicit, but it now seemed morally certain that our five hours of concern had been merely a mental exercise. I could feel my confidence in *Triton* resurging. With the fathometer fixed, the only problem now was Poole, and even he looked improved.

The first of March had been a long day, but we were snapping back. We were going to come out of this all right!

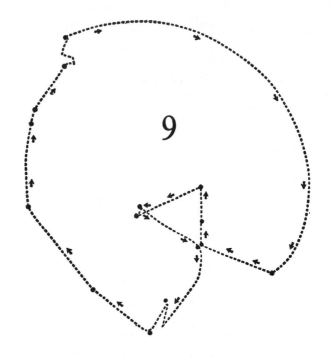

9

The first of March had indeed been a long day, and at two
o'clock on the morning of March second I knew that not all
our problems had yet been solved. Poole was having a second
attack.

As Jim Stark explained it, perhaps he did not pass the
stone a few hours before, despite indications that he had. As a
matter of fact, Jim wasn't really sure that the tiny speck we
had seen in the bottle Poole had produced for inspection was
a kidney stone. It might have been a tiny grain of sand or dust
that somehow had gotten into the bottle after it had been
carefully washed. There was always the possibility that Poole
had not actually passed the stone; another possibility was that
more than one kidney stone might have been involved. This

136

second attack was more severe than the first one, and Poole had to be drugged once more.

Under the morphine, Poole was not too uncomfortable. The question again: what to do? According to Stark, kidney stone attacks frequently clear up by themselves—as Poole's first one did—and then a second stone causes a relapse. In such cases, the discomfort of the second attack is compounded by the lacerations and swollen tissues resulting from the first. After an hour's earnest consultation with Jim, I decided we could continue running for Cape Horn. In the back of my mind, however, a firmly rooted thought had taken hold: the nearest help was the *Macon,* if my several-weeks-old information was still accurate. After that, it was Pearl Harbor or a foreign port. The problem would, somehow or other, have to be sorted out before we rounded Cape Horn.

I had hardly got back into my bunk, it seemed, when the Officer of the Deck sent a messenger to call me. There was a possible submarine contact on the sonar. I was on my feet in a moment, heading for the sonar room.

Some three hundred miles to the west of our course, on the coast of Argentina, lay Golfo Nuevo, a large landlocked bay with a small entrance where, within recent weeks, the Argentine Navy had had a first-class flap. According to the press reports, an unknown submarine had been detected in Golfo Nuevo by patrolling Anti-Submarine units of the Argentine Navy, which had subsequently made several attacks. The submarine, so the newspapers said, had once or twice surfaced in the gulf, and by its maneuvers was apparently damaged. Argentina blocked off the exit to the bay, and at about this time there came evidence of the presence of a second submarine in the same area. Shortly afterward, contact on both of them was lost.

The supposition was strongly supported in the South American press that the second submarine had rendezvoused with

its damaged fellow, either to render assistance or, as was considered more likely, to divert attention to itself while the
damaged one got away. In my own view, having had intimate
experience for many years with the difficulty of making and
holding contact on submarines I was not completely ready
to accept the story at face value. It is an easy thing for in-
experienced people to convince themselves they have made
a contact and then, in their gradually increasing excitement
and interest, to continue to deceive themselves for considerable periods of time. Whether or not there had actually been
a foreign submarine in Golfo Nuevo, however, one thing was
pretty certain: ASW units of the Argentine Navy had been
convinced of it.

Upon initial observation of our own sonar, it was not possible to tell whether the contact we had picked up was on the
surface or submerged. Our plot was busy with it, and there
was no question that it had movement of its own. It was not
bottom effect, that was clear, nor a sharp submerged peak.
It was something moving in the water.

I directed the Officer of the Deck to slow down to minimum
speed for a sonar investigation. Then, in a few minutes, following standard sonar investigation techniques, we turned
Triton's head around to the north. After a few more minutes
of careful checking, it was evident that we had a real contact.
The question was, what was it?

It could be a surface ship cruising about, but it was not
maintaining a steady course or speed, a fact suggesting that
it was not a merchant ship. It might be a vessel of the Argentine Navy, perhaps one of the ASW ships searching off-
shore. If this were so, her Captain's probable state of mind was
not apt to be relaxed. We certainly did not wish to create another international incident or, worse, have a depth charge or
two tossed toward us by some nervous skipper who might not
stop to consider that a submarine submerged three hundred

miles at sea is not the same thing as an unknown submarine in your inland waters. *Triton* should be able to evade Argentina's best ASW ship, but even so, I could well imagine the reports that might reach the US Navy Department and the questions that I would inevitably have to answer.

A second possibility was that this was another submarine. If this were true, it would almost certainly be confirmation of the submarine contacts in Golfo Nuevo. In that case, the matter would be of importance to the US Navy also, and we should probably find it necessary to send a message stating the situation.

A third possibility, one which submariners and ASW people have long since learned to be alert for, was that our contact was not a man-made vessel at all, but a school of fish. Large fish generally separate into several distinct contacts at some moderate range. A number of small fish moving about as a group can sometimes fool the most experienced sonarman.

At about 0300, *Triton*'s periscope broke surface for a cautious search around the horizon, followed by a radar search. Results of both were negative. There was no surface ship around. Back into the depths we went. It was either a submarine or fish. If the former, circumspection was indicated. Slowly and cautiously approaching the contact, we slowly relaxed, for the contact lost its sharp decisive contours, began to fade, and developed wavy outlines. Finally it broke into two parts, and we set *Triton* once more on the way to Cape Horn. No doubt the school of fish we had so gingerly approached was heartily glad this huge intruder was not hungry.

Some fishermen might have given a lot to have had *Triton*'s sonar at this point, for shortly after four o'clock that same morning we detected a second school of fish. Since the characteristics were identical, this time there was less difficulty in making a positive identification, and we were quickly rewarded by seeing the contact break up into numerous smaller blips.

Poole's condition was getting steadily worse, Jim Stark told me, yet there was nothing he could do for him but wait and see. Poole's senses, at least, were dulled by the morphine.

After seeing the patient at about five o'clock in the morning, my recollection is that I finally was able to get a little sleep. Upon awakening, I was astonished to find Poole dressed and once again on his feet in the radar department. As before, Jim Stark just happened to be only a few feet away, ostensibly looking over some of his medical supplies in the pharmacy. Jim could not be sure that the second stone had safely passed.

The only other event of this day was the receipt of our second babygram, for Chief Electrician James DeGange. Another girl, born March 1, 1960; the message from Admiral Daspit gave the further information that mother and Patricia Ann were both doing well.

The third of March began propitiously. We were still watching Poole carefully, but all looked well for the time being. He had been free of pain for some eighteen hours. Our course for Cape Horn had been laid out to bring us close to the Falkland Islands and permit us to run near Port Stanley, their biggest harbor. For drill purposes, we intended to make a photo reconnaissance; that is, take a series of photographs through our periscope. This was a technique submarines had developed during the war, by which important information was brought back to our Marine and Army landing forces.

The Falkland Islands are famous for the naval battle which took place there on the eighth of December, 1914. A month earlier, on November first, a strong German squadron of cruisers under Admiral von Spee had overwhelmed a weaker British squadron under Admiral Cradock off the cape of Coronel on the coast of Chile. The two biggest British ships, including the flagship, were sunk with all hands. Then Von Spee headed for Cape Horn at a leisurely pace, intending to capture the coaling station at the Falkland Islands, refuel, and head back to Germany. His big mistake was in moving so slowly, for when the English heard of the defeat of Cradock, they sent two of their battle cruisers, under Admiral Sturdee, from England direct to the Falkland Islands, with orders to coal at Port Stanley and then search out Von Spee. It was the ideal mission for a versatile British Navy and its new battle cruisers, as they were fast heavily armed ships which far outclassed Von Spee's armored cruisers in both speed and gunpower.

After a high-speed run the length of the Atlantic, Sturdee reached the Falkland Islands the day before Von Spee showed up. Von Spee's second mistake was in making his appearance at about eight o'clock in the morning, with a long summer day ahead of him. The *Inflexible* and the *Invincible* were coaling at Port Stanley when the German cruisers appeared on the horizon. Hastily casting off, Sturdee set out in pursuit. When Von Spee realized that the two big ships sortieing from Port Stanley were battle cruisers with twelve-inch guns, he turned and tried to escape. This might be termed his third mistake, for, with a fight inevitable, he should have got his own shorter-range guns into action while he could. Once lost, the opportunity never returned. Inexorably, the British overhauled him sufficiently to open fire—and then, when necessary, used their superior speed to stay out of range of Von Spee's guns.

One of the stories of that battle is that an old sailing ship which happened to be in the area suddenly found herself directly in the line of fire. Great ripping sounds were heard as the armor-piercing shells whistled overhead, but the extreme range of the British caused all the shells to pass harmlessly thousands of feet above her.

Von Spee's two bigger ships were the *Scharnhorst* and *Gneisenau*, both of which had held the Fleet Gunnery Trophy in the German Navy and were known as crack ships. But now the tables were turned, and in a few hours Von Spee, with his two fine cruisers, joined Cradock and his *Good Hope* and *Monmouth* at the bottom of the sea.

Scharnhorst and *Gneisenau* went down fighting; there were no survivors. They had not been able to inflict any damage of any kind on the British ships, any more than Cradock had been able to hurt Von Spee in the first encounter. But there was established a proud tradition in the German Navy, commemorated in World War II by some more recently remembered names of men-of-war.

According to Will Adams, we should sight the Falkland Islands at about ten o'clock in the morning. A little before this we came to periscope depth, put up the radar, and there, precisely as predicted, was a "pip" on the radar scope obviously made by land. The photographic reconnaissance party under Dick Harris, with cameras and equipment, was standing by in the conning tower ready for the initial approach, when Jim Stark sought me out. His face was like a thundercloud.

"What's the matter, Jim? Is it Poole?"

"Yes, sir. Worse than ever."

Thoughts of the impending reconnaissance vanished. "Let's have it," I said.

Choosing his words carefully, Jim explained that in his opinion Poole might still be having trouble with the original stone. It might not have passed at all. Temporary remissions of the type Poole had experienced were not unknown in such cases. On the other hand, it was possible that he had been passing a series of kidney stones and that this was the third one. In either case, said Jim, there was no telling how long this would continue, nor to what condition poor Poole might ultimately be reduced. While we had been heretofore running on with the idea that each attack would perhaps be the last, the Doctor felt that he could no longer leave it at that. As we talked, we neared Poole's bunk.

Poole himself, though obviously in great pain, was not

yet completely under the effects of the injection which Jim had been forced to give him. Sensing the reason for my presence, he croaked out a plea that we not turn back. "This is the last time, Captain. I swear it!" he said, but he was in such pain that he could hardly articulate the words.

I could both see and sense everybody staring at me. Their eyes said much, but nobody spoke a word.

A sort of hiatus descended upon the ship. In the conning tower, Dick Harris and his crew were waiting for the word to go ahead, but, having heard of Poole's new attack, simply stood by quietly.

With Adams and Stark, and Operations Officer Bob Bulmer, I went over the argument again. It was not as though I hadn't had plenty of opportunity to think it over before this. I had, in fact, already assumed that a decision must be reached one way or the other before we got to Cape Horn.

There never was a question of taking any chances with Poole's life. Both my orders for the trip and the traditions of the US Navy for peacetime operations categorically forbade it. On the other hand, we should not want to turn back and then have Poole's condition clear up by itself, as about three-quarters of all kidney stone attacks actually do. Yet we had already gone on for three days. No doubt we could still go on and hope the third attack would be the last. The salient point was that *Macon* could conceivably help us now, and if we passed her up, the nearest available medical help would be at Pearl Harbor, nearly eight thousand miles away.

Adams calculated how far we would have to travel to meet the *Macon,* and when. Somehow, it was almost as if there were dead silence in the ship. Not many felt like talking. A person becomes attuned to the mood of a ship, after serving in her a while. Our mood was solemn. Everyone realized what we were up against. Poole obviously had to have help, but to get it for him involved jeopardizing our mission. If, for any reason, the

Macon had been diverted from Montevideo, were not within reach, if no other US Navy unit could be sent to assist us— and I knew of none anywhere about—we should have to ask for diplomatic clearance for entry into Montevideo. Once the message was sent, we would be powerless to avert public disclosure of our mission. Unless we could carry Poole for two weeks longer, to Pearl, it had to be either *Macon*—with whose help we might yet salvage our continuously submerged record —or Montevideo. Success in our cruise meant a lot to all of us; only I had an inkling how much it might mean to our country.

Actually, although I technically made the decision and took the responsibility for it, there really was no decision to be made. Circumstances had made it for us. I picked up the wardroom telephone and dialed "O," which rings the phone at the elbow of the Officer of the Deck.

I held the receiver to my ear, waited until I heard a voice —it was "Whitey" Rubb.

"Officer of the Deck," he said.

"Reverse course, Whitey," I said. "Make your course zero zero nine degrees true and increase speed to Flank. Secure the reconnaissance party. We are heading for Montevideo."

Recessed into one of the wardroom bulkheads are dials showing the ship's speed, course, and depth. I watched as the gyro repeater rotated swiftly about until it finally settled at a heading just to the right of north. The speed dial also increased, until it indicated the maximum of which *Triton* was capable.

And then there was a feeling of frustrated despair for which there was no solution, except to carry on with what we were doing. I took a piece of paper and, with Jim Stark's help, composed a message stating our problem and asking for aid. It was almost as though I were writing finis to our effort and to the high hopes with which we had started the cruise. Finis, all brought to an end, because of a tiny calcified growth smaller than a grain of sand, which had lodged in the wrong place in a man's body!

It was very hard not to feel bitter against both fate and Poole.

There was a moment of comfort when I looked up the *Macon* in the Atlantic Fleet Organization pamphlet. I knew she was flagship of the task force in the South Atlantic, and I was pleased to see that the Admiral on board was listed as E. C. Stephan, my one-time Squadron Commander in Key West years ago. *Macon*'s skipper also was a very familiar officer, having been one of our most renowned and successful submarine commanders during World War II. I had never served with him and had last encountered him some years previously in the Pentagon, but everyone in the Navy knew of Reuben T. Whitaker and his dour, enthusiastic efficiency.

Not that friendship, per se, cuts any ice one way or another. But the tie of shared service certainly feels good when you're looking for help.

The question at this point was simply whether or not Rear Admiral Ed Stephan and Captain Reuben Whitaker would be able to help us.

Drafting a naval message—condensing it to say all that needs to be said with as few words as possible, and then encoding it—takes time. It was a full two hours before we were ready to transmit a final draft. We briefly described the medical facts, and announced that we were proceeding to the vicinity of Montevideo at maximum speed. We would arrive there by one o'clock in the morning of the fifth of March, we said, and, not knowing how else to state it, we put our plea for help in plain English: "Can *Macon* meet us and transfer Poole?" the message asked.

As we searched the chart for a suitable rendezvous, I was struck by the fact that not far off Montevideo there is a small relatively shallow spot in an otherwise deep ocean area. Probably merchant ships heading to or from the harbor would

When we took *Triton*
to sea on its initial run,
she was the world's largest submarine.   *General Dynamics*
Her 447½-foot hull was powered by two
nuclear reactors which propelled her at record speeds.

For the long voyage, we stowed
77,613 pounds of provisions, including 1,300 pounds of coffee. Here,
Ramon D. Baney, Commissaryman
Second Class, and Seaman Joseph
W. Tilenda load additional stores into an already jammed compartment.

Official U.S. Navy Photo

At the first of our four crossings of the equator, King Neptune (Chief Firecontrol Technician Loyd L. Garlock) came aboard with his cigar-smoking Queen (Torpedoman Second Class Wilmot A. Jones) and barrel-girthed Royal Baby (Engineman Second Class Harry Olsen); the pollywogs (sailors crossing the equator for the first time) were initiated by the Royal Court of King Neptune and, henceforth, were known as Shellbacks.

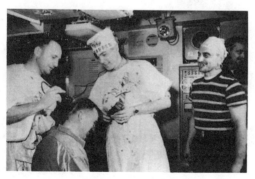

The ceremony initiation included a visit to the Royal Barbers, whose clippers shaved an erratic path across the pollywogs' scalps. Shortly after this photograph was taken, the Barbers clipped their own heads in self-defense. (*Left to right,* Chief Engineman Alfred E. Abel; Quartermaster Third Class Carl C. Hall; Lieutenant Tom B. Thamm; Gunners Mate First Class Peter P.J. Kollar; Photographer First Class Earnest R. Meadows.)

Photo by J. Baylor Roberts, © National Geographic Society

St. Peter and St. Paul's Rocks, looming starkly in the mid-Atlantic, marked the official departing and terminating point of the *Triton's* circumnavigation of the earth.

Official U.S. Navy Photo

If we were to complete our voyage within the allotted time, keeping on course was essential, and I had frequent navigation conferences with Lieutenant Commander Robert W. Bulmer, Operations Officer *(left)*, and Lieutenant Commander Will M. Adams, Jr., Executive Officer *(right)*.

While galelike winds and twelve-foot waves boiled the waters at Cape Horn, we sat safely sixty-five feet below the surface with a barely perceptible roll to hint at the strong currents and high seas.

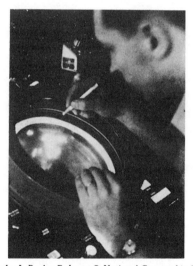

The radar in the Combat Information Center, operated by Chief Radarman Bernard E. Pile, clearly outlines the nodule shape of Cape Horn.

Photo by J. Baylor Roberts, © National Geographic Society

Hospitalman First Class "J" "C" Meaders checked the film badges of each crewman regularly to determine if anyone had endured excess radiation.

Photo by J. Baylor Roberts, © National Geographic Society

Part of our mission was a study of ocean currents, so Torpedoman First Class Robert R. Tambling ejected brightly colored bottles along our route. Within each bottle was a message asking the finder to report his discovery to the United States Navy Hydrographic Office in Washington, D.C., indicating the position and date of his find.

Lieutenant Milton R. ("Whitey") Rubb was our custodian of sea water. From each of the seven seas we gathered separate samples, and in one bottle we combined waters from each of the seas to present to the superintendent of the United States Naval Academy for use at the annual midshipmen's Ring Dance.

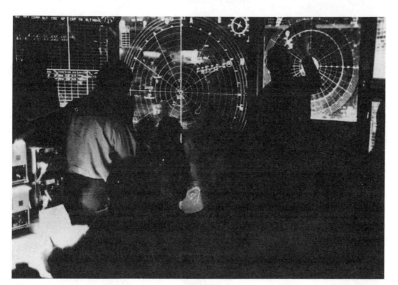

The nerve center of any ship is its Combat Information Center. Here is where we maintained our contact with the outside world and plotted the track of the *Triton*.

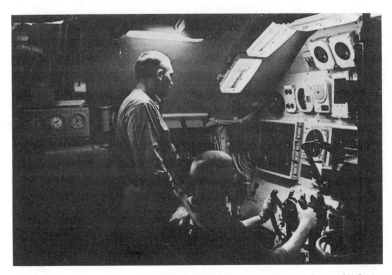

With this newly designed control panel, Seaman David E. Boe guides the ship in a manner similar to a pilot flying an airplane, while Chief Radarman Bernard E. Pile observes.

With precise instruments, such as our fathometer and precision depth recorder, we could chart our track across the ocean floor.

To relieve the tedium of the three-month voyage, some men played chess, others ate . . . (*Left to right,* Engineman Third Class Arlan F. Martin, Quartermaster Third Class Anton F. Madsen, Torpedoman First Class Stanley L. Sieveking.)

. . . and others formed a band with a makeshift horn, a pair of bongo drums, a guitar, and some willing voices. They might not have qualified for Birdland, but below the decks of the *Triton* they were a sensation. (*Left to right,* Chief Engineman Alfred E. Abel, Engineman Third Class James A. Steinbauer, Machinist First Class Colvin R. Cochrane, Fireman Raymond R. Kuhn, Jr.)

Photo by J. Baylor Roberts, © National Geographic Society

Dr. Benjamin B. Weybrew at work on his own very special chart, on which he recorded the varying emotions and reactions of the *Triton* crew members who participated in his psychological study.

Official U.S. Navy Photo

When we reached Guam, at the conclusion of the longest leg of our trip, I invited Steward Second Class Edward C. Carbullido to the conn. He was born on Guam, and through the periscope he saw his home town, Agat, which he had left fourteen years before.

We spent nearly six hours making a photo reconnaissance of Guam. Undetected, we observed Navy planes landing and taking off.

In Makassar Strait, this two-masted relic from the age of sail loomed clearly in the periscope lens.

While traversing Hilutangan Channel, we spotted this
Philippine boat with its triangular sail. In the distance
are the faint outlines of the mountains of Bohol Island.

In Magellan Bay I raised the periscope and looked at a young Filipino
in an outrigger canoe. He was the only unauthorized person to spot our
submarine during the voyage. Later, we were told he was nineteen-year-
old Rufino Baring of Mactan Island, and he was still convinced he had
seen a sea monster.

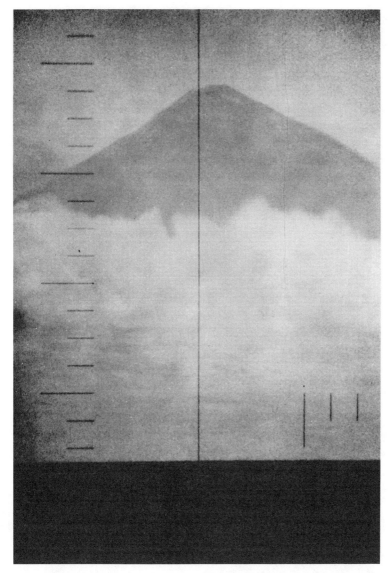

Through the Makassar Strait, across the Java Sea to Lombok Strait, where Mount Agung on the island of Bali rose majestically through the low-lying clouds.

The city of Santa Cruz on Tenerife Island in the Canaries, one of the most spectacular sights we encountered.

Photo by J. Baylor Roberts, © National Geographic Society

Photo by J. Baylor Roberts, © National Geographic Society

Wallowing along through the choppy waters of the Indian Ocean, just south of the Cape of Good Hope, this tanker was completely unaware that he had a visitor.

Photo by J. Baylor Roberts, © National Geographic Society

When we reached the coast of Spain, off Cadiz, the destroyer *John W. Weeks* sent out a long boat to secure the plaque we had cast for presentation to the Spanish government in commemoration of Magellan's historic voyage. Coming aboard a partially emerged submarine can be hazardous, as these dunked seamen discovered. It was a good thing we were hove to.

The inscription on the plaque reads:
"Hail, Noble Captain,
It Is Done Again."

To each of the crew members who participated in the *Triton's* voyage a commemorative medallion was presented. Here, Engineman First Class Walter J. Allen receives his medal.

Commissaryman Second Class Earl E. Bruch, Jr., sporting a voyage-grown set of handlebars, draws a doubtful twirl from his son after the ship docked at its home station in New London, Connecticut.

avoid it—a desirable factor. Should the weather preclude celestial observations, it also gave both *Macon* and *Triton* a fixed point of reference for navigation by fathometer. The spot we selected was smack in the center of the shallow area.

Midday is always a bad time to transmit messages, particularly over long distances, for it is well known that much greater range is possible at night. Time, however, was important, for we had no idea what sort of schedule *Macon* might be trying to keep. As soon as the message was ready, we slowed, came to periscope depth, and transmitted it to, of all places, the U.S. radio station on Guam, some eighty-three hundred miles away straight across the South Pole. Then *Triton* headed again for the depths and resumed maximum speed.

Our narrative for this period contains the following entries:

Since turning back, except for the time spent transmitting our call for help, *Triton* has been racing northward, deep beneath the sea, at the maximum speed that her two great propellers can drive her. There is no noticeable motion in the ship, not even vibration. All we note is a slight drumming of the superstructure from her swift passage through the water. Forward she is as steady as a church, as solid, and as quiet. Aft, only the powerful turbine roar gives away the tremendous energy she is putting into the water.

In the control and living spaces, the ship has quieted down, too. Orders are given in low voices; the men speak to each other, carry out their normal duties, in a repressed atmosphere. A regular pall has descended upon us. I know that all hands are aware of the decision and recognize the need for it. Perhaps they are relieved that they did not have to make it. But it is apparent that this unexpected illness, something that could neither have been foreseen nor prevented, may ruin our submerged record. If the *Macon* cannot meet us, if we have to go into the port of Montevideo to transfer Poole to medical authorities, we shall have to surface. We shall still, in that event, continue the cruise, for this would affect only our incentive factor. But that would be a big loss.

Naturally, there was no mention in the Log of any over-riding reason, other than our perfectly understandable desire for the trip to be entirely submerged all the way.

As we raced north, I gave a great deal of thought to what we should do when we reached Montevideo. There was the possibility that Poole would have another remission, and, in fact, there was always the possibility that this third attack would be his last. We would have a day and a half to find out, and it might even be possible, if *Macon* couldn't come to the requested rendezvous, to stretch things another few hours and wait and see. But I couldn't, in my heart, give much for our chances of not having to surface and enter port, if *Macon* could not get to us.

On the other hand, if *Macon* did meet us, we had a fighting chance. We could "broach" the ship—that is, get the upper part of the conning tower out of water—and convert the conning tower itself into a big airlock. *Triton*'s pressure hull and superstructure would remain entirely submerged. Only the upper part of the sail and part of the conning tower would in fact broach the surface—a maneuver submarines have performed for years—and this critical part of the ship would have been previously sealed off from the rest. Poole and the transfer party would be inside the conning tower, would be called to the bridge when *Macon*'s boat approached, and transfer across with ease.

The big "if" was the *Macon*. There was no doubt that she could do the job. The question was whether she was where I thought she was.

That night I wrote in the Log:

2300 Periscope depth. Maybe there will be a message for us—there could be, though it is probably too soon. . . .

2325   There is, indeed, a message for us from Admiral Daspit. Admiral Stephan is getting underway in the *Macon* and will meet us at the time and place we have requested.

For the second time in as many days a lead weight has been rolled off my chest. The news is immediately announced to the entire ship and at the same time we can now announce how we shall handle the rendezvous and transfer. We will not surface, at least, not fully.

All during that long day, Jim Stark and his Hospitalmen took turns keeping watch on Poole. His appearance was shocking. His face was swollen, eyes puffed up and half-shut, tears running down his nose and cheeks. He groaned continuously, sometimes in a low whimper, sometimes with startling loudness. From previous experience and Jim Stark's warnings, I knew that he had been pretty heavily loaded with sedation and was in fact totally out of his head. In a way, I had by now become steeled to Poole's expression, for apparently he had no recollection of the excruciating pain of his previous two attacks. But I became acutely conscious of the uncomfortable gazes and averted eyes of Poole's worried shipmates. During his first attack, I had thought of moving him somewhere, and similarly during the second. But *Triton* had no sick bay; outside of making it easier for Meaders, Fickel, Gladd, and Chief Williams, our four Hospitalmen, plus Jim Stark, all of whom were taking turns watching over Poole, the only other people who would really benefit from our setting up a sick bay would be those men who had to berth in the same area.

There was only one place in the ship which could be used for such a purpose without displacing a number of other people, and where, besides providing room for the medical equipment needed, Poole could be out of sight. The additional privacy would certainly mean nothing to him in his condition, but it would be highly desirable from the point of view of the rest of the men. After thinking it over, I gave orders that this time he be moved into my bunk. It proved to be a good decision, whatever else resulted, for it certainly demonstrated the truth of the adage that "out of sight, out of mind." Everyone perked up once Poole's sufferings were removed from public gaze, and we became positively cheerful after receipt of the Force Commander's encouraging message.

There were a number of preparations we had to make for the rendezvous. It would, for example, be necessary to communicate with *Macon* by short-range, ultra-high-frequency radio. Should our UHF antennas be out of commission because of their already prolonged submergence, which was a distinct possibility, some sort of stand-by system would be necessary. Years ago, in *Amberjack,* we had experimented with using the periscope to transmit messages at night by the traditional flashing-light technique. Now, I directed that a flashing light be rigged up for use in the periscope. It would work, I assured the slightly dubious quartermasters. Later on, I happened to overhear the irrepressible Bill Marshall telling his crew, "Listen you guys, did you ever hear of the charge of the light brigade? The old man says we're going to send blinker signals through the periscope, so we're going to send blinker signals through the periscope. Don't waste your time figuring it out!"

The metaphor was not exactly apt, for several obvious reasons, but I knew the gadget would work; so I chuckled inwardly, as I pretended not to have heard.

Another problem was that I did not know what instructions had been given to the *Macon,* other than to rendezvous with us and pick up a sick man. Her crew would probably be ashore in Montevideo on liberty immediately afterward and might be indiscreet. George Sawyer pointed out that the ship's identification numbers were painted in big white numerals on the side of our sail and would be visible to the *Macon* and her boat's crew when it came alongside. News of *Triton*'s presence so close to shore was bound to create intense interest in the city, should it become known.

We had no paint below decks, but there was some in a watertight tank in the sail. While we were awaiting the *Macon*'s boat, it was decided, a crew of men would hastily attempt to blot out the numbers with paint.

And, of course, there was Poole himself. He would have all identification removed and would have all the necessary papers attached to his person in a sealed packet to be delivered only to the Commanding Officer of the *Macon*. Included among them would be a request that he be segregated from the crew and protected from curious questioners. If he were to have a remission prior to the transfer, we planned also to spend some time briefing him, but if not, these provisions would satisfy the situation.

In describing the transfer of Poole to the *Macon,* which took place early on the morning of the fifth of March, 1960, I could not do better than to repeat verbatim the entries I wrote in the ship's official report of the incident.

Our rendezvous with *Macon* is for 2 A.M. At 0100 we slowed and came to periscope depth. *Macon* is out there waiting for us.

The rendezvous is perfect. She is heading south, we north, and the two ships meet at the designated position.

I was pleased to find that our UHF radio worked perfectly, despite the fact that it had been long under water and subjected to high speeds. Since we had built a gadget to signal through the periscope, however, I wanted to test it out. It was a dark night, with rain and poor visibility, but to my smug satisfaction and the expressed surprise of three quartermasters in the conning tower, we found ourselves able to exchange calls perfectly with the *Macon*. We had rigged a light inside a tin can with a wire and a sending key attached to it. By focusing the periscope directly on the *Macon* and holding the tin can tightly against the rubber eyeguard, we found it possible to send a perfectly readable signal to the bridge of the other ship.

The only trouble was that it took both of our periscopes to

perform this little stunt, inasmuch as one had to be used to receive return signals while the other one was transmitting; and after we had satisfied ourselves that it would work, and had tired of the performance, *Macon* kept trying to talk to us by flashing her light just when I wanted to use the periscope for other purposes.

0245   Approximately in position for the transfer.

0250   Broached on safety tank. Ship's depth gauge reduces to 42 feet, indicating that the top of the conning tower should be three feet out of water. All hands are ready; the lower conning tower hatch is shut. I hastily don a jacket and a cap and then direct Curtis K. Beacham, QM1 (SS), to crack open the conning tower upper hatch very cautiously in case the gauges at this shallow depth are not precisely accurate or if there is an inch or two of water above it—which indeed there is. A small cascade pours down through the barely opened hatch, and we jam it shut again. This is remedied by a short blast of high pressure air into our most forward tank, thus lifting the bow a foot or two more and giving a better drainage angle to the bridge.

A second time I direct Beacham to open the hatch, and this time no water comes in. We are out of water. He holds it at a quarter-inch opening for a minute or two to be sure that water is not sweeping over it. None does. It is definitely out. "Open the hatch!" I tell him. He flips it open, jumps out. I am right behind him. As I swing up the ladder to the bridge, one deck above, by pre-arrangement Beacham jumps below again and slams the hatch nearly closed, ready to shut it instantly the rest of the way should the bridge become swamped.

It is a lonely feeling to be the only man topside in an 8000 ton ship which is 99% under water. We have been very careful with our computations, but there's always the possibility that some miscalculation somewhere, or a sudden change in water density, might send her suddenly back down again. There is however not much time to dwell upon this, and besides there's every chance it will not happen. *Triton's* crew is too well trained, too intent on doing this thing correctly. Will Adams, Bob Bulmer and Tom Thamm are down below watching over this operation like old mother hens, and nearly everyone else is standing by his station just in case. There won't be any mistakes down there.

All looks well on the bridge, though I notice that one of the hand rails has been broken loose by the force of the water and will undoubtedly be a source of rattles in the future if it is not already. Otherwise, everything looks about the same as it did three weeks ago when we submerged. It is pretty dark but there seems to be fair visibility, despite a drizzle of rain. I fumble for the bridge command speaker, find the knob just where it is supposed to be. Pressing upon it, I call the conning tower and, to our mutual and infinite pleasure, Will Adams immediately answers from down below. We had pretty well expected this instrument to be grounded out from its prolonged submergence and it is a boon to find it in working order.

With communication once established, things are a great deal easier. I pick up the binoculars, scan the *Macon* and the water between us. We are lying to, stern into the wind, about five hundred yards downwind from her. She is broadside to us, her decks amidships ablaze with lights where her deck crew is hoisting out a motor whaleboat. All we have to do is receive their boat, when it comes, and keep a careful watch on the other ship to ensure that she does not drift down upon us. This will be easy, since our radar is constantly reporting ranges.

I reach forward, press the 7MC command communication button and call into it, just to make sure: "Control, Bridge; keep and log ranges to the *Macon* and report immediately when she commences to close."

The return from Bob Bulmer in the control room is immediate; "Range 600 yards, Bridge, and steady."—Then a minute later, "Bridge,—from the *Macon,* their boat is in the water heading toward us."

I acknowledge over the 7MC and direct my next order to Will

Adams in the conning tower. "Conn, Bridge—send George Sawyer and the topside line handling party to the bridge, through the conning tower hatch." We had already arranged that this group of people under our First Lieutenant and Gunnery Officer would be standing by with all necessary equipment. Upon the order they would proceed up one by one to the bridge and prepare to receive the lines from the *Macon*'s boat when it comes alongside.

Two of them had been directed to break out paint pots and brushes and carry them down with them to slosh paint over the number on the side of the sail, after which the brushes and pots would be discarded overboard. I had not been too keen on this idea when it was first suggested, but had allowed myself to be talked into it. It did have merit, of course, but I found myself wondering how these men were going to manage paint can and brush in one hand and hang on to the handrail on the side of the sail with the other.

Will Adams' answer from Conning Tower comes back immediately. "Line handlers are standing by. We will open the lower conning tower hatch as soon as ready."

A few minutes later, "Bridge, Conn—request permission to open the bridge hatch and send line handling party topside." I press the speaker button and respond, "Bridge, aye. Permission granted."

In a moment George Sawyer's determined voice resounds from the bridge, "Line handlers on the lower bridge, sir, Sawyer and four men."

I have been looking over the side to decide which is the better angle for the boat to approach from; the starboard side looks a bit better; besides, the access door from our sail is on that side. "Stand by to take them alongside the starboard side, George," I call down to him, "I'll signal the boat to make our starboard side."

"Starboard side, aye aye," from Sawyer. The four people with him are Peter P. J. Kollar, Gunner's Mate First Class; Wilmot A. Jones, Torpedoman's Mate Second Class and recently King Neptune's Royal Consort; Thomas J. Schwartz (the profile), Torpedo-man's Mate Third Class; and David E. Boe, Seaman.

The noises emanating from the lower bridge indicate that Lt. Sawyer and his men are breaking out the necessary gear, stored there in a watertight tank, to receive the boat alongside. Each man has on an inflatable life jacket with attached flashlight, and a safety belt with traveler.

The latter device is the result of an accident several years ago in northern latitudes, when the US Submarine *Tusk* rescued the crew of the sinking submarine *Cochino*. In preparation for the rescue, *Tusk* rigged lifelines on deck forward. Nevertheless, a huge sea came aboard, swept the people on deck off their feet against the lifeline and broke it, plunging them all into the sea. Herculean efforts on the part of the *Tusk* got most of them back aboard, but a number lost their lives in the freezing water.

As a result of this accident, a safety track similar to a railroad rail was installed on the decks of all submarines. Anyone going topside in bad weather or under hazardous conditions wears a strong canvas belt, with chain and traveler attached. The traveler clamps over and slides along the safety track, and may only be put on or removed from the track at certain places. This arrange-ment permits a man to move back and forth on deck and still re-main firmly attached to the ship by a short length of very strong chain [with a "quick release" snap-hook in case of need].

When two people want to pass each other, the technique is to seek a safe moment and quickly exchange travelers by unsnapping the chains from one's own belt and snapping the other man's into it.

I am well aware of all of these historical matters as I look over the side and ponder the advisability of letting George and his peo-ple go down on deck. Seas are sweeping freely across our deck aft, but that is of no particular importance at the moment. Our bow is staying about a foot out of water, but around the conning tower, where I am looking over the side, the deck is frequently inundated.

The night is cold and dark, completely overcast, and a light drizzle is falling. The sea feels warm.

With a little luck, George and his men will very likely have no difficulty under conditions as they are. But the risk looks a little too great. With a low freeboard the transfer is aided, provided it isn't so low that there is risk to your deck crew. Besides, even though Poole is at the moment having a remission, partly with the help of morphine, transferring him under any but the best conditions for his health and safety is out of the question.

Again, there is really no decision to be made at all. Technicalities about staying submerged have got to give way to the realities of the situation; the safety of the people involved in this operation is more important than anything else. We will have to come up a little higher. I push the button energizing the microphone to the control room.

"Control, Bridge, blow forward group for one second."

"Forward group, one second, aye aye," from control. Almost simultaneously, I hear air whistling into the tanks forward. It blows for a second, stops abruptly.

The effect is most apparent. The ship having previously been carefully brought to perfect trim, addition of a thousand pounds or so of buoyancy in the forward section lifts her until the displacement [not weight] of *Triton's* above-water volume equals that of the water displaced by the air in the tank. The superstructure, being entirely free to flood, displaces very little water, except for the conning tower itself, and the forward section rises several inches. The main deck in the area of conning tower and sail is now fairly clear, only an occasional wave slapping over it.

Sawyer's voice from below, "Permission to open the access door and go out on deck, Captain?"

"Open the door, but do not go out on deck until I give you permission."

This is just to keep control to the last before letting him go. I can hear the sound of the fastenings being opened up and the door swinging wide.

George again: "Looks all clear topside, Captain, permission to go out on deck?"

"Affirmative!" I yell back.

In the distance, the lights of the approaching motorboat are visible coming around our stern. Down below, in the flickering semilight cast by their flashlights, the men of the deck force reach through the open access door, affix their travelers to the track, and then, holding their safety chains taut, step swiftly forward on the main deck. Two men quickly turn to on a collapsible cleat just forward of the sail and rotate it upward. This is the point where we plan to take the boat's bowline. Two other men, carrying paint pots, move aft along the sail and hurriedly commence daubing at our starboard side block numbers.

Possibly some unknown vagary in water density or wave action has commenced to affect us as *Macon*'s boat approaches. Two or three seas roll over the foredeck. George has his men by this time arranged alongside the sail, gripping the handhold bars, and of course holding on to their safety belts. Gazing intently over the side of the bridge in the misty darkness, I am unable to see any evidence of paint pots, a fact which does not surprise me, is on the contrary something of a relief. As I watch them anxiously, a larger than average sea mounts up the side, and all of them are momentarily buried up to the neck. George shouts "hang on" as the water rises about them. All were already pretty well soaked and the danger is more apparent than real, but we can't let this continue, "Blow the forward group for one second," I again order the control room, and again there is the welcome blast of high-pressure air into the tanks. This brings the deck up again and we motion the boat alongside.

In the meantime, Jim Stark and John Poole have been waiting in the conning tower. We have used the last few hours, during which he has been free from discomfort, to brief Poole thoroughly on what he can say and not say, once departed from *Triton*. His transfer papers and other official documents are made up in waterproof bags and attached firmly to his person. He himself is so bundled up and swathed with protective clothing and life jackets that he can hardly get through the hatch. At the word from Stark that all is ready, I order the two men to the lower bridge. Our good-byes have already been said. There is no time for more than a last hasty "good luck" to Poole.

The boat is alongside, bow painter around the cleat and held by Wilmot Jones. Two men in the boat hold her off from our side with reversed boat hooks. Chief Fitzjarrald and Sawyer steady Poole and a couple of the men in the boat stand by to catch him. Seizing a moment when the gunwale of the boat is level with the edge of our deck, Poole steps easily and quickly into it. It is a standard Navy motor-whaleboat, evidently *Macon*'s lifeboat, manned with a crew of about 5 people. It is a pleasure to watch the boat's coxswain maneuver his frail craft alongside. There is no doubt that he knows his business. Poole hasn't even gotten wet, and the boat's gunwale has only once touched our side.

In a moment, the riding line is cast off. The men with boat hooks push hard, the engineer guns the engine, and they are away. Another moment suffices to get George and company back on the lower bridge.

"All clear on deck, Captain!" shouts Sawyer. "We didn't get any painting done though. The first wave flooded the paint pots. Anyway, the paint wouldn't stick, and the old paint is pretty well stripped off by the water anyhow." This was a point we should have thought of, but all's well that ends well. Then they are below, hatch shut behind them.

While waiting for further word from the *Macon*, Machinist's Mate Bob Carter is busy with a hacksaw, taking off the loose bridge guardrail we had noticed. In a few minutes the welcome word comes from our Communications Officer, Lt. Bob Brodie, in Radio: "Bridge, Radio—from the *Macon*—Poole safely on board."

Among the papers Poole has with him are personal letters of appreciation to Admiral Stephan and Captain Reuben Whitaker. More than our thanks for their help, there is little information we can give them about our trip. They must be bursting with curiosity. We send a final message of thanks and then, with topside clear and hatch shut, I order Dick Harris, Diving Officer of the Watch, to return to periscope depth. The air bubble in our tanks is released, and gently *Triton* eases her sail into the warm sea. The total time with the bridge above water has been less than an hour. With a deep feeling of gratitude for the way the Navy has come through, we shape our course at maximum speed southward.

Now that we have successfully solved the difficult problem about Poole, the atmosphere in our ship lightens considerably. With everything wide open, *Triton* is again heading for Cape Horn. This time we will save time by passing to the west of the Falkland Islands and head for Estrecho de le Maire, a small strait between Staten Island [familiar name] and the main part of Tierra del Fuego.

We calculate that we will have gone 2,000 miles out of our way on this mercy mission, and it has cost several days. The distance is almost equal to an Atlantic transit.

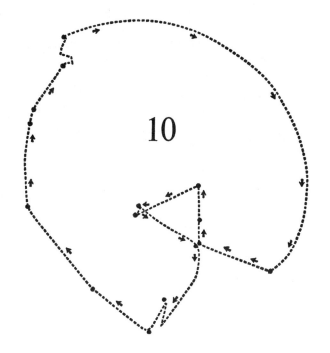

10

Sunday, March sixth, was a day of rest, well deserved by all hands, and it was noteworthy for a special reason. Our growing concern over our fathometer had caused us to keep a closer-than-usual watch over it and over our regular search-sonar equipment, too. Searching out ahead, to our great pleasure, the latter at 1610 detected something that looked like a fifty-foot peak, or boulder, on the bottom. A moment later, as *Triton* herself passed over the spot, the fathometer registered the accuracy of the information. It was a comforting thought to know that our search sonar, designed to detect other ships and submarines, might be depended on to give us adequate warning of the approach of shoal water.

For two days, *Triton* roared toward Cape Horn, driving to

make up lost time. On Monday, the seventh of March, we reached the storied Land's End of the western hemisphere.

I had been giving some thought to how we should make proper observance of our passage from the Atlantic to the Pacific and finally hit upon a simple idea. In the *Triton Eagle,* I occasionally wrote a column called "The Skipper's Corner," to say things which it seemed might best be handled informally. On the seventh of March, therefore, the following entry appeared in "The Skipper's Corner":

As for Cape Horn, *Triton* will make a photographic reconnaissance on it, and then Mr. Roberts will make a National Geographic reconnaissance. Following this, as we cruise by for the 3rd or 4th time, I intend to require every man on the ship to come to the conning tower for a look. It is not a usual thing for a sailor to round the Horn these days. Many spend a lifetime and never do. By far the majority of US Navy sailors have never done it. Quite obviously, if you ever brag about having been around the Horn, the next question will either be, "Did you see it?" or "What does it look like?"

We intend to take a picture and I think it will be possible to make enough copies for all hands. But more than this, I want every man aboard to be able to say he's seen it. Note: there will be no muster taken. If you don't want to see the Horn, no one will force you. But you'll wish you did later, because you'll probably never get the chance again.

And then, that morning, I let it be known that in the old days, when a sailor went around the Horn, he hoped not to see the fabled Cape. If anyone aboard an old sailing ship, bucking wind and tide to double the Cape, sighted the forbidding promontory looming through the haze, it was considered that bad luck would follow very soon in the form of shipwreck on one of the most inhospitable coasts in the world.

More modern traditions, I announced, were different. A sailor who gazed upon Cape Horn deliberately would experience good luck for the rest of his seafaring career. Not only that, but all sailors who rounded the Horn automatically attained certain privileges denied ordinary mortals (one I did not recommend was that we might all have a pig tattooed on the calf of the right leg). Tradition has it also that sailors who have rounded the Horn may with impunity throw trash and slops to windward, and because of their great victory over the forces of the wind, none of it will ever be blown back into their faces. They also have the traditional right to wear their hats on the side of their heads instead of square above the eyebrows, as is required by Navy regulations (no one may wear it on the *back* of his head).

We made no muster, but we did keep an unofficial count of the persons coming into the conning tower for a look, in some cases to photograph the famous landmark with their own cameras (which they had been permitted to bring provided all film was turned in for checking). Every man wanted a look, and it was necessary to go back and forth five times in front of the Cape before all hands had had their view.

Triton's Log for the passage may give some idea of the conditions the old-timers faced in the days of sail.

Our observations of the conditions make it quite clear why it was such a tremendously difficult thing for old-time seafarers to weather this famous Cape. In the first place, though we are safely submerged and comfortable, *Triton* is rolling rather heavily. There is an unusually rough sea topside. Lt. James C. Hay, recently reported aboard from West Milton, has already established himself as a most competent diving officer—but he is having difficulty in maintaining ordered depth today. Good practice for young officers, and planesmen, too. We estimate the waves as 10 to 12 feet high and the wind about 25 knots from the west.

There are occasional rain squalls and the cloud coverage is rather low to the water. It is also noticed, after a few navigational cuts, that we are being set backwards, to the east, by a current of some 3 knots. Under such conditions it is easy to see how an old wind-jammer, trying to beat her way around the Cape, might find it almost impossible. Heavy winds and a strong current were both dead against her. Even a steamer would have her troubles at a time like this.

Although the conditions we have observed could hardly be called a storm, there is no doubt that any ship riding around Cape Horn on the surface today would be having a rough and uncomfortable trip. By contrast we are comfortable and snug.

Joe Roberts had spent practically his entire life as a photographer, and was one of the *National Geographic*'s best. He also happened to be endowed with a genial personality which generated real affection on the part of officers and crew alike. An illustration of this was an incident that occurred in the conning tower as we passed Cape Horn. After taking his *National Geographic* pictures with half-a-dozen expensive cameras which he had slung around his neck, Joe had been about to make room for others by going below, when a sailor with a box camera appeared in the conning tower. Photographing through the periscope is by no means a simple procedure and Joe put down his cameras and other paraphernalia and turned back to help.

Sailor after sailor—and some officers, too—came to the conning tower with cameras, and to each one Commander Roberts patiently showed the tricks of the game, helped calculate and adjust the periscope diopter setting for the particular camera, plus the camera settings for the type of film and the outside light. Money could not have purchased the instruction and assistance these men were getting for nothing, and I wished I had had the sense to bring my own camera.

We had hoped the passage to Easter Island would be uneventful, after the rather strenuous navigation around the Falkland Islands and Cape Horn. I looked forward to a twenty-five-hundred-mile run through deep water, few problems, and a chance to read Thor Heyerdahl's book, *Aku-Aku,* in which he describes his search for the origin of the Easter Islanders and his re-erection of one of the stone monoliths. It was, unfortunately, not to be so.

The tremendous capability of the nuclear power plant and the many changes in submarine operating procedures which it requires were brought firmly home the day after we passed Cape Horn, when we held a "loss of all main power" drill. All naval ships are required to carry out such exercises, for the obvious reasons that they develop the crew's ability to cope with the problem should it occur in battle or as a result of some mishap.

Triton had, however, traveled some two thousand miles at great speed since she had last "gotten a good trim," as submariners say. She had, moreover, changed from Atlantic waters off the River Plate to Pacific waters on the far side of Cape Horn, and was well on her way toward Easter Island. Our instruments, and those of Nick Mabry from the Hydrographic Office in Washington, gave us some idea of the change in salinity of the sea water—generally speaking, the Atlantic side of South America was saltier. We had taken aboard a good deal of water for various purposes, including running our evaporators and keeping our fresh water tanks full, and we had pumped varying amounts of water overboard to compensate for our computed decreased buoyancy.

Prior to the test, Tom Thamm sought me out.

"Captain," he said, "my calculations show us to be pretty heavy by the time you consider the reduced salinity and the changes which have taken place in our internal weights."

"Yes?" I said.

"According to these figures we ought to pump out about seventy thousand pounds before we have the drill . . ."

"Tom," I interrupted, "aren't your Diving Officers and Diving Chiefs keeping up with the trim as we go along?"

"Yes, sir, but I made a special computation because of this drill coming off, and that is what the figures show."

This would be an opportunity for a good lesson, I thought. "Permission not granted, Tom," I said. "The sort of casualty that we're simulating might happen at any time, and we would have to face it with the conditions existing at that time. Suppose we really were to lose all power right now, rather than an hour from now after you get all this water pumped out?"

I had Tom there and he knew it, though I could see that he did not fully approve. "Aye aye, sir," he said. "I'll stand by in the control room just in case."

I grinned at him. Tom was a perfectionist who didn't want to have anything go wrong in his department. If the ship were too badly out of trim, a short blast of high-pressure air in the main ballast tanks was the quickest way of expelling a lot of water and stopping her descent. Then, the air in the tanks would have to be vented off—partly, at least—as we came up. Otherwise, with reduced external pressure as the ship rose to shallower depths, the air in the tanks would expand even more, thus still further lightening her. Blowing precisely the right amount to balance exactly could not be guaranteed, and several blowings and ventings would undoubtedly be required before the trim pump could get rid of enough water. And later, Curt Shellman's carefully tended air compressors would have to perform considerable extra work to recharge the air banks.

In the unlikely event that Tom was wrong, that the ship was light instead of heavy, water would have to be taken in rapidly in order to keep her from broaching surface; but with the aid of sea pressure, this is always a much easier thing to do than to pump it out.

The particular problem that faced us had almost never been experienced in battery-driven submarines, for these normally operate at minimum speed while submerged in order to conserve their vitally important batteries, and any divergence from a perfect submerged trim is instantly evident. As a consequence, all old-fashioned submarines automatically stay in perfect trim, practically as a reflex action, whenever they operate submerged. Being even slightly out of trim causes difficulty in maintaining depth at slow speed. But at our sustained high speed, a few hundred tons of extra weight, or buoyancy, would be unnoticeable—until we slowed down.

Everyone in the ship was up and around during the drill period, late-sleepers among the off-watch section having been jolted into consciousness by the daily test of the ship's various alarm systems, which had been programmed for fifteen minutes prior to the beginning of the exercise.

At the agreed-upon time, I, too, was in the control room, as were Will Adams and Tom Thamm. At my signal, Will picked up the telephone and spoke briefly to Don Fears, who, naturally enough, just happened to be in number one engine room.

Immediately, a strident voice bellowed on the ship's general announcing system. "Control, this is Maneuvering One. We've lost all power, both shafts."

I watched the engine-order telegraph indicators on the Diving Control Panel shift swiftly from "ahead full" to "stop."

For a moment, nothing else happened, though I knew our propellers were now only pinwheeling with the ship's motion through the water. Dick Harris, who had the Diving Officer's watch, stepped a few inches closer to his planesman; all three were intently scanning the instruments in front of them. Seated on the padded tool box in front of the fathometer, Tom Thamm was doing the same, while two feet farther aft, Chief Engineman E. C. Rauch had squared himself away in front of his Diving Panel and crushed out his half-smoked cigarette.

Elsewhere in the ship, wherever there was a critical station, I knew that the men on watch were standing by to take whatever action might be necessary, and because this was a scheduled drill, at every station there also stood, as observers, the off-watch personnel, the senior petty officer in charge, and the officer responsible.

We had been making just under twenty knots. As the ship slowed, I knew that both Dick and Tom were watching the depth gauges and the plane-angle indications for the first sign that we were, as everyone suspected, considerably heavier than the water we displaced. We waited a long minute, as *Triton* slowed and her bow and stern planes gradually lost effect. Suddenly, Harris reached his hand out behind him, motioned toward Rauch. "Pump auxiliaries to sea!" he snapped.

I had not seen yet any indications of the ship's being heavy. "How do you figure we're heavy, Dick?" I asked.

"Mostly intuition I guess, Captain," he replied. "There's really no sign here yet, but I know darned well she's heavy."

Another minute passed. We had slowed perceptibly and now it became evident that to hold the ordered depth, the planesmen were required to maintain up angle on both bow and stern planes.

"We are heavy, all right," I said.

From Harris my response was a tight-lipped smile, but it was Third Class Quartermaster Roger A. Miller, standing watch on the bow planes, who put it into words with a deep-toned whisper which caromed off the deck and bulkheads and brought amused smiles to everyone within earshot.

"This old hog sure has lead in her ass!" said he, as he lifted the bow planes another five degrees.

As speed dropped off rapidly, bow and stern planes soon were at the maximum angles of elevation and then, inexorably, *Triton* began to sink. In the meantime, Rauch, checking the rate-of-flow meter, was monotonously calling out the amount of water we pumped overboard: "5,000 out—7,000 out—10,000 out, sir—12,000 out—15,000 out."

Dick made no motion to stop him. *Triton*'s speed through water had by now dropped to only three or four knots; she was still on an even keel, but the depth gauges were showing a gradually increasing speed of descent.

It was apparent soon that we should not be able to get enough water out of the ship before she had exceeded the maximum depth to which we were allowed to submerge her. Deliberately I waited as long as possible, then finally nodded to Dick, "I guess we won't be able to catch her, Dick. Blow tanks."

"Blow forward group! Blow after group!" Dick had the orders ready.

So did Rauch, whose fingers were already on the main ballast blow valve switches. With two quick motions, high-pressure air was roaring into *Triton*'s main ballast tanks. Dick waited until he saw our downward motion perceptibly reduced, then gave the clenched fist signal to Rauch at the same time as the order, "Secure the air!"

The noise of air blowing stopped. We had lightened the ship by several hundred tons, and *Triton*'s involuntary dive stopped well above the allowed limit. But this was not the end of the episode.

The depth gauges now started going in the other direction. *Triton* was rising to the surface, slowly at first and then with increasing speed. We had placed a large air bubble in our main ballast tanks which, like uncorked bottles inverted in the water, were open at the bottom and closed at the top. It was impossible to gauge the amount of air that had to be blown into the tanks so as to put the ship precisely and exactly in equilibrium at a given depth.

Having put enough air into the tanks to stop the descent, it was apparent that the ship would now rise. As she rose, however, the size of the air bubble increased as the sea pressure reduced; and as the air bubble increased in size, it pushed even more water out through the bottom of the ballast tanks, thus making *Triton* still lighter. In this condition, we would continue to lighten and rise faster until we reached the surface.

Once, during the war, with the old *Trigger* leaking badly and surrounded by Japanese destroyers listening for us to start our pumps, we had survived just such a situation by putting an air bubble in one of our tanks and then either venting it slowly into the ship (we dared not use the main vents, which would have loosed a betraying bubble of air to the surface) or blowing it carefully. With the desperate skill of emergency, for fifteen hours Johnny Shepherd maintained precise control of our depth, as the accumulated leakage of water gradually made us heavier and heavier, until finally we outlasted the enemy. We had not dared to relieve Johnny.

The situation here was far less tense. There was no enemy; we could afford to let air bubbles come to the surface. Our only problem was to control the size of the bubble in our tanks to keep from broaching surface on the one hand or going too deep on the other.

As *Triton* ballooned upward, I watched silently for signs of the required action. It is for situations like this that men are qualified in submarines. With approval, I saw Rauch keeping his eyes on Harris, his hand already resting lightly on the controls for the main vents. Thamm was watching, too. *Triton* rose at an ever-increasing pace and finally Dick gave the order: "Open main vents."

I could hear the vent mechanism operating and all of us heard the rush of the entrapped air as it escaped from the tank. But Dick was still watching the depth gauges, "Shut main vents," he ordered. His objective was to catch some of the air still inside the tanks in order to retain some of the resulting buoyancy. In the meantime, with approval, I noted that he had not ordered Rauch to stop the trim pump, that we were still pumping water from the midships auxiliary tanks to sea.

Triton's rise toward the surface ceased rather abruptly. By this time, we had no forward motion through the water at all. With the ship badly out of trim, she was controllable in depth only by the constant buoyancy of her great hull, plus the variable buoyancy of the expanding and contracting volume of air in the ballast tanks. Undersea ballooning was an apt simile.

But Dick had let out too much air, for *Triton* was now heavy and began to sink once more; as she sank, the air bubble remaining in the ballast tanks would be further and further compressed, with the result that the ship's buoyancy would continue to reduce and she would now progressively descend faster and faster—though slower than the first time. Dick was ready for this, however, and after we had sunk some little distance, he again ordered that tanks be blown, but for a considerably shorter time than before. Again, *Triton* halted her descent and began to rise; and, as she neared the surface, Dick opened the ballast tank vents and allowed most of the air to escape.

In the meantime, we had continued pumping water out of the ship. Gradually, our wild gyrations lessened as we got her correctly trimmed. With ballast tanks again full of water, no air trapped in them, *Triton* finally hovered, motionless, balanced precariously with her internal weight exactly equal to that of the water displaced.

It might be well to explain at this point a fact that submariners know well, but which may not be so well known to others: it is impossible for a submerged body to be so delicately trimmed or balanced that it will remain indefinitely static, neither rising nor falling. Despite fanciful tales written by people who do not know their physics, things cannot just sink part way. A submerged submarine has no reserve buoyancy; that is to say, she gains no additional buoyancy by sinking a little deeper in the water (a surface ship, passing from more-dense to less-dense water, increases imperceptibly in draft). If an eight-thousand-ton submarine is one pound heavier than the water she displaces, she will slowly sink. The deeper she goes, the greater the pressure; even the strongest hull will be slightly compressed, thus reducing the volume of displaced water and increasing the disparity between her weight and that of the water displaced. She will go all the way down until she reaches the bottom. Conversely, a submerged submarine one ounce light will ultimately broach the surface. The only exception to this rule occurs when there is a layer, or stratum, of heavier water underlying a lighter layer. In this case, the submarine can "balance" on the boundary between the two, as long as the dissimilarity continues to exist. This is known as "riding a layer."

It is true that a submarine almost in perfect trim—as near to perfect trim as it can possibly get—might very very slowly sink in water of a certain density until it reaches a layer of water considerably cooler or more saline than the one for which trimmed, and there she will stay for a while. Ships have been known to ride thus, suspended between two layers of water of dissimilar densities, for many hours. There have even been stories about balancing a submarine so skillfully that the slight increase in displacement gained by raising a periscope would cause her slowly to drift toward the surface, and sink slowly when the periscope is withdrawn inside its bearings, but, practically speaking, such situations are rare and highly temporary.

The submarine riding on a layer will maintain depth so long as all the factors affecting her equilibrium remain exactly the same. But they never do. Considering the many changes constantly taking place in the weight of the submarine, due to leakage through propeller shaft glands, to name one unstoppable source, or water taken in by the evaporators, for instance, it is certain that within a short time the sub's trim will change. In all cases, the change is in the direction of becoming heavier and, without the intelligent hand of man, she will shortly resume her descent. Nothing, in other words, can float without control between the surface of the sea and the bottom.

Davy Jones might have been perturbed had he observed *Triton,* the world's greatest submarine, slither to a halt and commence a series of astonishing gyrations in depth, accompanied by a frenetic blowing and venting of air and grinding of pumps. He would indeed have been justified in suspecting something to have gone seriously wrong. Such was, however, far from the fact. We were well pleased with the results of our drill, which showed that we had more than adequate control of our huge ship, even under the hazardous conditions which result from a complete loss of power; and after a short time, the mock-casualty restored, *Triton*'s great propellers began to turn purposefully once more and she settled down on her course to the northwest at a speed faster than any submarine had ever traversed these waters.

According to *Triton*'s Log, it was next day, at about ten-thirty at night, when a calamity of very real proportions confronted us. Intimation of the problem came when Don Fears called me on the ship's service telephone in my room. For a few days we had had a severe leak around the starboard propeller shaft, which had been growing steadily worse. Now, as Don put it, it was no longer incidental, but of some magnitude. Fears and Curt Shellman were both in the lower level of the engine room, and I got there as soon as possible.

Spotting the leak was easy. Great sheets of water were spurting out around the periphery of the flange and gland through which the propeller shaft passed into the sea, driving a solid white spray perpendicularly outward from the shaft itself around 360° of its circumference, soaking the overhead of the platform deck above, the curved side of the ship outboard of the shaft, and the tiny walk deck. A heavy canvas dropcloth had already been rigged to protect the machinery near the leak, while Curt Shellman and three of his engineers, all of them drenched, were struggling perilously close to the rapidly revolving propeller shaft in their effort to stem the flow of water.

The tremendous racket produced by the hydrantlike force of water striking deck plates and other structures in the engine room made it almost impossible to talk. I put my mouth next to Don Fear's ear and shouted, "Good Lord, Don, how long has it been this bad?"

Fears looked serious and shouted into my ear in turn. "This is why I called you, Captain. The leak we had before was getting slowly worse and I was thinking of calling you anyway, then suddenly she broke loose."

"What is the trouble?" I yelled.

Don shook his head. "Don't know for sure, sir. Curt and his people have been right on it, though. Maybe we'll have an answer pretty soon."

"You can't handle this with the drain pump, Don," I shouted, enunciating slowly and carefully above the din. "We can't let these bilges get too full!"

Don nodded understandingly. "We have the drain pump on the line already, Captain, but I think you're right. The pump won't be able to keep up with this flood!"

Quite apart from the ultimate safety of the ship herself, if this huge leak could not be stopped, there was a lot of electrical equipment and other delicate machinery in the engine room which would be damaged if the water level rose too high.

"Don," I said, "we'll have to stop the starboard shaft. That will help some. At least it will let Curt get closer to the problem. I don't like him working around the shaft like that while it's turning."

Don nodded, shouting in my ear. "Maybe we could come to a shallower depth, too, Captain. That would reduce the pressure and cut down the leak some."

I assented. It took but a second to dash up the ladder to the upper level, find a telephone, and call the Officer of the Deck. In a moment, the starboard propeller shaft began to slow down, and at the same time the ship angled gently upward. In deference to the amount of water already in the bilges, which would all be concentrated in the after end if too steep an angle were assumed, I had told the Officer of the Deck to bring her up handsomely—that is, slowly and steadily, with good control.

As the outside water pressure was reduced, the leak correspondingly decreased. Shellman cast me a grateful look. I beckoned to him. "Curt," I said, "we are locking the shaft so that it can't turn. This will let you get closer to it, at least."

Shellman was mopping his face with a rag. "Thanks, Captain. I was about to ask if we might do that. I'm afraid to put somebody outboard of the propeller shaft because there's not much clearance between it and the skin of the ship."

He did not need to say more. There was perhaps a foot-and-a-half clearance between the propeller shaft and the curve of *Triton*'s pressure hull or skin. As I watched the propeller shaft come to a complete stop, there came into view a great bolted coupling by which two sections of the shaft had been joined together. The huge coupling had been rotating previously in a sort of a blur, its machined edges a lethal hazard while the shaft was turning.

With the shaft at a complete halt, Curt and Chief Engineman Fred Rotgers climbed on top, braving the reduced spray of water, while "Rabbit" Hathaway, a compactly built Engineman, squirmed under the shaft and into the confined space.

Several minutes later we had the answer. The spit of anger in Rotgers' voice as he reported the basic cause of the problem was not all due to the salt-water bath he had just experienced. "The _____ nuts on the far side of the gland are so loose you can turn them by hand," he spluttered.

"How about the locking washers, Chief?" asked Shellman.

"I sure didn't see any. That's why they loosened up!" Rotgers glared as he spoke. It was evident that whoever had installed these bolts would have fared badly had the powerful Rotgers been able to get his hands on him at that moment.

"There are locking wires on the inboard side of the gland," reported Shellman, after a brief inspection.

Further investigation showed that loose bolts were not the end of the trouble. The propeller shaft water seal had been improperly installed, that is, not made tight, either because of the difficulty in reaching some of the bolts or through lack of locking devices. Under the vibration and stress of continual high speed, complication had followed upon complication. Looseness of the bolts on the outboard side had permitted the packing gland to become partially cocked on its seat, and now, tighten the bolts as we would, it remained jammed in a cocked position and could not be straightened. We heaved on the nuts with the biggest wrenches aboard, to the point where Curt feared further pressure might distort or damage the parts even more, but there was no stemming the leak.

Not sure, in fact, whether or not some improvement might have been made, we eased *Triton* down again into the depths, and the resulting effect, with the greater pressure outside, was striking, to say the least.

We had obviously not solved the problem. The next step was to put an emergency clamp around the leak, utilizing three damage-control clamps which had been designed for small patches, not for anything as massive as this. Down we went for a test again, but the pressure of the water was so strong that it simply pushed the clamps apart.

Midnight had long given way to morning as Curt Shellman, Fred Rotgers, Clarence Hathaway, and others struggled with the leak in the confined space. The watch had changed at midnight and again at four o'clock, but Shellman, Rotgers, and company stayed on the job. Two solutions were decided on: first, we would try to reinforce the three damage-control clamps which had failed; second, we would design an entirely new clamp, sacrificing for the purpose a section of molding from the wardroom passageway, which happened to be made of corrosion-resisting steel and was, by good fortune, of sufficient size for our use.

By breakfast time the first try was in place, damage-control clamps with backing plate for reinforcement. It had been a long, back-breaking job, performed in tight quarters under the most unfavorable conditions, with water squirting in under pressure the whole time the men worked. When we unlocked the propeller shaft for a full-fledged test, Curt Shellman's naturally haggard face assumed an even more worried expression, the deep circles under his eyes standing out almost as though the difficulty had caused him physical suffering. But all went well; the leak did not increase beyond manageable size, the drain pump was able to take care of the water leakage without difficulty, and Shellman permitted a half-smile to wrinkle the deep bags under his eyes. At noon, Fears reported that the modified clamp would hold, for the time at least, and that our newly manufactured one would be held in reserve.

Entry from the Log dated 12 March, 1960:

0020   Our fathometer is out of commission again. This is bad news. It has been giving us trouble off and on for the past several days. Each time, however, we have brought it back into operation. This time, as our electronics technicians and sonarmen check it over, they actually record the gradually decreasing installation resistance in the head. It appears to be flooded.

Ever since the initial difficulty with the fathometer, "Whitey" Rubb and Dick Harris had been giving me daily reports as to its condition, and I was well aware of their increasing fears as to its performance. All the instruction books we had on board for the fathometer had been pored over, and in anticipation, we had checked over the stock of electronic spares on board the ship, the back-up for all the complicated electronic-control equipment with which *Triton* was fitted. All spare parts which could conceivably be used in the fathometer—tubes, resistors, crystals, power amplifiers—all, no matter what type of equipment they were originally designed for, had been located, so that we could substitute as necessary.

As the careful watch over the fathometer continued, our worries increased. The receiver crystals had again burned out, and our new transformer had gone, too. Both were abnormal casualties, and it appeared that the basic trouble was not in the electronic hookup of the fathometer, but in the installation of the fathometer head itself. This, unfortunately, was something with which we could not cope, even were the ship on the surface. We could, and did, take resistance and capacitance readings of various components through the electrical connections inside the ship to which we had access. But so far as inspecting the head, possibly eliminating a leak or replacing a bad component with a good one, we were completely helpless.

By 0200, complete loss of the fathometer was confirmed. Another set of crystals, just replaced in the receiver, had immediately burned out, and there was no question that the fathometer head itself was the cause. Chief Sonarman George McDaniel reported that while he was measuring the resistance to ground he recorded a rapidly reducing resistance to the point where the sonar head was completely grounded out.

All submarines are plagued with inability to maintain topside wiring free of water. A great number of cables must come through the pressure hull and therefore, over some percentage of their length, must be exposed to full sea pressure. Despite great care in installation, there are always some that flood, either through an unsuspected fault in the pressure sealing of the cable itself or because of improper installation. New ships, because of their miles of cabling, always have the greatest difficulty keeping their wiring dry.

Realizing that we would have to complete the rest of our cruise without a fathometer, a serious period of self-analysis faced me. Could we safely finish the trip without danger of running aground on some uncharted shoal or damaging the ship by striking bottom in one of the restricted passages we would later be required to navigate?

It was not as though this had suddenly become a consideration at four o'clock on the morning of the twelfth of March. I had been thinking it over ever since the first difficulty with the fathometer had arisen, and had generated some experiments with our search sonar and Mike Smalet's "monkey in a cage"—our name for his gravity-metering gadget.

Even before it finally broke down, I had become convinced that despite the loss of the fathometer we could still proceed along our way. Our search sonar reliably detected shallow water ahead and on either side, and particularly gave us immediate warning of sudden changes in the depth of the ocean bottom. Smalet, who was as anxious as anyone that the trip proceed successfully, had advanced the theory that although unexplained anomalies in the earth's crust had an effect on gravity, it was also true that gravity was fundamentally a function of mass and distance. A perceptible increase in gravity should therefore coincide with a reduction in the depth of the ocean, and vice versa. We had been trying out his theory whenever there was an opportunity, and to our delight found that there was indeed some such correlation.

However, a more subtle question had to be answered: should I report our trouble?

By this time, we had passed into the operational control of ComSubPac, whose headquarters were in Pearl Harbor. What would be his reaction upon receiving a message from the *Triton* stating that her fathometer was out of commission? What indeed would be the reaction in the Pentagon? It was in a sense my duty to report our problem, but would I not, in so doing, be passing on responsibility I should assume myself? How could any admiral in Pearl Harbor or Washington or New London evaluate the situation as well as I could? Unable to see the situation at first hand, might they not be obliged to adopt the cautious course?

In short, if I simply reported the loss of the fathometer without all the amplifying considerations we had so laboriously developed in the past week and a half, was there not a good chance that we should be ordered to cancel the remainder of our trip and proceed directly to Pearl Harbor for repairs?

This question, with all its nuances, was the big one. In final analysis, I felt continuation of our expedition depended as much upon my decision at this point as on anything we had done to date. Well I knew the Navy tradition; on the Captain rests the responsibility for the right decision. And well I remembered what had happened to Father after the *Memphis* had gone aground in Santo Domingo harbor. The cause had been a tidal wave—unpredictable, therefore something against which one could not have been prepared. Pacing the deck of his ship on a warm, pleasant afternoon, at anchor with awnings rigged, gangways down, and liberty parties ashore, he had been the first to see danger. Within forty minutes, mast-high breakers swept in from the peaceful sea and *Memphis* was cast ashore on a coral reef, a total wreck. Father was exonerated of all blame for the catastrophe, except the impossible responsibility for not having anticipated a tidal wave. (Technically, "not having been ready to get underway immediately.")

This was, in fact, the major contention upon which his court martial eventually turned. In the crux of the decision, which the court, true to Navy tradition, could not but render against him, was the statement that nothing could divest the Commanding Officer of the ultimate responsibility for the safety of his ship. A comparable responsibility now burdened me.

Breakfast was served as I wrestled with the problem. This was not something that anyone else on board the *Triton* should be concerned with, but the more I thought of it the more certain I became that here, even more surely than off Montevideo, success or failure of our voyage lay in the balance.

Much has been written about the so-called "calculated risk," but one of the considerations or calculations which cannot be neglected is that if failure is encountered, the penalty is no less severe than if the risk had been assumed without forethought.

All the training the Navy had given me, all the background of the Naval Academy and my years at sea, could lead to only one conclusion. As in Father's case and in every similar case, the final responsibility is on the Commanding Officer. I had to make the crucial decision, and it had better be the right one.

I resolved not to report our difficulty. Come what might, we would carry on and complete the voyage. Furthermore, I could not permit our situation to be fully appreciated by anyone else aboard. This load, like that of our special mission, could not be shared with anyone.

At 0105 on the morning of March thirteenth, our search sonar made contact with a submerged peak. Without the fathometer or the precision-depth recorder—which received its data from the fathometer—we were unable to determine the minimum depth of water over this peak.

We could not, consequently, predict how much water we had to maneuver in. In accordance with instructions, the Officer of the Deck slowed and changed course to avoid. We did so with ease, passing the shallow area well abeam and continuing on our way. Probably our caution was excessive, but my confidence in our ability to detect and avoid shallow water was confirmed.

At five o'clock in the morning, we brought *Triton* to periscope depth. Easter Island should be dead ahead.

From the Log:

0512   Radar contact on Easter Island at bearing and range predicted.

As we approached land, to my gratification our search sonar indicated a gradual shoaling of water as we moved steadily toward the island. Because of loss of depth of water information and in deference to the three-mile limit, we had decided to stay well clear of land.

From the Log:

0706   Commenced photographic reconnaissance of northeastern coast of Easter Island. About 0930, after careful search of the area, Thor Heyerdahl's statue is located, right where he said it was. Several other old stone heads have been sighted, none clearly identifiable from a distance, but there is no doubt about this one. The word is passed throughout the ship that anyone wishing to see a stone statue had better come to the conning tower.

In no time at all there is a regular procession of men coming up for periscope liberty, as was the case off Cape Horn. The statue faces inland and not much can be made out of its features, but the morning sun glints in orange and crimson upon the angular granite—and many details are filled in by our imaginations, reinforced by Heyerdahl's book.

In the meantime we have been carefully searching the shore and slopes of Easter Island to detect any movement of people or any possibility of our periscope being spotted. The possibilities are remote; not many island people spend much time gazing at the unchanging landscape of the South Pacific ocean. Nevertheless it is a possibility—but search as we may, not a single moving creature is seen on the island. A number of habitations are seen, one, not far from the statue, consisting of a small but attractive pink stucco house surrounded by well-tended foliage and an apparently nicely graded dirt road.

1116   Took departure from Easter Island enroute Guam, 6734 miles distant.

This was Sunday, and it was my turn to be the leader at the Protestant church services. I had never led any type of religious meeting before this, and put in a considerable amount of preparation. I called my "lesson" "Shipmate means sharing," and tried to describe in simple terms the duty I felt was owing from one shipmate to another.

My little talk appeared to be well received; under the circumstances it could hardly have been otherwise, but I could not help feeling that the events of the last few days had proved not all things could be shared.

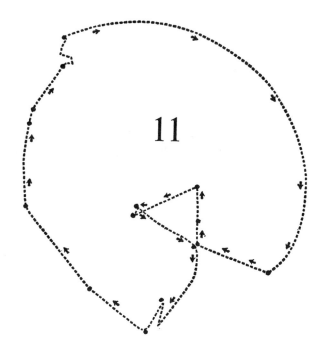

11

From Easter Island to Guam would take us about two weeks. Aside from the necessity of threading rather neatly between the outlying reefs of one or two archipelagos, we foresaw no need to slow down, except for such maneuvers as we might ourselves decide on. But I remember having a feeling of concern which I could not shake, as we began this longest leg of our trip.

The passage from Cape Horn to Easter Island had turned out to be full of very real difficulties. Fortunately, all had been successfully remedied, with the exception of the fathometer, but the experience boded ill for the future.

We could use a fathometer in the Pacific, for it had at least as many peaks as the Atlantic, but there was one difference. Most of these were coral formations instead of volcanic in

181

origin. They should, therefore, be less precipitous, more gradual in slope in both directions, inherently less dangerous. As we moved along our course, we gained assurance in the various methods we had devised to get substitute depth readings, now that the fathometer was no longer working. Every day we became more certain of our ability to detect shoaling water under any circumstances. More and more, I knew that my decision to press on had been the right one.

As for our equipment, however, the trans-Pacific leg of our voyage began in a manner by then uncomfortably all too familiar. On the seventeenth of March, in the early morning, George Troffer, *Triton*'s Electrical Officer, stood solemnly outside my door. One of the air compressors which supplied the air pressure needed for certain automatic control systems had gone out of commission. As George explained it, the electric motor had apparently been slowly failing in its resistance to ground and, overworked as it was, had finally given up the ghost. Inspection of the motor had disclosed that the armature windings were entirely burned out.

This was disquieting news. Although we had stand-by controls for all essential systems, this would necessitate increasing the watch squad in certain areas. It might also, at the same time, result in some sluggishness in the automatic controls. I listened gravely as the technical tale of woe was unfolded.

"What about a jury rig, George?" I asked.

George nodded. "I was going to suggest one, Captain," he said, "but I don't know how you'll like it . . ."

"Shoot," I said, motioning him to the tiny built-in stool under my folding wash basin.

Troffer carefully perched on the stool, which had now been dubbed, so I had discovered, "the one-cheek hot seat."

"We can get air from the ship's main air system, though not at the right pressure," Troffer explained. "But we do have some pressure-reducing valves among our spares, and I think we can rig them up. We'll have to use two reducers in tandem and the pressure won't be quite the same, but I think it'll work."

"Sounds good," I said. "Where will you get the air from?"

"Well, maybe we can take it from the ship's hundred pound service air main," he said. "That would be the simplest, provided we can get the right reducing valve arrangement. Otherwise, we might have to take it from the four hundred pound air-pressure header."

"You'll need a pretty good length of hose or copper tubing to run it over to the control air system," I said. "Do we have enough?"

"We may have to rob something else, but I think it'll be OK," George said. "If we have to take it straight off the four hundred pound header, it will be a pretty long run, though."

"Well," I said, "it looks as if we don't have much choice. See what you can do."

Troffer nodded. "I figured the same thing, Captain," he said. "We've already started—one of the troubles, however, is that if we have to use the four hundred pound air system, we'll have to run it through a watertight door. This will reduce our watertight integrity, because we won't be able to shut the door if we should have to."

"Not so fast," I interrupted. "If you have to run a line through a door, let me know before you do, and at all times while that line is through the door, there'll be a damage-control ax and a heavy set of wire cutters standing by. That's easy."

George's face cleared as he stood up. "Aye aye, sir. That's just what we'll do."

As Troffer disappeared down the passageway back toward the engine room, I could not help but reflect upon the tremendous competence *Triton* had working for her. One way or another, her control system would be working again soon; and I also knew that in due course the reason for the failure of the air-compressor motor would be discovered; its cause eliminated. Shaking out such bugs is always one of the objectives of a shakedown cruise, and *Triton* was at the moment indubitably on hers. The only difference was that an ordinary ship on a shakedown cruise is unperturbed by minor casualties, even if they temporarily reduce her operability. No one expects a brand-new ship to function perfectly the first time. We, however, had a mission to complete. Not only was the Navy depending on us, but there was also a tradition that no nuclear submarine had yet failed on a mission to which she had been assigned. No doubt it was this confidence in the dependability of Admiral Rickover's ships which had inspired this voyage in the first place. We would not be the first to break the tradition.

I knew that this spirit and outlook had permeated our crew. But even so, I was surprised, a few hours later as I was wandering through the engineering spaces, to discover a group of toiling men, conspicuous among them Chief Electrician's Mate Herbert F. Hardman—the same who had happily announced achievement of a thirteen-year's ambition at the crossing-of-the-line ceremony—struggling to remove the ponderous inoperative electric motor from the control air compressor to a workbench some distance away.

"I thought I understood that we had no spare armatures for this thing, Hardman," I said.

"We don't, sir, but this damned motor shouldn't have broken down. First, we're going to find out why, and then we're going to rewind it."

"Rewind the armature!" I expostulated. "I've heard of Navy Yards and tenders doing that with all the extra equipment they have, but I know darned well we don't carry any of that kind of gear!"

Hardman, as I had reason to know, was a man of great positiveness, as well as being an efficient Electrician's Mate. His whole bearing spoke determination as he answered, "This damned motor is my piece of gear, and it's going to be running before we get back." His jaw muscles bulged slightly as he snapped out the last few words.

I remember wishing at the moment that I had had some appropriate rejoinder worthy of the occasion. All I could think of to say was, "Good!"

But if I was surprised in the engine room, what I saw that same day in the electronics technician's storeroom was astonishing. Electronics Technicians G. E. Simpson, M. F. Docker, and N. L. Blaede had started constructing a new fathometer! A stainless-steel cooking pot had been commandeered from the galley, and a number of stainless-steel rods, plus considerable small, fine copper wire from the engineering and electrical spare parts petty officers. The technicians had calculated the resistances and impedances and were busily engaged in constructing a new sound head.

"Certainly it'll work," said Docker. "The question is whether it will be powerful enough to do the job for us, and whether we can find some way to put its signal into the water."

Another project they were working on was the conversion of one of our general announcing speakers into a sonar transmitter, a conversion that involved developing a means of making it both watertight and pressure-proof at the same time, and yet able to transmit and receive sonar signals. A third, and much more primitive idea, beating on the bottom of the hull with a hammer, was ready for trial as soon as we happened into shallow water again. All these projects were based on the hope that we might be able to catch an echo on one of our other sonar sets and, by timing it, ascertain the depth of water.

I could only marvel at the ingenuity of the American sailor. These experiments might not work, but all three were certainly worth trying.

The last-named idea required no special preparation other than finding the best spot for hammering on the hull, a suitably heavy hammer, and a brawny sailor. Years ago, when the submarine S4 lay sunk on the bottom of Cape Cod Bay, communication had been maintained with the survivors by means of hammering against the hull. It was just possible that enough energy could thus be placed in the water for our modern and acutely sensitive sonar to pick up a returning echo from a nearby shoal.

When it came time to make the test, Torpedoman Second Class Wilmot A. Jones drew the assignment of being the human fathometer. The forward torpedo room bilges, beneath the torpedo tubes themselves, appeared to be the most suitable spot for the effort. Armed with a heavy sledge hammer, Jones crawled down into position.

The number of hours poor Jones spent at his task, hammering with prodigious force upon the unyielding structure of *Triton*'s hull in the hopes that somehow a faint return might be heard, are unrecorded. We heard him clearly inside the ship, but no matter how hard he hammered or how shallow the water, no echo was ever picked up.

Had we been able to project all the sounds straight down through some sort of a diaphragm or sound-channeling arrangement, better results might have been achieved, for, after all, that is the principle upon which the fathometer itself operates. But this was not possible, and the only tangible result of Jones's efforts was a cartoon which appeared the next day in the *Triton Eagle,* showing a section of the forward torpedo room bilges with an idiotic-looking sailor sucking his thumb and crouched below a set of torpedo tubes. He was labeled "Jones," to be sure he would be properly identified, and with his free hand he was swinging a hammer and pounding on the hull. The balloon above his head held the words, "Da Da Da, Whee—I'm a fathometer."

Nevertheless, we had a good idea of the depth of the water. As we approached the charted shallow areas, our search sonar detected shallow water ahead and to port, where we had expected it. In the meantime, Mike Smalet, our gravity-meter expert, noted definite changes in the gravity readings recorded by the "monkey in a cage." While the change in gravity might have resulted from some other cause, its correlation with the search sonar could not be ignored.

Crossing the Pacific from Easter Island to Guam took us two weeks, and it was during this trip that Will Adams decided the greatest danger of boredom existed. The same trip took Magellan three months, during which he and his crew nearly starved to death. Our desire to emulate his feat did not extend to culinary duplication, and the various breaks in our monotony which Will devised were to a large degree dependent upon food (Poi, near Hawaii, for example).

On Sunday evening, the twentieth of March, *Triton* reached her closest point of approach to Pearl Harbor, and we held a ship's party in honor of the occasion. Naturally, it had to be a Hawaiian Luau. My memories of such an occasion stemmed from the war years, for I had not been in Hawaii since then. But Will had, and so had Ship's Cook First Class William "Jim" Crow. In fact, Will had given the matter some forethought, and one of the announcements before departure from New London was that all hands were advised to bring along some sort of sports togs or shirts (he had been very cute about this), similar to Hawaiian "Aloha" shirts, for our expected ship's party in the Bahamas. He had also suggested that anyone who had a musical instrument bring it along.

Bob Fisher and Will Adams spent considerable time on the Luau menu. And even though I had been pretty well prepared for what I was to see at 1800 when the party started, I was amazed at what they had done. A coconut tree, bearing two large brown coconuts garnished with great purple leaves, "grew" out of the deck. A number of Hawaiian leis were strung about the overhead, some looking suspiciously like the commercially manufactured article made with bits of colored plastic paper, others obviously homemade. On the bulkheads were drawings of Hawaiian scenes. Having seen some of Tom Thamm's work before, I had no doubt that a great deal of this was due to him. There were brightly colored shirts and two or three battered but gaudy straw hats. There were even hula skirts, made of cloth strips and string. And the food, with the exception of Will Adams' poi, was uniformly excellent. There was no octopus, the Navy standard menu having no provision for serving octopus in any form, but we did have raw fish garnished with some sort of hot sauce, French-fried shrimp and ocean scallops, sweet-and-sour pork, fruit, salted nuts, and iced punch.

To my surprise, even the ersatz poi had a number of takers, although so far as I was concerned, it was just like Hawaiian poi: paste without taste. And when the meal was over, and a large, specially baked cake cut and passed around, we all relaxed for an hour, singing songs of the Navy and the submarine force dating back to the war years and before.

From the Log:

Monday, 21 March 1960   Shortly after midnight, as we came to periscope depth for celestial observations, it was discovered that the sextant built into our new periscope has gone out of order. This will be a serious blow if we can't fix it, ameliorated only by the fact that running continuously submerged as we are, we find that our dead-reckoning is most phenomenally accurate. Rarely has our estimated position deviated from our actual observed position by more than a mile or two. It appears that currents and other forces affecting surface ships during transits are much less a factor during submerged runs. To paraphrase an aphorism, "deep waters run still."

0531   Periscope sextant is back in commission as the result of some rather inspired work by L. L. Garlock, FTC (SS) and W. E. Constantine, FT1 (SS).

Our submerged navigation was accomplished by several methods. One consisted of regular observation of the SINS mechanism, a system so new, however, that it was in effect an experimental model, full of bugs and therefore not dependable. Celestial observations through our special periscope proved to be far more accurate; and to Will's satisfaction, dead-reckoning also surpassed the SINS. Since the celestial observations were by far the most accurate of the three methods, loss of the periscope equipment would have been serious, despite the stand-by system which, thanks to George Sawyer—who had put long hours into having it ready in case of need—we could have placed in service.

From the Log:

Midnight, 21 March   A double babygram: an 8 pound 7 ounce girl [Frances Ann] for Leonard F. Lehman, Electrician's Mate First Class; and 6 pound Kari Jeanne for Richard Brown, also Electrician's Mate First Class. Birth dates respectively 15th and 18th of March. Mother's and Father's copies of babygrams are duly delivered. Fathers are honor-bound to bring the one with the cupids home to their wives.

Wednesday, 23 March 1960 0834   Crossed International Date Line from west longitude to east longitude at latitude 10° –36′ North. As this significant milestone was achieved, a message arrived from King Neptune informing us that because of our highly satisfactory conduct on 24 February, when we first crossed the equator, all hands were automatically, without further examination, taken into The Royal Order of Golden Dragons and so recorded in his log. There will, however, be a severe price.

Thursday, 24 March, is dropped from our calendar. This day, a full day from the lives of all hands, has been exacted from us in tribute for crossing the date line [technically speaking we advanced all clocks twenty-four hours]. Additional penance consists of working the ship for 24 full 25-hour days before we will be home again, although it should be noted that a number of these 25-hour days have already been worked off enroute to this area.

Still from the Log:

1733   The gravity meter indicated a rise in the ocean floor. There is no indication from sonar for 5 minutes, until 1738, when sonar detects a ledge from dead ahead around to port to a bearing of south.

1834   Gravity meter and sonar together show a dropping away in the ocean floor.

1933   First trial on our hand-made fathometer transducer: Unsuccessful.

The new fathometer transducer, the product of much inspired work by the Electronics Technicians gang under "Whitey" Rubb, had at last been completed, and had passéd a successful test. In the Electronics Technicians' workshop, a sonar signal set into the transducer was clearly heard outside it, even though the frequency response was theoretically in the inaudible range. The thing was worked in reverse also and was proven sensitive to the reception of noise beamed at it by radio or tape recorder at an approximately correct frequency. The problem now was to find some means of getting this sound into the water and catching it on the return.

Steel is a good conductor of sound. Our theory was that if we could send out a sufficiently strong signal, it might pass through the steel of our pressure hull and carry to the ocean floor, there to be reflected, hopefully, in sufficient strength to be detected either on the transducer itself or on one of our external hydrophones.

Another of our problems was that the pressure hull was the inner of *Triton*'s two hulls. When Jones had gone to work with the sledge hammer, we hoped that the water between the two hulls would carry the signal. But this experiment had been completely unsuccessful; in order to get the maximum possible chance of success with our handmade fathometer transducer, we had to do better.

There was, fortunately, a way to reach the outer skin of the ship itself, through the forward trim tank. Located in the space between the pressure hull and the outer hull, the tank had been built to withstand full test pressure and to meet the highest specifications of shock resistance. It also was accessible through a manhole cover at the bottom of the torpedo storeroom.

Tom Thamm adjusted the trim of the ship so that all water normally carried in the forward trim tank could be pumped out of it and into the midships auxiliary tanks. (Balance fore and aft was maintained by pumping an equal weight of water to auxiliaries from the after trim tank.) Then the tank was opened and tested for gas. After it had been pronounced clear, Lieutenant "Whitey" Rubb and Machinist Phil Kinnie descended into the heretofore sealed space, carrying our jury-rigged transducer with them.

Placing the new mechanism carefully against the skin of the ship, alongside the internal keel, they quickly made a connection to a cable from the fathometer transmitter nearby. After all was in readiness, we began the first test.

For a moment, we were greatly encouraged. We actually heard a sharp click, as the outgoing signal sped through our handmade transducer. But there was no returning echo. Various combinations were tried, including partially reflooding the forward trim tank so as to submerge the transducer and thus increase its ability to transmit through the bottom of the trim tank and to the water outside. But in the end, we were completely disappointed. The effort was unsuccessful.

"Whitey" was dejected. "I'm satisfied this isn't going to work, Captain," he said. "But I'd like to keep trying."

The only bright spot of the day was receipt of our fifth babygram. A boy, Donald, Jr., for Engineman First Class Donald R. Quick.

From the Log:

Sunday, 27 March 1960 1349 We will soon be passing through our nearest point of approach to the presumed location at which the first *Triton* (SS-201) was lost in action during World War II. As a matter of interest, this took place almost exactly seventeen years ago, and by a strange coincidence the first *Triton* departed on her last patrol from Brisbane, Australia, on the same day (16 February) as we, her namesake, departed from New London on this voyage. *Triton* I is presumed to have been lost as a result of depth charge attack by three Japanese destroyers on 15 March 1943, in a position almost exactly 800 miles due south of where we are now.

At that time I was engineer officer of *Trigger,* also lost in action later in the war, and LCDR R. S. Benson, USN, was skipper. On 15 March 1943, as it happened, we were on patrol in the same general vicinity as *Triton* I. Correlation between the known facts of *Triton*'s loss and *Trigger*'s report of the events of that date indicates that the two ships may have attacked the same convoy. *Trigger* believed she had sunk one ship and damaged a second, and *Triton*'s results were unknown. We were depth charged, though not severely. But afterwards we heard distant depth charges for approximately an hour. Japanese records indicate that the depth charging heard by *Trigger* most probably accounted for the loss of the old *Triton*. Their report of the action contains the notation that a large amount of oil came to the surface in the center of which floating objects were found bearing the label "Made in USA."

It was *Triton*'s sixth patrol, but the first for her new commander, LCDR George K. McKenzie, Jr. Besides her skipper, she had on board an unusual array of talent in LCDR John Eichmann, Executive Officer, and LCDR Jack R. Crutchfield, who was, I believe, Engineer. Eichmann had been with the *Triton* since she was commissioned in 1940. His name is engraved upon *Triton*'s old commissioning plaque, presented to us last November 10 by

Mrs. Lent, widow of the late Rear Admiral W. A. Lent, *Triton* I's first skipper. The plaque is now mounted in the passageway outside our wardroom.

Without too much fact on which to base my supposition, I have always assumed that John Eichmann had been slated for transfer to his own command, possibly to be brought back to the States for a new construction submarine as was the custom for people who had spent a long time in the war zone [and later happened, in time, to me], and that he had either been pursuaded to remain for one additional patrol, or very likely had volunteered to do so in order to provide some kind of continuity for the new skipper.

I had met Eichmann in 1939 when, as an Ensign, I spent a day at sea with the S-25 to which he was attached. Without conscious intention I had kept track of his whereabouts ever since. A year after the loss of *Triton,* after I had been Executive Officer of the *Trigger* for some time, I also agreed to stay for one extra patrol because *Trigger* had unexpectedly received a new skipper. In my case, *Trigger* survived the most serious depth-charging of her career and returned triumphantly to Pearl Harbor. But all during the ordeal, I kept hearing the parting words of the chap who left *Trigger* in my place: "You'll be sorry you didn't go, Ned—you'll be sorry—you'll be sorry." The Japanese depth charges' "click— WHAM—swish" said the same, and I kept thinking of Jack Eichmann.

Lt. McDonald and I put considerable thought into preparation of the service. We decided that a version of the committal service would be most appropriate, although we could find no reference or description of exactly what we wanted. Improvisation is the order of the day in submarines at sea anyway.

The services were announced at 1340, with directions that all hands not on watch assemble in the crew's mess, the air-control center or the officer's wardroom. At 1345 the services were broadcast throughout the ship, begun by the playing of Tattoo. This was followed by the National Anthem and a scripture reading from Psalm 107.

Following the scripture reading, a short prayer similar to the committal service was read, followed by reading of the tribute, which could hardly be called a eulogy but which was an attempt to put the significance of the occasion into words for our own better inspiration and understanding: The sacrifice made by the first *Triton,* and all the sacrifices by all the people lost in all the wars of our country, sanctify the service of those who follow in their footsteps.

Rendering of proper honors gave considerable occasion for thought, and it finally was decided that the only salute a submarine can fire is actually the most appropriate one anyway. Upon command, *Triton's* course was changed to due south and the Officer of the Deck was directed to stop all engines. The entire ship's company was then brought to attention, and all were directed to face forward. This was, of course, possible even at their regular watch stations. Then, with the entire crew silently at attention, the forward torpedo tubes were fired three times in rapid succession.

We could hear the resounding echo of the water-ram and feel the fluctuation of air pressure on our eardrums. Three times the harsh war-like note traveled through the ship; and as the last air fluctuation died away, the clear notes of Taps sounded in proud and thoughtful tribute.

The moment of reverence was a real one, truly caught. Everyone on board felt it; and though their response was by command, their personal participation sprang from deep within themselves and was given willingly.

When the memorial services were completed, we resumed our base course and speed. Next day, we were to pass between Guam and Rota islands in the Marianas.

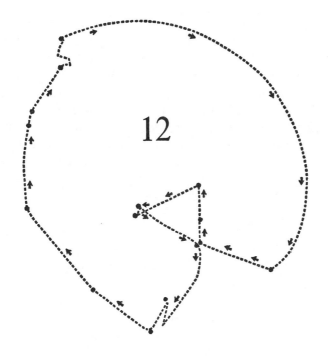

12

During the trip across the Pacific, *Triton* employed two sets
of navigators. The regular team, consisting of Executive Officer Will Adams and Chief Quartermaster William J. Marshall,
was backed up by team number two: Operations Officer Bob
Bulmer and First Class Quartermaster Curtis K. Beacham.
Will, I hoped, would soon have his own command, while Bob
was preparing for a chance at nuclear training. We would be
bound to lose one of the two officers and possibly one of the
quartermasters besides. It was just as well to be ready to make
a shift in assignment.

As a consequence, the landfall on Guam was made by the
combined efforts of both navigating teams, and at 0726, on
the twenty-eighth of March, with the whole day ahead of us
for a careful reconnaissance of this once-beleaguered Pacific

195

bastion, *Triton* came to periscope depth. Guam was dead ahead and Rota lay due north. It was another perfect landfall after sixty-seven hundred miles of submerged travel.

We planned to work our photographic reconnaissance for the northwestern coast of Guam as closely as we could. We would have no problem with the three-mile limit, for Guam was a US possession. Nevertheless, so far as we knew, none of the American authorities on Guam were aware of *Triton*'s trip, and from our point of view it would be as embarrassing to be detected by our own personnel as by any other nationality.

We had two complete photographic teams. Team One consisted of Commander Joseph Roberts, USNR, helped by Photographer's Mate First Class Earnest R. Meadows, who were specially attached to *Triton* for the voyage. Team Two consisted of Lieutenant Dick Harris and Chief William R. Hadley. Though the teams naturally competed with each other, both had full access to the special skills and techniques which Joe Roberts had developed during a lifetime in the business. In addition to everything else, Joe had been assigned as "pool press photographer," which meant that all his pictures would be equally available to the entire newspaper and magazine media of the country.

As the water shoaled, while we were working into position, we had an opportunity to test our latest, do-it-yourself fathometer in relatively shallow water. By this time we had two homemade fathometer heads, or transducers as they are technically called. One had been built from scratch and very neatly finished off by Phil Kinnie and Chief Engineman Alfred Abel, both of them accomplished stainless-steel welders—which is, by the way, one of the most difficult phases of the welder's art. Commandeering one of Jim Stark's stainless-steel medical containers, they had cut it down and welded it around the entire jury-transducer which Electronics Technician's Mates Docker, Simpson, and Blaede had manufactured under "Whitey" Rubb's direction; it looked like a most professional job. The second transducer was a conversion from one of our regular announcing-system speakers, waterproofed as well as we were able. While not so rugged as the stainless-steel one just described, it had the theoretical advantage of being superior in frequency response.

But as ingenious as the new heads were, they still could not transmit a signal with enough strength to pierce the outer hull and return to the ship. Our efforts, again, were a complete failure.

However, there was one way, short of cutting a hole through the bottom of the hull of the ship, to project our transducer directly into the sea and by-pass the rugged steel plating. This was through our garbage ejector. If we could operate it with the inner door closed and the outer door open, the signal would at least have an unimpeded path through water. Whether we would be able to hear an answering echo on our sonar receivers, which were located quite some distance forward of the garbage ejector, was a matter for conjecture. And whether we could devise some means of getting electrical energy into the transducer through the closed breech of the garbage ejector was a technical hurdle as yet uncrossed. But the idea was at least worth a try.

From the Log:

During the approach to Guam, we have remained at periscope depth and have observed considerable activity on shore. Several aircraft are landing or taking off and a helicopter can be seen hovering over the airfield. We can see the planes being maneuvered about the hangar and people walking on the roads, cars driving back and forth, and other signs of activity. There is one housing area which is very clear indeed on top of a near hill with slope toward the sea. We can see the green grass plots, and brown areas where walkways and driveways have been carved out. The houses are white or creamed stucco, surrounded in most cases by flowers and shrubs.

As we prepare for our reconnaissance our vision is occasionally obscured by a succession of torrential downpours which come marching in from the north. At times the rain is so heavy that it is impossible to see more than a few hundred yards in any direction. Our photographic efforts therefore are under an unusual difficulty—that of predicting the showers so that the part of the island we wish to photograph is for the time being clear. During one period there were as many as three localized thunderstorms on different bearings, with clear visibility between.

Today is a big day, too, for Edward C. Carbullido, SD2 (SS), USN. Carbullido was born on Guam and has youthful memories of the period of Japanese occupation during the war. Subsequently, when old enough, he enlisted in the US Navy and has been in the Navy for 14 years, during which he has never returned to his home island. Today is, in fact, the closest he has ever been. We wish it were possible to let him go ashore for a few days, and we shall do as much as we can for him.

Carbullido's father is a Chief Quartermaster in the Navy, now retired and living here. He has recently built a new home in the town of Agat, just to the southward of Orote peninsula, around the point of land from Apra Harbor and Agana, the main city of Guam.

Many a father would like to have a son like our Carbullido. During the Japanese Occupation, the father was away. This was good luck, of a sort, but during this period there was no support for his family. Edward Carbullido, the oldest, worked for the Japanese to support his mother and the younger children. After the war, as soon as old enough, he joined the Navy, and during the subsequent 14 years he has sent home every cent he could spare, a total of several thousand dollars, to help pay for a new house and the education of his brothers and sisters. Carbullido's ambition is to return to Guam after completing 20 years of service, 6 years from now. One can hardly believe that he is actually well into his 30's; he looks 10 years younger.

We spread a map of Guam on the wardroom table and ask Carbullido to pinpoint, as accurately as he can, the exact spot where his parents' house is. In "The Skipper's Corner" I have explained that today, after we have carried out our scheduled drill photographing the Island of Guam, we shall expend a few hours giving Carbullido the best possible look we can through the periscope at his home town. This seems to suit everyone.

After we finish photographing the town of Agana, we go through the same procedure at Apra Harbor. Behind the breakwater we can see a floating dry dock, a Navy barracks ship or barge, and what looks like a small seaplane tender. We then pass close around the tip of Orote peninsula, periscope raised, looking very carefully at the signal station out on the end of the point. We don't want to be detected; therefore it receives a searching investigation. The place is deserted.

1445 We have rounded Orote Point and changed course toward Agat. The water is deep and the sea calm, although large rollers are sweeping down past Orote Point. They do not affect us in the lee of the land.

Carbullido is ready a full hour early in the Conning Tower, wearing a clean suit of dungarees and grinning self-consciously. As we approach Agat, he gets his turn with the periscope alternately with the Executive Officer and myself. His eagerness is evident as we approach closer and closer, and the objects on shore become clearer to him.

During our times at the periscope Will Adams takes navigational cuts, and I am constantly sweeping the near shore against any possibility that someone might be there by chance looking out to seaward. People ashore rarely look to sea, however, and I doubt, even if there were anyone, that there would be much chance of their seeing our periscope. Nevertheless, we are cautious with it, exposing only a few inches for brief seconds.

It is touching to see the intense eagerness with which Carbullido peers through the periscope, looking for the house he has helped to buy but has never seen. With a big grin, he announces that Agat is very different from the way he remembers it. "Many more people," he says, "many more houses." It is, indeed, an attractive modern-looking town. As we draw closer, we insist upon Carbullido identifying his father's house, which he feels he can do from the descriptions and pictures he has received by mail. Finally, with a wide smile, he has it spotted, and we all eagerly take turns to look it over. Even with the periscope at high power and the ship as close to shore as we can bring her, the house Carbullido has selected is only a tiny spot in the distance. It is situated as he had described it, on a fairly high piece of ground, near the water but high enough to be free of flooding.

We stay a long time at slow speed in Agat Bay, in order to give Carbullido the maximum periscope liberty possible. At one time I draw Carbullido to the periscope with the idea that I can see a person or people near his house. After a long look Carbullido confirms this, but still I am not sure. It would be nice to say that he actually did see some member of his family, but we are too far away to be positive. Whatever it is I saw, it was motionless much too long.

1630   We have been in Agat Bay an hour and ten minutes; it is time to go. Regretfully, I tell Carbullido that we must put the periscope down and get under way for the Philippine Islands. Carbullido's eyes are shining as he thanks everyone in the conning tower and starts down the ladder into the control room.

One of the things which has impressed me from the beginning of this episode is the consideration and kindness of the rest of the crew and the conning tower personnel for their shipmate. So far, at every landfall we have made, there has always been a number of men wanting to come up for a look; off Cape Horn and Easter Island there had been a determined effort to get as many people as possible to the periscopes so that they could say that they had seen them. In this instance, not a soul has asked for permission to come up and take any of Carbullido's periscope time; and if he had been the Captain of the ship himself, he could not have received more attention or assistance from the quartermasters with regard to focusing the periscope, aiming it in the right direction, setting his bearings, etc. As Carbullido's grateful face vanishes below the conning tower hatch to the control room, Chief Quartermaster Bill Marshall puts into words the thought which has occurred to all of us: "Wouldn't it be great if we could figure out some way to get him to Guam for a real leave? Fourteen years away from home is a long time." We have already been gone a long time, too; a month and a half. To Marshall's words, there is general nodding assent.

A few hours later, I went Marshall one better and categorically promised Carbullido that some way, somehow, we would get him to Guam. It was a reckless promise, but I felt a way would turn up to make it good.

So far as we could tell, we had passed close aboard the island of Guam, had held the periscope up for a lengthy period, and had even spent considerable time in Agat harbor with the periscope going up and down almost continuously without stirring any noticeable reaction on shore. That night, however, I suddenly was not so sure. We had been at periscope depth for a short time, to make our normal celestial observations and ventilate the ship, when flashing red and green lights were detected on a bearing northeast by east, in the general direction of Guam, approximate altitude 30°, closing on us with a steady bearing.

I snatched the periscope when the report was given and made a long, searching inspection. There was no doubt about it. Lights were flashing red and green, and the bearings did not change. It must be an aircraft heading for us.

"Down scope," I barked. "Secure ventilation. Take her deep."

If it was indeed an aircraft coming right for us, possibly inspecting the surface of the water for want of anything more interesting to look at, we didn't want to show the white froth of our propeller wake which would reveal the fact that something unusual had been there in the sea. I waited a perceptible time before giving the next order. "All ahead two-thirds."

I could feel *Triton* angle downward gently and our speed begin to increase. Deliberately, I waited until the depth gauges showed there was a concealing cover of water over our screws before ordering, "All ahead full."

Down we went into the friendly depths, on our way toward the Philippine Islands. I was somewhat disturbed that the aircraft had showed no signs of flying by, instead it had zeroed directly in on us.

From the Log:

Tuesday, 29 March 1943   Coming to periscope depth for routine night evolutions including ventilating and celestial observations.

1946   Aircraft contact bearing 070° true. Flashing red and green lights. Two nights in succession; maybe we have been detected. Who could be so persistent? Has he figured out our routine? Only a submariner could do that—maybe Admiral Benson, my ex-skipper and now ComSubPac, is playing games with us; or maybe the fliers in Guam have some extra gasoline to expend. Possibly they suspect a non-US submarine.

Two weeks before, we had received a message informing us that my old wartime skipper in USS *Trigger,* Commander (now Rear Admiral) Roy S. Benson, had taken over as ComSubPac. Our acquaintance had dated from my midshipman days, when he had been my instructor in seamanship and navigation, and well did I remember his propensity, as both instructor and skipper, for an occasional witticism at the expense of one of his less alert students or subordinates. There never was a sting to any of Admiral Benson's humor, and usually there was a lesson to be learned. There was, for example, the day I navigated the old *Trigger* directly under the sun.

When the sun passes dead overhead, its altitude measures 90° no matter in what direction one looks, and a special type of observation known as a "high-altitude sight" must be worked out for a position. A running fire of semicaustic comment from Benson, to the effect that modern navigators didn't know how to handle a high-altitude sight, that no Executive Officer of a submarine today, myself included, would know what to do about this situation, had impelled me to a rather searching investigation as to just how the situation *was* to be handled. When the calculated time came, I stood on the bridge and took shot after shot of the sun as we approached and passed through the subsolar point, finding later, to my astonishment, that I had been there for an hour and a half of continuous observation. Then, still fascinated with the unique navigational problem, I spent another couple of hours computing the results. When I was finished, I had produced a beautiful set of curves showing exactly where we had been during the entire period, all defined by a series of tiny intersecting arcs.

As nearly as I can now remember, Captain Benson's comment, when I proudly showed him the results of my work, was something to the effect that any navigator worth a damn would have done the same. But the pleased look in his eyes gave my confidence a terrific boost.

In my own mind I knew that if Admiral Benson, ComSub-Pac, had learned that an unknown periscope had been detected off Guam, his aircraft would be sent out to find us. As officer in charge of all US submarines operating in the Pacific Fleet, he would have our basic itinerary and would know exactly where to send his planes. Their orders, couched in officialese though they might be, would be designed for the express purpose of "teaching that young fellow Beach how to run a submarine."

Extreme caution with the periscope was thus in order. I recalled all my techniques of the war years, leaving the periscope up for short periods only, crouching as I used it so that only one or two inches of it were exposed. We had *Triton* making minimum speed, in order to create the smallest possible periscope feather in the dark waters. Under these conditions, even the best antisubmarine radar would have difficulty detecting the tip of our scope, while I looked carefully at the airplane in an effort to learn more about it. Once again, the bearing of the aircraft appeared to be nearly constant, and the thought flashed across my mind that it might be merely a regular commercial airliner flying between Guam and the Philippines. The alternately flashing red and green lights tended to bear out this theory. But after a few careful observations, spaced some time apart, it became apparent that the distance to the flashing lights did not seem to have changed perceptibly. Furthermore, there was something just a little strange about the alternations of the red and green lights. . . .

Just as someone in the darkened conning tower, possibly Will Adams, commented that perhaps it would be a good idea to check the *Nautical Almanac* or the star charts, my brain which subconsciously had been trying to give me the right information all along, suddenly supplied the answer.

We had been fooled by a star millions of miles away! No wonder both the range and the bearing had seemed so nearly constant! I stood up from my half-crouching position and ran the periscope all the way up to the top.

In a few moments, the confirmation came from Chief Quartermaster Marshall, below in the chart room. Our visitor of two nights in a row was a navigator's friend, the red star Arcturus, which, according to the *Nautical Almanac,* should have the altitude and bearing of our supposed aircraft at that very moment. The green light which had apparently alternated with the red was no doubt simply a refraction effect on the damp surface of our periscope lens.

My only comfort, as we laid aside our anxieties and went about the business of the night's periscope depth routine, was that more than one submarine has dived for a rising star. During the war, three times in a row the ace submarine *Tirante* had dived when Venus came over the horizon—in one case, according to the excited lookout who saw it, accompanied by whirling propeller, machine-gun bullets, and the leering face of a Japanese pilot.

Thursday, 31 March, 1960, from the Log:

0545 As we cross the Philippine Trench, the bottom rises precipitously to the 100-fathom curve. Our echo-ranging sonar picks it out like a brick wall as we come up on it, and once again the gravity meter indicates a rapidly shoaling bottom.

A glance at any chart of the ocean depths will show that one of the deepest spots in the Pacific Ocean is the so-called Philippine Trench, lying on a north-and-south axis just to the east of the Philippine archipelago. As *Triton* approached the Trench, I remember looking with interest at the repeater scope of our search sonar. We were in a sea of nothingness. The limits of the huge trench were well beyond the range of sonar, the bottom so far away as to be like a void.

Our objective was Surigao Strait, and according to our chart the depth of water would reduce suddenly from thousands of fathoms to less than one hundred, if we were able to pick the spot accurately where the Strait entered the Philippine archipelago. If we missed the mark, the vertical wall of the Trench implacably stood in our path.

Silently and at reduced speed, our great ship glided toward the barrier, probing for the relatively small notch at the top which would be our entry point. Our navigation was accurate; that we knew. We had learned to have considerable faith in it over the weeks since we had left New London. But even so, there might be some unexpected current, some unexplained drift of the ocean waters which would sweep us a little bit one way or the other and cause us to miss the tiny V-shaped notch in the top of the wall toward which we were bound. Faced with the massiveness of nature, the hundreds and thousands of cubic miles of material deposited here, almost as though by design to bar our way, even the powerful and mighty *Triton,* the supreme effort thus far of man's competition with his environment, suddenly appeared insignificant.

As we approached the barrier, my concern rose and little feelings of anxiety pricked at my subconscious. What if the channel we sought were not there? How could we retrieve the shattering catastrophe of striking the barrier, rather than passing over it?

My brain always did have a tendency to be overimaginative, I thought, as I pushed the unbidden doubts to the back of my mind. We had slowed our headlong pace, were cautiously and carefully searching for the passage. It was there, and we would find it.

Again, Will Adams' navigation held true. The low spot in the massive wall ahead of us which was Surigao Strait showed up beautifully on the sonar, and correlation with our previously calibrated indications showed us a depth, at the entrance, of well over a hundred fathoms. Not much, surely, compared with the nearly six thousand-fathom depth only a mile or two to the east, but more than enough for us.

At 0743 on the morning of March 31st, *Triton* entered Surigao Strait.

From the Log:

We have been taking water samples of the various bodies of water through which we have passed during this voyage. One of the things for which the water samples can be used is the Naval Academy's annual Ring Dance. Part of the ceremony for the Ring Dance is to christen the class rings of the new senior midshipmen in the waters of the seven seas. As can be appreciated, getting an authentic sample of water from a remote spot of the world is sometimes difficult. We may, at least, help them out. Additionally, the class of 1945, less than a year ago, donated a small-boat navigational light to the Academy and named it the *Triton* Light, without realizing, apparently, that their light and our ship have something very much in common. So we shall also send USS *Triton*'s own unique tribute to the *Triton* Light.

Here, in Surigao Strait, there is a special reason for collecting water, and a special sample of it is going to be sent to Admiral Jesse P. Oldendorf, USN (ret.). Admiral Oldendorf had command of a squadron of cruisers, destroyers, and elderly battleships, which, it will be remembered, "crossed the T" at the Battle of Surigao Strait. It was here that the repaired and regenerated *California, Tennessee, West Virginia, Maryland,* and *Pennsylvania* returned the wounds they had received at Pearl Harbor on the day the war began. It was probably the last time the "T" will be crossed in battle.

"Whitey" Rubb [additional duty as water collector] assures me that there are indeed great streaks of rust to be found in the Surigao Strait water—and that, upon close inspection, it is indubitably identified as rust from old and long-sunk Japanese warship hulls. We think Admiral Oldendorf will appreciate a sample of this body of water, and though he may not have the precise instruments Whitey and I do for detection of the rust streaks, I am sure he can devise an adequate test of his own.

At this point, with the opportunity before me to write a fuller history of *Triton*'s pilgrimage, it must be admitted that our tests for rust in the Surigao Strait water would hardly stand up against careful laboratory examination. As a matter of candid fact, they existed only in Whitey Rubb's and my minds, for the entire episode was one of sentiment, not science.

1105 Came to periscope depth for an observation and sighted a small fishing boat under sail on our port bow. We watched with interest as the fishing craft passed along our port side about a mile away and disappeared astern. No indication that anyone on board saw us, though we took a number of photographs with the consequent necessity of leaving the periscope up too long.

1300   Have passed through Surigao Strait and entered Mindanao Sea. As we enter Mindanao Sea, we pick up a sonar contact bearing 345° true, which upon careful checking is classified as a medium-to-heavy single-crew ship.

1307   Sonar contact in sight bearing 347° true—a moderate-size freighter, single stack, two masts. This is an opportunity we have been looking for. We have been drilling our approach party but have not had a moving ship to actually work with. As a matter of fact, even if we had, we would not have been able to play with any ship, until today, long enough to get much good out of the exercise. Now the situation is different. We are not in so much hurry, and here is a nice big ship heading our way.

1308   Manned tracking stations. We need not approach the target very closely, and we shall be particularly careful to give no indication that we are present. Submerged submarines are always the burdened vessels in such cases. They must never annoy other ships, and they must never forget that no one can identify the nationality of a periscope at sea.

1332   We have had an excellent drill. The ship has gone by at a good range, identified as a World War II Liberty ship in excellent condition. She is nicely painted with black hull, white stripe and white superstructure. No colors visible, and we were much too far to read the name. But she gave us a fine workout; and we are much the better for it.

One unusual thing developed in that the ship's actual course never did check with my observations. Through years of practice I knew my angles were not that far off, and as a matter of fact, when they were exactly 90°—which is easy to tell because the front and rear sides of the bridge line up exactly—they did not check at all with our plot of her track. We think we know the reason for this phenomenon, and at 1417, obtaining an accurate position from bearings and ranges on land, our suspicions are confirmed. We have been subject to a rather strong current, apparently well over 2 knots. Our friend has been steering a course deliberately calculated to allow for the drift.

Our track leads us down Surigao Strait, across the Mindanao Sea and around Bohol Island to the west and into Bohol Strait; thence northward to Mactan Island. This is not the same track followed by Magellan, who went east of Bohol Island to the Camotes Sea and thence southward to Cebu. That route is much too shallow for us. Mactan is a very small island, lying close to the much larger Cebu and terminating Bohol Strait. On the western side of Mactan is Cebu Harbor, with north and south approaches through the channel between Cebu and Mactan. To the east of Mactan lies deep and straight Hilutangan Channel, joining Bohol Strait and the Camotes Sea.

The place we have come to see is Magellan Bay, on the north shore of Mactan Island. Having survived the most extreme privation, not to mention the mutinous acts of a disloyal fleet, Magellan had brought his three remaining ships through unknown and uncharted waters to the Far East. He had achieved his objective— of this there was confirmation in the chance encounter with a Malay trading vessel. The fabulous Spice Islands, at most, could be but a few more days' sail away! Parr's book, *So Noble a Captain,* well describes the exaltation and religious fervor which filled Magellan's soul. He died in the shallows of the bay now bearing his name, having landed with only forty-eight men to bring Christianity to fifteen hundred hostile warriors by force of arms, trusting in a divine miracle the equal of the one which had brought him there in the first place.

The *Sailing Directions* and the chart of the area show a spot on the north shore of Mactan, in Magellan Bay, which is marked "Magellan Monument." To traverse these historic waters and sight this monument constitutes a high point in our cruise, already 19,700 miles long.

Tonight we received our sixth babygram: a girl for Chief Engineman Clarence M. Hathaway, Jr.—the only man small enough to crawl outboard of our starboard propeller shaft—Inge Mae, born March twenty-fifth. Mother and child are well.

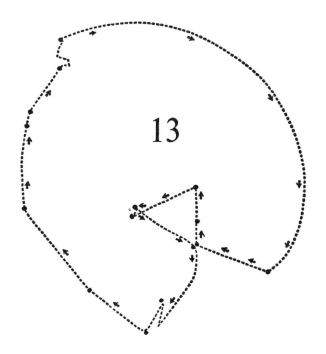

13

Friday, 1 April, 1960, from the Log:

We have been slowly working our way up Bohol Strait toward Mactan Island all night long, occasionally coming to periscope depth where radar and periscope observations have assured us as to our safe navigation. We have likewise seen, or heard on sonar, numerous small fishing vessels and a few coastal-type freighters or passenger ships. All are brightly lighted.

0428 Periscope depth. Sighted a small coastal freighter to the eastward about 4,000 yards away. Had held him previously on sonar.

0430 Sighted Lauis Ledge Light on the southern shore of Mactan Island. Commenced maneuvering in the approaches to Hilutangan Channel to the eastward of Mactan.

0608   Ejected hydrographic bottle number MT-71. Like the others, the paper inside is filled out in our code, except that on the back is written in English, "Hail, Noble Captain, It Is Done Again," for which Dr. Parr can take most of the credit. It is, of course, the translation of the Latin inscription on the plaque Tom Thamm designed to commemorate our submerged circumnavigation. We hope we shall see it delivered to the starting point of Magellan's epochal voyage.

There is much sonar activity, ships on all bearings, all classified as small light vessels.

0623   Sighted two small merchant ships at range of about 1 mile, steaming in close contact and apparently headed for Cebu. As we cautiously dunked the periscope, they passed within about 1,000 yards and proceeded on their way.

0722   Heard the first of a series of explosions—seven in all during the forenoon—apparently coming from the vicinity of Mactan Island. There is no visual dust or smoke cloud to confirm the source of the explosions, but we assume it is blasting in connection with some harbor work.

As we approach Hilutangan Channel, we are much interested in some of the fishing boats and other small craft which are all about. One of the first sighted is nothing more than a small raft with a sort of wooden tripod built on one end upon which branches of trees have been placed, apparently haphazardly. Usually these crude rafts have only a single passenger, who appears to be steering them. Our impression is that they are simply blown across the channel by the sail effect of the branches and twigs on the tripod [all were going east]. Possibly this is merely an easy way to get logs from one side of the channel across to the other.

A number of other types of craft, many of them old and decrepit, are around also. As we approach Hilutangan Channel, the number of boats decreases. Most of them are concentrated in the approaches to Cebu, before we get there.

0800   Entering Hilutangan Channel. Speed, 4 knots, at periscope depth. Tide and current tables indicate that we should receive a pretty strong set to the northward, in the direction we want to go. This indeed proves to be the case, since our speed over the ground is about 3 knots faster than our speed through the water.

As we enter the Channel, we are much interested in the picture presented by our echo-ranging sonar. The sonar-repeater in the conning tower gives an actual picture of the shape of the Channel. The depth of water is in many places greater than a hundred fathoms and the shore is steep-to. As a result, the area of shallow water near the shore is very clearly outlined on the face of our conning tower repeater. With this kind of gear we could easily go deep and proceed at high speed. Not knowing, however, exactly what we will find at the other end, we shall go through at periscope depth; perhaps on the return trip we can transit the Channel at deep depth.

During the passage through Hilutangan Channel, numerous small boat contacts are made. In one case a very decrepit boat with an outrigger on both sides and a large canvas awning, propelled by an ancient one-lung engine, came across our bow, distance a few hundred yards. It looks like a ferry, probably plying back and forth between Mactan and one of the islands on the eastern side of Hilutangan Channel. Numerous passengers can be seen, and none give the slightest evidence of seeing us. After all, who would expect a periscope here?

One of the passengers is a rather attractive Filipino woman dressed in a faded pink print dress of some sort and holding, I thought quickly, a small child on her lap. Her face is placid and emotionless. She is looking in our general direction but thinking of something else. To her left stands the steersman of this strange craft, paying attention to his business. Most of the other passengers are faced ahead or toward Mactan, on the other side of the ferry.

From here on, as we proceed up Hilutangan Channel there are increasing numbers of boats, most of them pleasure craft. In the distance, in the Camotes Sea far beyond Magellan Bay, more fishing boats may be seen. The pleasure boats, outrigger canoe types with a large and very colorful sail, I would judge to be anywhere from 12 to 20 feet long, narow of hull and mostly white or gray in color. They have a single mast with a cross arm on which a triangular-shaped sail is mounted with the point at the bottom. There are usually one or two occupants lolling around comfortably, perhaps fishing, although few fish poles or lines are in evidence. Most likely they are out enjoying themselves. Some sun helmets are in evidence on both men and women. The sails are most colorful, being decorated with half-circles, half-moons, triangles, diagonals, and so forth. None of the occupants appear to take the slightest notice of us, although at times our curiosity and the desire to get a good photograph cause us to leave the periscope up longer than I should have liked.

To ensure that all craft are avoided by a safe distance, our periscope observations are frequent and carefully timed, so as not to be too long.

Upon one occasion as I raised the periscope [invariably first looking ahead for fear of striking a log or a small boat], I caught a glimpse of a canoe drifting swiftly by. It had two occupants; a small and elderly woman with her back to us, and at the other end of the boat, facing me as I looked at him with my solitary eye, a rather portly gentleman, bare to the waist and heavily tanned, even for a Filipino. As I looked, he lifted his hand and waved at me in a manner almost as if he were saying to his companion, "Now as I was saying, that could almost be a periscope. It looks just like that, and it sticks up out of the water just like that thing over there." —at which point I quickly lowered it.

The portly gentleman did not appear particularly disturbed at our periscope and in fact probably did not recognize what it was, unless, indeed, he is a retired US Navy Steward.

1057   With the help of a strong current, we have made a remarkably fast passage through Hilutangan Channel.

1100   We are past the north end of Mactan Island and enter Magellan Bay. This Bay also has very deep water extending well inside the points of land which form its two extremities, though it is very shallow close inshore. [Magellan was killed here fighting in water up to his knees.]

Not having our fathometer, we approach cautiously. But our sonar picture shows a bottom contour that corresponds closely to the chart, and we have complete confidence in it by this time. *Triton* is, however, a pretty big ship to take into this tiny Bay, and our navigation is rapid. There are, fortunately, several clearly defined landmarks as well as a couple of lighthouses upon which to take bearings. In the distance, over the end of Mactan Island, can be seen the buildings of Cebu marching up into the hillside, with the dome of the Provincial Capitol etched white against the verdant hillside. Near the waterfront several large modern structures can be described; one in particular, which would not be out of place in any modern setting, is three to five stories high and approximately three hundred feet long.

Our foray into Magellan Bay is complicated somewhat by the discovery of three tall tree trunks sticking out of the water. Apparently they are ballasted to float vertically and are anchored to some sort of bottom structures, since they have no supporting wires of any kind. Maybe they delimit fishing areas. At all events, we carefully avoid them and the rock piles and anchor cabling they may mark.

1120   We have been carefully, without much luck, searching the south shores of the Bay to determine whether the Magellan monument can be seen. About this time, as I scrutinize the shore, it finally comes into full view. Without any doubt whatever, I announce to the conning tower party, "There it is!" The water is too shallow for us to approach close enough to get a really good photograph, but we take movies of what we can see of it from as many angles as it is possible to get them. It can be seen clearly from only one bearing, probably straight front, where trees and foliage have been cut away.

The monument is apparently made of masonry, probably recently whitewashed; it gleams white in the sun. There are dark objects in its center which might be one or more bronze tablets or possibly openings into the interior. It is a rectangular pedestal with long dimension vertical, straight sides and a slightly curved top, standing on a set of steps or a base. The impression is that it may at one time have supported a statue or been intended to, but what we see consists, in that case, only of the statue base.

1125   Sighted aircraft resembling a twin-engine DC-3 making a landing approach near the city.

There are numerous small boats in Magellan Bay, and we would not be surprised to find they are contestants in a sailboat race. Most of them are brightly colored pleasure craft.

One of these in particular intrigued me. Occupied by a single relaxed-looking gentleman, dressed in gay clothes and a broad hat, the boat was about fifteen feet long, painted white, with a white mast and white outrigger. The sail was red, with a large blue half-moon design on it, and like all sails of this type was a simple triangle mounted on a single crossed yard near the top of the mast, its pointed foot secured to a single cleat or snap ring at its base. Two "braces"—as Stephen Decatur would have called them—led from the yard-arm ends to the rear or cockpit of the boat, where its comfortably slouched owner handled them with one hand while he operated a rudder with the other.

At most, the boat had room for only two people, being a faithful replica of the narrow dugout canoe which had been its inspiration. Stability, in face of the lofty pressure center of the sail, was achieved by a narrow pontoonlike float held on outrigger arms half the boat's own length on the starboard side. The rig was obviously speedy, shallow of draft, and extremely steady in any wind. A particular advantage which would appeal to many a sailboat buff was the untrammeled visibility in all directions.

She would be a pleasure to sail, I thought, and I wondered why no US boat builders had ever tried a similar model.

Enthralled, I counted fourteen gaily decorated sails of different hues and patterns, and half as many slatternly ones, which we took to be fishing boats. At the same time, we made frequent observations all around for the many navigation checks demanded by Will and to detect in good time any sailboat approaching too close. Our photographers, led by Joe Roberts and Dick Harris, snapped as many pictures as they could. This was something of a chore, for to take a picture I had to aim the scope, permit it to be defocused to a predetermined setting, then duck my head while the photographer held his camera against the eyepiece and fired away. Demands on periscope time were heavy, and I was conscious that we were leaving it up too long and raising it too often.

1146 Upon raising the periscope I am looking right into the eyes of a young man in a small dugout, close alongside. Perhaps he has detected the dark bulk of our hull in the relatively clear waters of the Bay, or he may have sighted our periscope earlier. He and I study each other gravely. His boat is a small dugout, perhaps 12 feet long, devoid of any paint and without mast or sail [which is why he got so close in on us]. He has a paddle with which he easily maintains a position abeam of us at our present slow speed. He looks ahead and looks behind, looks down in the water and maintains position about 50 yards abeam with occasional muscular sweeps of his paddle.

Down goes the periscope. At my startled comment, everyone had pressed in closer to it.

"Can we get a picture?" Joe Roberts asked.

"No. We can't fool around with him." But the look on Joe's face would have melted a much harder heart than mine.

"You ought to let us snap him," he begged. "Later on you'll wish you had . . ."

"OK," I yielded. "No time to argue. Up periscope!"

I fielded the handles as they came out of the periscope well, put my right eye to the eyepiece, rose with it to nearly its full extension, then stopped it with a sudden signal to Beacham.

"There he is—here!" The picture in the eyepiece blurred out of focus. I drew my head to the side, felt the warmth of Robert's face near mine, his arm pressing on my shoulder. "Click" went the camera, then "click" again, and a third time.

Our friend is a dark-complexioned moon-faced young man with a well-fed physique. His clothing is tattered and he wears some kind of a battered hat for protection from the sun. Our photographic party obtains several pictures of him which will be interesting to look at later.

"Down periscope!" The steel tube slithers down into its well as I describe the scene above to the people in the conning tower. They would all like to get a look at him, but that isn't too practical.

I motion for the scope to slide up once more. Sure enough, there is our friend impassively leaning on his gunwales and staring right at the periscope as we raise it barely two inches out of the water. "We've played with this gent long enough," I mumble inaudibly. Spinning the periscope around for one last cut on the now-familiar landmarks and to say aloha to Magellan and his intrepid spirit, I sight a fair course between the nearest set of tree trunks, take a final look at our friend in the dugout canoe, and snap up the periscope handles as a signal for it to start down.

"All ahead two-thirds. . . . Right full rudder!" This is something our swarthy friend won't be able to handle. *Triton* slips neatly ahead of him and away to the right. Upon slowing for a look a few minutes later, I spot the dugout many hundreds of yards away, being paddled rather strongly in the wrong direction.

For some reason, the concern I had expected to feel if some unauthorized person saw our periscope did not come. We had, it is true, discussed this possibility at that long-ago conference in the Pentagon. Our entry into Magellan Bay would expose us to detection, but the decision to go ahead had been made nevertheless. Though nothing more had been said, I remember feeling that Admiral Beakley was not too concerned over the possibility.

Still, there *was* a risk that some notice would be taken of our presence, and I might have worried more had not some of our more perceptive conning tower crew unconsciously said exactly the right thing:

In the conning tower, the irrepressible Bill Marshall says aloud, "Wonder what he is going to tell his friends in Cebu tonight." Quartermaster Second Class Russell K. Savage probably has the right answer: "They won't believe a word he says."

As *Triton* eases slowly out of the Bay, checking her position every two minutes or so because of the swift currents we have encountered, we are all aware that today will go down as one of the high points of our trip. We have come more than halfway around the world to see this spot.

While a midshipman at Annapolis, I had a classmate named Carlos J. Albert, a Philippine national, who has had quite a career since our Naval Academy days. He went back to the Philippines upon our graduation in 1939 and was commissioned in the Philippine Navy. During the war he was a thorn in the side of the Japanese, narrowly escaping death on several occasions. More recently, with the rank of Commodore, he was assigned to the post of Armed Forces Attaché at the Philippine Embassy in Washington, D.C. There, I came to know also his lovely wife, Mila, a charming, willowy Filipino girl with a beautiful and expressive face. Carlos is now in Manila—or was. Lately I have not heard what Carlos is doing, and the temptation is strong to write him a note for transmission by hydro bottle, possibly on the hydro paper itself, requesting the finder to communicate with Carlos and receive a reward. I even have the absolute authentication so far as Carlos is concerned, for all I need to do is write "What about '39?" and he will know that it is genuine.

With a sigh, I am forced to the conclusion that this is one of those ideas which will have to be enjoyed only in the imagination. I can write Carlos a letter later on. When well clear of Magellan Bay, we release our second hydro bottle of the day, bearing a paper in no way different from the earlier one except for the serial number.

1320   Entered Hilutangan Channel headed south. This time we will proceed well below periscope depth at higher speeds than before.

1324   With the outline of the channel clear as print on our sonar visual repeater, changed depth to 150 feet and ran down the channel at 10 knots.

1407   More blasting in the distance.

1434   Clear of Hilutangan Channel, set course down Bohol Strait, increased speed to 15 knots, increased depth to 200 feet.

1504   Increased depth to 300 feet, increased speed to 20 knots.

2035   Entered Sulu Sea. Will spend the rest of the night and tomorrow morning crossing the Sulu Sea enroute to the Celebes Sea and departure from the waters of the Philippine Republic.

I have in a way also fulfilled a personal mission in this trip to the waters of the Philippine Republic. In 1898, my father was a Lieutenant in the *Baltimore* when Admiral Dewey defeated the Spanish Fleet at the Battle of Manila Bay. Subsequently, Dad spent several years campaigning against the Filipinos in their hopeless and heroic insurrection. From their point of view, they were fighting an American imperialistic scheme to take over where the Spanish had been forced to leave off, and although he fought against them, Father's personal sympathies were always with the embattled Filipino farmers and their high-minded leaders. He became, in fact, acquainted with the head of the Philippine insurrection, Emilio Aguinaldo. As a boy, I remember the arrival of occasional letters to Father from this quondam national hero.

Although I am not very sure of the details, my recollection of the story is that during the initial confused stages of the insurrection, Father in some manner had arrested or captured a party of Filipinos, among whom was a young woman who turned out to be the wife of Emilio Aguinaldo. The rest of the party were apparently her protectors and servants. I am sure the United States government has long since forgiven Father [if indeed it ever knew of it] for the manner in which he handled this gratuitous "prize-of-war." He escorted the entire party to the nearest Filipino post and bade Señora Aguinaldo a sweeping and courtly good-bye. Sometime later, Father was captured by Filipino guerrillas and detained for several hours, until peremptory orders arrived from some highly placed official that he be restored immediately to the American lines, which was done.

It should not be inferred from this yarn that the Filipino insurrection was a comic-opera war, for it was not. The Filipinos had been fighting the Spanish colonial government [a direct relic of Magellan's landing] for several years before we got into the fight. They welcomed us with great joy, thinking our plans were the same for them as for Cuba, and that their independence was but a short time away. When they discovered that this was not our intention, at least, not at this time, with grief by some and fanatic fury by others, they commenced to fight against their erstwhile comrades. And yet, the Filipinos—most of their educated leaders anyway—knew that they were fighting the best friend their country ever had. If either war was a comic opera, it was the Spanish War, with its fake "assault" on the fortifications of Manila, not the Philippine insurrection, which was in deadly, pathetic earnest.

Saturday, 2 April 1960   0047   There is severe oscillation in our gyro repeaters, probably caused by something wrong with one or more synchro amplifiers. Shifted to direct gyro input to the helmsman and began to check out the synchro amplifiers. After some moments, the oscillations ceased and the situation reverted to normal. This may be a warning of trouble to come. With the oscillation gone, we are for the moment unable to determine what is the precise cause of the difficulty.

0135   Sonar contact on the starboard bow. A large ship, from the heavy beat of his propeller. Left him astern and lost contact after tracking him for some thirty minutes. He faded out as though a thermal sound layer had come between us.

0859   At periscope depth to fix our position prior to passing through the Pearl Bank Passage and then through Sibutu Passage into the Celebes Sea. Locating and passing through Pearl Bank Passage is somewhat like threading a needle. There is a difference, however. Should we miss the deep water hole between reefs, we have an excellent chance of digging a groove in the coral with our bow. The land is very low-lying hereabouts and it is difficult to detect by periscope or radar. A complication develops when a ship is sighted hull down on bearing 076° true, approximately 8 miles away. From course and speed it is quite possible that this fellow may be the one we detected on sonar seven hours ago. If so, we have run right past him. Very likely *Triton* and he are trying to thread the same needle. Proximity of the ship prevents us from raising our periscope as high as we might like, or using our retractable radar to fix our position accurately. The sea is nearly glassy; any unusual activity in the water would attract notice. Went deep, increased speed and headed for the presumed position of Pearl Bank Passage.

1130   Periscope depth again, land in sight more clearly, and we are now obtaining a rough position. Changed course to head for the presumed location of Pearl Bank Passage when again we sight the same ship, range now only seven miles, bearing 030° true.

1245   This ship is going to give us trouble. He is much higher out of the water than we, therefore can see better, and very likely he knows this area thoroughly. Although we have the speed on him, we must proceed slowly and with extreme caution, to be sure of our position before we try to run through the narrow Pearl Bank Passage. With no such problems, he has been overhauling us for the past several hours.

We believe we have Pearl Bank Passage pretty well defined now, bearing due south; and we have been steering south for about 45 minutes. We should, however, remain at periscope depth as we pass through the channel because of variable currents which the *Sailing Directions* say we may expect. Besides, Will says he still is not fully satisfied with the accuracy of our position. After thinking things over, it is apparent that our best bet is to let the ship precede us.

We therefore reverse course to the north to let him go first, exercising extreme caution with our periscope and swinging wide. Commander Joe Roberts and photographer Ray Meadows are in the conning tower ready to take pictures should any opportunities develop. The merchantman, a Victory freighter of World War II with black hull, white superstructure and a black-and-red shape on his funnel, goes by at range 3300 yards. We are able to take a few pictures as he passes.

1311 Changed course to 180° true to follow behind the freighter. This makes it easy.

1417 Sighted Pearl Bank Light bearing 234° true and obtained the first really good fix of the day.

1436 Commenced transit of Pearl Bank Passage.

1450 We are inside Pearl Bank Passage, taking occasional checks on our position by bearings of the lighthouse on the right and a point of land on the left. We are well behind the freighter and can use our periscope with relative freedom.

The first indication of trouble came when Chief Quartermaster Marshall suggests the situation may be propitious for obtaining a sun azimuth. Will has been doing this every day he can. It is good business to check the accuracy of our gyros and determine their errors as often as possible. The error can vary and there goes your dead-reckoning capability.

A low whistle from Marshall. "This can't be right," he comments. "This shows the azimuth is 6° off." Calling to the navigator in the forward end of the conning tower. "Mr. Adams, are you sure you read the bearing right on the bearing repeater?"

"I think I did," calls back Adams. "Maybe it is not following freely. Helmsman, mark your head!"

The helmsman, one of our new men, answers immediately, "Mark! One nine one, sir." With the periscope aimed dead ahead, the bearing repeater should read exactly the same—and it does. Suddenly the pieces fall into place. I shoot a quick look at the rudder angle indicator alongside the helmsman. He has 20° right rudder on, but the ship's course has not changed!

"Our gyro has gone out," I call out.

Lt. George Sawyer happens to be officer of the deck. He has reached the same conclusion. "Up periscope!" he shouts.

The handles at the base of the steel tube come up; he grasps them; shouts "Lighthouse—bearing, mark! Left full rudder!"

There is no need for me to look through the periscope to know what George is seeing. When he called "Mark!" he was looking dead ahead. We are at least 90° off our course already, in a narrow channel. George is understandably startled by seeing the lighthouse in front when it should have been on the beam. The urgency in his voice tightens us all up in the conning tower.

With the ship once more on approximately the right heading, we shift steering control to the control room where the helmsman can use the master repeater, the only remote gyro indication we can trust right now.

It is a good lesson to all hands, one which I take pains to expand on in night orders later that same day. It is our normal practice to check our gyro repeaters against the master and auxiliary compasses every 30 minutes. Yet the rapidity with which the situation developed shows us how much trouble we could have gotten into even with this procedure. We were fortunate that we caught the difficulty so quickly, but it was strictly accidental that Marshall thought of taking a sun azimuth at the time he did. Apparently he caught the incipient error when we had only gone six degrees off our course.

The real error was on the part of the helmsman, who should have realized that the ship cannot help turning if 20° rudder is put on. If you have 20° rudder on and you are not changing course, either your rudder or your gyro compass is not working, or something else very unusual is happening. The helmsman must become accustomed to seeing the ship respond ever so slightly to a tiny amount of rudder one way or the other; and if she does not, he should immediately initiate a check to see if anything is wrong.

In this instance the ship was never in danger, since we discovered the difficulty so quickly, and because our sonar equipment has been indicating the shoal water on both sides of Pearl Bank Passage, as it did in Hilutangan Channel; thus we would have known that we were approaching shoal water long before we got in trouble. Even so, the episode has a sobering effect.

1517 Cleared Pearl Bank Passage heading for Sibutu Passage and entry into Celebes Sea.

1856 Entered Sibutu Passage.

2036 Passed Sibutu Island abeam to starboard at about 7 miles.

2200 Passed into Celebes Sea; departed from waters of the Republic of the Philippines.

Sunday, 3 April 1960 1147 Entered Makassar Strait. Departed Celebes Sea.

1330 Sunday Service on schedule, led by Will Adams. Our attendance has increased somewhat—an encouraging sign. Will's talk, "Have Made Passive Search, Hold No Contacts," refers to the sonarman's report made just before we bring the ship to periscope depth. He uses it to illustrate the point that life demands more than a passive search, and the lesson sinks home.

1422 Crossed equator for the third time this voyage at longitude 119°—05.1′ E. We are old hands now, and King Neptune just waves us by as we speed through his domain.

Monday, 4 April 1960 0613 Sighted a sailing vessel to westward. Joe Roberts' eyes glisten as he evaluates the report. This is the kind of sailboat he has been hoping to photograph, a Makassar inter-island merchantman. As he passes nearby, Joe obtains what should prove to be excellent pictures.

0930 Completed photographing the Makassar merchantman. The vessel in many ways resembles a Chesapeake Bay schooner of a type I had seen many times from my room in Bancroft Hall at Annapolis. It is about 50 feet long, painted white, low in the water with a cargo resembling deck lumber. She has two masts with heavy booms and gaffs. There was also a rather heavy bowsprit and two good-sized jibs—a topsail was rigged between mast and gaff on both fore and main masts. At the stern of the ship was a rather strange outrigger affair, a sort of structure built well out from the stern to which the mainmast backstays are secured and from which the ship is steered. Two men could be seen aboard —one man standing aft on the outrigger, apparently steering the ship, and the other, evidently a deck hand, up forward. Neither one seemed to be aware of our presence, although during our photographic interlude they had passed rather closely and we were able to inspect them carefully.

Strangely, I seemed to recall having seen this schooner somewhere. It soon came to me: in an intelligence photograph taken in this very area during the war. It was indeed quite possible that this was the same sailing vessel, for some of them have been known to survive for a century or more. Steamers are a nondescript lot that wear out in a few years and change mightily in the process. But sailing ships seldom change, their rig seldom varies, until near the end. This is why old sailors can recognize without fail old sailing ships which they know well.

1700   Having come to periscope depth to get a fix on Balalohong Island Light, observed up ahead a great deal of splashing in the water; thought for a moment that we might have found the mythical sea serpent. It next appears to be a tide rip similar to one observed earlier today, but upon closer inspection it is evident that these are big fish and little fish, and that the little fish are having a hard time. Maneuvering to close and take pictures of the operation.

There are evidently at least three kinds of fish present. Nearest to us is a lazy group of porpoises swinging along and gamboling among themselves. Up ahead it is evident that the predatory fishes are probably porpoises also, and we cannot understand why the band close aboard is so unconcerned with the battle royal going on just ahead. Perhaps this is a different tribe. Try as we can to approach close enough to get a look at either group, however, we are unable to do so. Apparently they consider us an unwanted witness to whatever is going on. The lazy band of frisky porpoises avoids us by adroit maneuvers at the right time, while up ahead the fighting fish move steadily away and even the ones being eaten seem to co-operate in keeping us at a distance. It is a thrilling sight to see the sleek black bodies of the porpoises flashing around in the water. With their tremendously powerful tails working back and forth like pistons, they dash about at speeds reportedly between 20 and 30 knots. No telling how fast these lads are going, but they certainly seem to have a lot in reserve.

1749   Resumed base course and speed. Now transiting Flores Sea.

Tuesday, 5 April 1960   This morning, as we passed through the last shallow water areas before Lombok, a final try was made to fix our fathometer. Results were both success and failure—success on the theoretical plane, failure on the practical. Our second transducer, converted from a general announcing speaker, indeed produced a signal, and it did receive sounds transmitted through air or water. But like its predecessor, it could not penetrate the heavy steel of the ship's hull.

We do, however, have one hole in the bottom of the ship—the garbage ejector. To use it, we first have to secure the fathometer head inside the garbage ejector, then shut the upper cap and open the lower door. Our first homemade transducer had been too large to fit into the garbage ejector, but our second attempt, constructed out of one of the ship's regular announcing system speakers, fits into it neatly.

No luck at all, not even theoretical, attended this attempt. The speaker was put into the garbage ejector, connected up. All appeared well; but when the inner cap was secured, it dislodged the speaker, causing it to fall to the bottom of the garbage ejector where it became wedged sideways. For a time could neither fish it up nor get rid of it, and it looked as though we might have lost use of our garbage ejector and gained nothing. The situation was retrieved with expenditure of a great deal of effort, and the garbage ejector given a normal flushing, after which inspection showed that the modified speaker now rests somewhere in the Flores Sea.

0650   Approaching Lombok Strait to enter the Indian Ocean.
Lombok Strait was one of the principal submerged highways for
submarines based in Australia during the war. Situated between
the islands of Bali and Lombok, it is one of the widest straits
through the Malay Archipelago and is spectacular in that it has
precipitous volcanic peaks on both sides. The water in the Strait
is deep, but treacherous because of strong currents. During the war,
there were reported cases of submarines spending hours at maximum sustained submerged speed only to surface at night and find
that they had been going backwards. The Japanese knew that Lombok Strait was "Submarine Highway" and made efforts to close it.
Generally, you could depend upon at least two patrol vessels being
somewhere in the area and frequently there were more than that.
Toward the end of the war, before the Japanese were pushed out of
this area, they took to flying patrol planes back and forth also.

The last submarine sunk in the war, USS *Bullhead,* commanded
by my Naval Academy and submarine school classmate and good
friend E. R. (Skillet) Holt, Jr., was most likely destroyed here on
6 August, 1945. This was "Skillet's" first patrol as skipper, after
a number in lesser capacity. He had been ordered into the Java
Sea, just north of Java, and was due to transit Lombok Strait and
enter his assigned area on the 6th of August, 1945. On that day,
in position 8°—20′ S, 115°—40′ E, a Japanese patrol plane attacked a submarine, claiming two direct hits. The report went on
to say that for ten minutes or more air bubbled to the surface and
the water was slick with oil.

1030   Our position is exactly 8°—20′ South, 115°—40′ East.

The last time I saw "Skillet" was when we both graduated from
submarine school on 20 December, 1941. Our careers paralleled
each other; we arrived at the submarine school and achieved our
first commands at approximately the same time. We departed for
our respective first command patrols within a few days of each
other; both of us were due to report to our new stations on the
6th of August, and on that very day both patrols were, in effect,
terminated by bombs. In my case it was the bomb on Hiroshima.

While transiting Lombok Strait, we sighted several ships of various types. One was a small sailing ship similar to the one we had seen yesterday in Makassar Strait, except it had only a single mast. Later, at 0950, sighted 3 ships, apparently small Naval or Coast Guard craft, heading north up Lombok Strait.

In attempting to determine the course and speed of these last-sighted vessels we experienced considerable difficulty in fixing an accurate angle on the bow. Every time the periscope was raised for an observation, they seemed to be heading in a different direction. There was no indication of a search pattern or deliberately erratic steering, but no two of them ever got together on a course, and they were never seen heading in the same direction twice. Finally, after some time, they steadied out and proceeded past us up Lombok Strait on a steady course and speed. We forgot the problem until later.

During a period, relatively free from near contacts, the opportunity was seized to inspect Bali carefully. Bali is a spectacular volcanic mountain, now extinct. Viewed from Lombok Strait, it is perfectly symmetrical, in many ways similar to Mt. Fuji in Japan, but without a snow cap. According to the chart, however, Bali Peak is not quite as symmetrical as Fuji, for the northwestern side was blown off by an eruption a long time ago.

On the eastern side of Lombok Strait there is another mountain, even higher than Mt. Bali: Mt. Rindjani. Both shores could be seen clearly. A village was visible at the foot of Mt. Rindjani on Lombok, but none on Bali, which only had terraced hillsides up a goodly portion of the steep sides of the volcano.

Although there were also many bare spots, Bali was bright with green verdure and held promise of many lovely valleys tucked away here and there amid the crags and outcroppings worn by centuries of weather and covered [in most places] with a skin of fertile soil. One could well believe the many stories told of the delightful living conditions and handsome, friendly inhabitants. It looks like a good life.

1029   In connection with our hydrographic and oceanographic work, of which very little can be told in this report, we seized the opportunity while in Lombok Strait to obtain deep-water samples, measure the general density, and observe temperature and other characteristics of the water. One of the simplest ways of measuring density is by behavior of the ship herself, since she will be considerably lighter in denser water and heavier in less-dense water. Correlation with known constants can give us a very good measure of the actual water conditions. To this is added careful analysis of the sample itself.

Upon going deep in Lombok Strait there were two distinct layers where the temperature changed rather rapidly, and at maximum submergence *Triton* was some 20 tons lighter than at periscope depth. This was easily understood, for directly to the south were the cool, deep waters of the Indian Ocean, while to the north were the warmer, saltier and shallow waters of the Sunda Sea and Flores Sea.

The heavy currents reported to exist here at various depths we can also well believe, and we have measured them. The existence of these currents bears out theories regarding the meeting of the Indian Ocean and the Flores Sea, and the resulting water density changes.

1215   Sighted ship bearing 205° true, at 7000 yards. Once again, in tracking the vessel, it proved difficult at first to determine his angle on the bow because he was continually changing course. Finally, he straightened out as the others did earlier today, and came by us at a reasonable range, steady course and speed. The vessel was a small but beautifully maintained trawler type. Probably a fisherman, possibly a government vessel or even a small yacht.

1300   Through the periscope sighted ahead a ridge of water several feet high, apparently caused by the confluence of the waters sweeping down from the north through Lombok Strait and those of the Indian Ocean coming up from the south. About this time the Diving Officer [Jim Hay] was having difficulty maintaining periscope depth at ⅓ speed. ⅔ speed was ordered to give him a little more control. In spite of this, and with a slight up angle, the ship slowly drifted downward. We thought all the time this would shortly stop, when suddenly the depth gauges began to spin; depth increased to 125 feet in the space of 40 seconds. Standard speed was ordered to pull out of the involuntary dive, and we steadied out at 125 feet, shortly thereafter regaining periscope depth with an entirely new set of trim readings.

In reconstructing the incident, it would appear that a strong northerly current of less dense Indian Ocean water had been setting in to Lombok Strait for some time, but that a current from the north was also making up. This would account for the apparent ridge or "wall" of water which we had seen ahead, for the variations of the water density when we went deep not long before, and for the erratic courses of the ships we had been watching.

At the point where we experienced the sudden change in depth, it would appear that there must have been a swirling of water, perhaps a downward current, as the Indian Ocean current met the Lombok Strait current.

Nick Mabry, the Hydrographic Office representative for oceanography, confirms our hypothesis as being a probable one. It was as though we had hit a hole in the water which acted on us as a down draft would act on an aircraft. Under the circumstances, *Triton*'s size, tremendously strong hull and great power pretty well eliminated any danger, especially since we had tight control of the ship at all times; but the situation of a wartime submarine with a weaker hull and only battery power must have been less comfortable.

I had experienced changes in water density many times before, but never one of this magnitude, nor this suddenness. There had been wartime reports of British submarines in the Mediterranean having somewhat the same experience, and some of the hard-to-believe stories of the period laid heavy losses in "the Med" to this phenomenon.

1313   Sighted an outrigger canoe with a sail bearing 144° true.

Approached and photographed same. It appeared to have a whole family aboard.

1400   With all contacts pretty well out of sight, periscope liberty was announced for those who might be interested. Approximately 75 crew members came into the conning tower to say a fond hello and sad farewell to Bali of the beauteous damsels. They will at least be able to say they have seen it.

1630   Entered the Indian Ocean. Next stop—Cape of Good Hope.

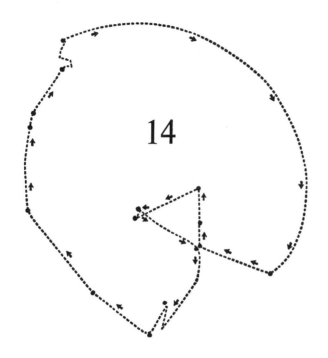

14

From the Log, Wednesday, 6 April 1960:

There is one bit of good news to report today. Using substitute materials exclusively and manufacturing all the special tools needed, Herbert Hardman has rewound the control-air-compressor motor. It became, in fact, a special project, dubbed "practical instructions for electricians." Under Hardman's tutelage, George Bloomingdale, Jessie Vail and Herbert Zeller, all Electrician's Mates First Class, have really turned-to in their off-watch hours, and all four deserve much credit. It was a mean job, the motor being a 10 horsepower 3-phase type. Merely digging out all the ruined windings and cleaning up the stator took over a week. When assembled, the motor ran perfectly the first time it was tried.

During the past several weeks our urgent need for a fathometer has been somewhat allayed because of the very fine performance of the active ranging sonar equipment; so the complete lack of success of our intensive efforts to devise a new fathometer is philosophically accepted. At this point, my biggest regret is the disappointment the failure must be causing to Simpson, Docker and Blaede, who have put so many hours into the project. When we get back to New London, we'll give their sound head a thorough evaluation, just for the experience of seeing it work.

2339   As we make this observation, our sense of well-being is shattered again: the active sonar is reported out of commission; cause not yet determined. It is the report I have been dreading most. We still have thousands of miles to travel through not-too-well-sounded waters. Without a fathometer, it is essential that we keep our active sonar in commission.

Thursday, 7 April 1960   0050   A thorough check of the active sonar has revealed that a tube has failed from long continuous usage. With a new tube installed, the equipment is functioning as well as ever, and Will Adams, Bob Bulmer and I are greatly relieved. Bob, having officially relieved Will as Navigator when we left Lombok behind, finally feels light hearted enough to accuse his mentor of having deliberately caused the sonar failure to take place at this precise moment. Will grins. "Of course I did," he says. At which point I don't know whether to believe these clowns or not.

Sunday, 10 April 1960   0000   Ventilation secured after a thorough sweep-out of the atmosphere of the ship. One of the requirements of the cruise is to conduct a sealed-ship test under controlled conditions for observation of certain phenomena. Our time with a sealed atmosphere will not approach that of *Seawolf* in 1958, mainly because of the expense of all that oxygen, nor does it need to, so far as this test is concerned. But since we are a brand-new ship, this is one of the things we need to accomplish merely to develop our own techniques and limiting factors.

Until now, except for short periods for testing of our equipment, it had been our practice to come to periscope depth every night for about an hour, and run up the ventilation pipe for a sweep-out of the bad air and replacement with fresh sea air. Life under these conditions had its rigorous aspects. Little by little, during the day, the oxygen content of our atmosphere was reduced as the 183 men on board *Triton* slowly consumed it. Toward the end of the day, it usually had become oppressively low.

We were not concerned about the accumulation of carbon dioxide, for one or more of the carbon-dioxide-removal apparatuses was run continuously and we had no difficulty in keeping the carbon-dioxide content under control. The average consumption of oxygen by active persons, however, is just under a cubic foot of oxygen per man per hour, and a very close correlation was immediately found to exist between our oxygen consumption and the days of the week. On Sundays, when there was very little going on beyond normal ship cruising routine, the oxygen consumption per man approximated seven-tenths of a cubic foot per hour. Friday was Field Day, with all hands up and turning to, and the average consumption this day was always about one cubic foot per hour. As a consequence, one of the disadvantages of our Friday Field Days was the labored breathing which afflicted all hands the last few hours prior to running up the snorkel pipe.

We discovered other phenomena, too. For example, increasing the pressure of the ship's internal atmosphere had no effect upon the percentage of oxygen it contained, but it did have an effect upon the total amount of oxygen in each cubic foot of atmosphere. Thus, deliberately increasing the air pressure in the ship by a pound or so per square inch greatly improved the ability of our laboring lungs to draw in oxygen, and consequently everyone felt better. The difficulty with this scheme was that as soon as we began ventilating to the atmosphere, the pressure would reduce to normal. If we luxuriated in hyper-pressure atmosphere for too long a period, some of us might temporarily be exposed to an atmosphere below the minimum allowed oxygen content before our ventilation blowers had managed to sweep out the bad air.

It is remarkable how much stability the human body requires within the wide range of the possible conditions of nature. Ideally, man should be in a temperature of around 70°; by various stratagems, he is able to exist over a temperature range of perhaps 120°, centered on the 70° midpoint. But temperatures in nature can go down to a minus 459° F—which it does in outer space—or up into the thousands of degrees.

Man is acclimated to twenty-one percent of oxygen in the air at normal pressure. He suffers acutely if the oxygen percentage drops only a few points, to seventeen percent, for example, or rises much above twenty-one percent. At the time that we in *Triton* began to feel distressed, we would have consumed only one-sixth of the available oxygen in the atmosphere of the ship. Were the oxygen percentage to rise above the norm of twenty-one, we should probably experience most of the effects of ordinary intoxication.

There was really nothing unusual in these "discoveries" which we were making; submariners have known and applied the principles for years. But there is no substitute for experience, which opens many new avenues of inquiry.

For example, there was the question whether gradual oxygen reduction each day for a prolonged period would have any damaging consequences on us. The effects of depriving the human body of oxygen all at once to an excessive degree are well known. But what about minor deprivation for many days? No observable deleterious effects have been noted, but many highly qualified medical people have recently been devoting considerable research to this question. The problem ranges from the physical to the psychological, from an environment of oxygen deficiency to one in which the entire atmosphere is mechanically controlled and stabilized at some optimum point.

From the Log:

The Medical Research Laboratory in New London has been pursuing this particular project for a long time, the first announced test being Operation Hideout in the mothballed submarine *Haddock* in 1953. Doctors Ben Weybrew and Jim Stark have been discussing the sealed-atmosphere test for several days, and finally have proposed a procedure. We will remain sealed for approximately 2 weeks, running various physical and psychological tests among selected volunteers from the crew. Somewhere during the mid-point of this period we will put out the smoking lamp for an extended time. Careful checking of all factors will continue for several more days before terminating the study.

The purpose of the no-smoking test was partly psychological, but there was a question of atmospheric research, too. Smoking, nuclear submariners had discovered, was their only source of carbon monoxide. In a completely sealed atmosphere, accumulation of carbon monoxide could not be permitted because of its deadly brain-damaging tendency. Expensive equipment had been devised and installed to convert it into carbon dioxide, so that it might be "scrubbed" from our atmosphere along with the carbon dioxide exhaled from our lungs.

One of the questions raised was whether or not this equipment was worth the cost; or whether it would be better to prohibit smoking in a completely sealed atmosphere, instead of going to the added expense and trouble of installing the carbon-monoxide removal apparatus purely because of the psychological satisfaction that some men got out of smoking. All this, of course, has a direct bearing on the endurance of submarines at sea—their ability to cope with the various problems they would undoubtedly encounter, and the efficiency with which they might be expected to operate under various severe conditions. The data that we were helping to gather would become available to our first space pioneers also.

Everyone on board was determined to go through with the test in good heart and spirit, but as the dread day for putting out the smoking lamp approached, various reactions were noticeable among crew members. The nonsmokers were lording it over the others, describing with great relish how the test would have no effect whatsoever on them, and there was an aura of apprehension among the habitual smokers. Even before we put the smoking lamp out, the witticisms had an edge to them, and some of the protestations that "smoking don't mean that much to me" developed a noticeably defensive tinge.

One saving feature in the eyes of many was the fact that both doctors on board, Commander Jim Stark, who dabbled in psychology, and Dr. Ben Weybrew, professional psychologist attached to the Medical Research Laboratory, were themselves inveterate smokers. Weybrew created quite a stir, therefore, the evening before the test was scheduled to begin, when he casually tossed his pipe into the garbage ejection chute. He, at least, was ready to make his sacrifice for science, and it was said that he whistled happily as he prepared the charts and the graphs he would draw as a result of our sufferings.

One thing we did notice as soon as we sealed up the ship: maintaining our atmosphere at a common standard level of oxygen content was a far more comfortable way to exist. Among other things, the air conditioners had less work to do; once the humidity was brought to the optimum level, it was easy to maintain. Previously, and by contrast, the fresh air drawn in from just a foot or two above the surface of the tropical seas was extremely humid and salty, dampening the entire ship for a few hours until the air-conditioning machinery had caught up with it again. To illustrate a second advantage: perhaps I personally had become accustomed to the daily deprivation of oxygen, or perhaps I had simply been unaware of my reduced efficiency. At any rate, I found myself more alert, more alive, and less tired when breathing the artificial atmosphere than when we were taking daily snorts of fresh air.

Everyone on board, I believe, had a somewhat similar reaction. We settled down quickly to the pleasantest period of the entire trip and, deeply submerged, crossed the Indian Ocean without physical contact with the outside in any way.

The Indian Ocean, by the way, is to the US sailor one of the least-known oceans. Yet it was one of the better-known waters of Renaissance days. According to the chart, it is uniformly deep, its bottom scarred by relatively few of the peaks and valleys familiar to the Atlantic and Pacific. In color, the water seems somewhat bluer, more transparent, with less marine life and less natural or artificial flotsam and jetsam.

During the war, the southern part of the Indian Ocean was especially active with German surface raiders and the British task forces set out to intercept them; and there were German, Japanese, British, and Dutch submarines on patrol in the area as well. So far as America is concerned, however, it is one of the oceans we still have to discover. Now that knowledge of the sea is of greater importance to our country than ever before, it is probably time we learned some of the intimate details of this great and unexplored body of water.

Monday, 11 April 1960 A message from ComSubPac relays information from ComSubLant announcing prospective promotion of Chief Petty Officers Bennett, Blair, Hampson, Hardman and Loveland to the rank of Ensign, and of the following First-Class Petty Officers to the rate of Chief Petty Officer: Hoke, Meaders, Lehman, Mather, Pion, Stott, Bloomingdale, Flasco, Fickel and Tambling. There is jubilation among the lucky advancement winners and good sportsmanship among the others. But this can't be the entire promotion list, since examinations for all rates down to Third Class were held before departure. More information should be forthcoming soon. Five Ensigns and ten Chief Petty Officers is a tremendous haul for any single ship, particularly one with a crew of only 159 enlisted men. It is a tribute to the overall capability of our crew, and to the hard effort of the men themselves. The fact that their tests were taken during an extremely heavy watch-standing schedule, to which was added strenuous overtime preparation for an unusual cruise, adds to the accomplishment.

The opportunity for hazing some of the lucky ones is too good to be missed. One by one they are called before me to be asked, in a grave voice, "What have you done to cause ComSubLant to send a message to us about your actions?" The look of incredulity on the faces of the first ones to arrive was real enough, but all ships have a sort of extra-sensory communication among the crew, and I doubt if the last few were particularly perturbed by my feigned severity.

Tuesday, 12 April 1960   Seventh babygram—sixth girl, 9 lbs., born 8 April; father, Bruce F. Gaudet, IC3. Both mother and baby fine. Poor Gaudet had been getting a little worried, but he feels fine now.

Six days a week all during our cruise, the *Triton Eagle* had faithfully come out in the early morning hours, composed directly on the duplicating machine paper by editor in chief Harold J. Marley and laboriously run off on the printing machine, with the ship's office swept up afterward, by Audley R. Wilson, Radarman First Class, who comprised the entire staff of the paper outside of the editor. Except for one memorable day when Editor Marley took all his news from a three-year-old edition of the New York *Times* (detected by very few people, surprisingly), we had managed to get up-to-date news. Every day or so I managed to come up with a column of some kind for the paper—either "The Skipper's Corner" or another, which I fondly hoped was a humor column, supposedly written by an unidentified person named Buck. Buck was an unregenerated sailor, butt of all jokes, apt only in hiding from work and the "OM" (myself, the "Old Man"). Theoretically, nobody knew that Buck was the "OM" himself.

There was a moment of concern early in the game when I realized that Lawrence W. Beckhaus might equate *Triton*'s Buck column with a similar one in *Salamonie*'s *Bunker Gazette*, but a sharp sally from Buck, in which Larry was admonished to keep his mouth shut, had, I supposed, the desired result.

Had one never experienced it before, the large share of our daily lives occupied by this little two-page newspaper might have appeared surprising. To me it was not, for I had seen the same thing before on long, uninterrupted cruises. The moment the ship gets to port, however, there is no further interest, and the ship's newspaper may as well cease publication until you are once again at sea.

The highest point of the *Triton Eagle*'s journalistic achievement was probably reached during our traverse of the Indian Ocean, when it published daily reports on an extended controversy involving a mythical "two-gauge goose gun." Tom Thamm and Chief Petty Officers Loveland and Blair were arraigned on opposite sides of the argument, which ran for several issues, and everyone had a lot of fun with it.

From the Log:

Friday, 15 April 1960   0000   Out goes the smoking lamp, eliciting many unfavorable comments from the smokers, a great air of superiority from the nonsmokers.

All hands have been carefully briefed for some time as to the purpose of the test and how it is supposed to be run, but we have avoided giving any indication as to the intended length, stating only that the operation order prescribes it shall not exceed 10 days. Ben Weybrew tells me privately that it will not have to be nearly that long, but that he wishes to avoid any complications from anticipation of an early "relight." In preparation for it LCDR Bob Fisher (SC) USN, [the only supply corps officer attached to and serving on board a submarine] has laid in a stock of candy and chewing gum. It is shortly discovered that some of the men had apparently also brought along a supply of chewing tobacco, which introduces an unforeseen variable into the experiment. Some of the volunteer subjects had neglected to mention their intention to chew tobacco in place of smoking during this period. It was noted, too, that cigars are at a premium since they can be cut into short lengths and chewed also.

Saturday, 16 April 1960   The smoking lamp is still out and the psychological reaction building up is surprising. Although I had not felt repressed by the atmosphere in any way previously, there is to me an indefinable but definite improvement to it. It feels cleaner, somehow better, and so do I. Will Adams agrees, being also a nonsmoker, but nobody else does. Tom Thamm announces that the limits of human endurance had been reached in the first 3 hours, so far as the smokers of the ship were concerned, and the remaining time of the test is purely a sadistic torture invented by Weybrew, Stark and myself.

Thamm is a tall very blond type whose meticulous and precise approach to everything conceals a highly developed artistic nature. He is Auxiliary Division Officer and, as such, works for Don Fears, our Engineer. Tom is in charge of most of the auxiliary systems and appliances throughout the ship, such as hydraulics, air conditioning, carbon-dioxide removal equipment, auxiliary diesel engine, main vent mechanisms and the like.

We have nearly crossed the Indian Ocean. Tomorrow, we expect to arrive at the Cape of Good Hope. It has been a pleasant trip, unmarred by submerged peaks or other alarms. The water is as uniformly deep as anywhere we have seen, not too cold, but cool and beautiful through the periscope. It is one of the least known oceans, bounded on the north by the subcontinent of India, on the west by Africa and on the east by the Malay Archipelago and Australia. Its southern boundary is Antarctica. One of its noticeable characteristics, at least so far as we have observed, is a consistently heavy sea condition, and in this it resembles the Atlantic. Every time we are at periscope depth for observations, it appears that a state 3 to 4 sea is running [corresponding to wave heights from 5 to 10 feet], enough to make surface ships uncomfortable.

A matter of note: LCDR Adams, now relieved from navigational chores, is concentrating full time on administrative matters, with intent of having desk cleared for the avalanche of paper work we expect upon arrival in the United States. There has been a steady flow coming out of his desk anyway, but since Lombok Strait it has tripled. And all of us dread the blizzard of paper awaiting us in New London.

So far as the no-smoking test is concerned, Weybrew and Stark contend that they have enough now to fulfill the requirement laid upon them by Medical Research Laboratory. It is also apparent, according to them, and I must confess having noticed something of the same myself, that the test has gone on just about long enough. Overt feelings of hostility are coming to the fore, expressed in a number of small ways, and there have been instances of increasing irritability. Deprived of a normal intake of mild stimulant, there obviously have been mild withdrawal symptoms among the heavier smokers in the crew.

The same is evident in the officers. Most noticeable, to me, are signs of forced gaiety, frequently with a sharp edge to it. Jim Stark, himself a heavy smoker, enjoys egging his wardroom buddies on— and this, in my opinion, is *his* compensation.

One night during this period, I recall asking the cause of a large red welt across the top of Jim's baldish head. The explanation, given with suppressed mirth by his wardroom mates, was that an hour before he had been demonstrating his complete freedom from any reaction to the enforced abstinence from smoking by showing that his physical co-ordination had been unimpaired. The test he chose, hopping on one leg, might have been a good one had he taken the trouble to check his surroundings first. Without thinking, he hopped through the wardroom doorway and attempted to ram his head through the heavy aluminum beam which forms the top of the door frame.

From the Log:

These were expected manifestations of adjustment and are cause for no particular notice, but there are also one or two cases where evidence of heightened nervous reaction is accompanied by relatively poor adjustment. In a ship's company of 183 people, something of this sort is bound to turn up. But answering my question as to what the ultimate results might be in the most severe cases, if the smoking lamp could not be relighted, the savants spread their hands expressively, "Who knows?" they say. "Most likely, if the man recognizes that it is impossible to smoke, he will psychologically adjust to it with relative ease. Symptoms will disappear or maladjustments will work themselves out."

The point is that here in *Triton* the only reason for prohibiting smoking is for a test. Everyone knows it requires but one word, and the smoking lamp will be lighted. Were we in a dangerous situation where safety of the ship or life of personnel were involved, as for example in an explosive atmosphere, the entire situation would be different.

Easter Sunday, 17 April 1960   We are approaching the Cape of Good Hope. Many people will be surprised to learn that the Cape of Good Hope is not actually at the southernmost tip of Africa at all. This honor is reserved for Agulhas Point, a little more to the south. Agulhas is not, however, a prominent landmark like the Cape of Good Hope. The story goes that when a storm blew Bartholomew Diaz around the southern end of Africa, he saw nothing and actually went quite some distance northward on the east side of that continent. On his return voyage, he bestowed the name "Stormy Cape" on the most distinctive point of land in the area; it was King John of Portugal who thought of "Cape of Good Hope."

Between Cape of Good Hope and the southern tip of Africa is a bay called "False Bay," possibly so-named for some early maritime mishap, and a few miles to the east and south is Agulhas Point. The chart also indicates another reason why no ship is anxious to make landfall on Agulhas Point. Agulhas Bank, immediately to the south, is shallow and extends a good many miles to sea. There is also a strong prevailing current setting the sailor in toward land. In the old days, anyone sighting Agulhas Point was already in trouble, much as in the case of Cape Horn.

0600   Periscope depth to fix position with regard to Cape of Good Hope. The sky is overcast and weather not too favorable for the photo reconnaissance which we had planned. Went deep and continued running.

1136   At periscope depth with contact on Hangklip Point, South Africa. Resumed base course and speed heading for Cape of Good Hope. As we enter the Atlantic Ocean again, we observe a noticeable drop in the water temperature. At the same time, we are most anxious to notice whether there is any definable current. Charts and *Sailing Directions* indicate that this is the case, probably setting us to the northeast. Without a fathometer, we are staying well clear of possible shoal water in anticipation of this effect.

1330   Held Easter Sunday services. Pat McDonald brings new life to the Easter Story. The little mess-hall chapel is nearly full.

1400   At periscope depth. Cape of Good Hope is in sight through the periscope, bearing 348° true about 10½ miles. It was named thus to be a good omen for men, and we take it as such.

1408   Sighted a ship bearing 308° true about 8 miles away. Stationed the tracking party. The ship is a 6,000 to 8,000 ton tanker with a nice clipper bow, but her counter stern, tall stack and large rabbit-ear ventilators belong to a vessel of older vintage. She may pass close enough for us to obtain periscope photographs, provided she remains on her present track. Joe Roberts is standing by, itching to get a picture, and I am beginning to worry over the fact that the ship, evidently making for the Indian Ocean, may change course toward us in rounding the Cape. We will embarrass him if he sees our periscope near his intended track. In such a case, it is quite possible he might precipitantly turn in such a way as to endanger himself or us. We must remain doubly alert where probability of a course change exists, to detect the change and go deep in good time.

I always worry through all these difficult possibilities almost by reflex; and in the meantime, as the ship passes safely by, Joe Roberts has an ideal opportunity to get a picture. The ship has a black hull, clipper bow, counter stern, a white stripe below the gunwale. [The third ship we have sighted this voyage with this distinctive feature.] Her superstructure and upper works are white with black and red trim. Her foremast is painted all white and her mainmast is white for the lower one-third and black above, where her stack smoke would blacken it anyway. Both masts are stick masts. We are almost, but not quite, able to read the name on the stern.

She has no colors visible and therefore we have no knowledge as to her nationality, but she is obviously not an American, for American ships rarely present this good an appearance.

1540   Weather conditions near the Cape are going to prevent our photo reconnaissance from being as successful as we would like, but we shall close in a bit and get what we can. Mt. Vasco de Gama on the Cape of Good Hope reminds me of Diamond Head, having somewhat the same shape and dimensions, though not quite the same rugged characteristics. Possibly Good Hope is a considerably older formation. Little foliage or natural growth is visible, something of a surprise for this temperate latitude [33°S].

1618   Periscope depth once more for photographic reconnaissance. There seems to be a haze in the distance and we are unable to focus clearly upon the Cape of Good Hope. After a careful sweep panorama, we call it a day.

1721   With Cape of Good Hope bearing 117° true, distance 8 miles, took departure for St. Peter and St. Paul's Rocks in the mid-Atlantic. We will arrive there on the 25th of April.

Monday, 18 April 1960   0000   Smoking lamp is relighted. Maybe I am a bit sadistic: no one was expecting it; so instead of directing that the word be passed to relight the smoking lamp, I strolled about the ship smoking a cigar, blowing smoke in the faces of various people and inquiring in a pleasant conversational tone, "Don't you wish you could do this?" It took some 37 seconds for the word to get around.

As in any group, there were probably a few of our people who secretly welcomed the no-smoking edict as a crutch to help them make the break from the habit. By far the majority had no intention of stopping; and it is noticeable that few, if any, have continued their abstinence after the smoking lamp was once lighted. An exception is Tom Thamm, who had entered into a no-swearing pact with his two friends, Chiefs Loveland and Blair. Terms were that the first man to breach the rules would continue to abstain for another day after the smoking lamp was relighted. There may have been some collusion in this case, for, shortly after the terms had been agreed upon, Jim Stark appeared on the scene and yanked a yellow hair out of the middle of the Thamm chest while the others distracted his attention.

Thamm's yelping malediction toward the good Doctor was witnessed with glee by all three plotters; and now Thamm sits grimly in the wardroom inhaling second-hand smoke, mumbling at the faithlessness of all shipmates, vowing that he will carry out his part of the wager, come what may, and swearing by the few remaining hairs on his chest that Messrs. Stark, Blair and Loveland will regret the episode.

1105   We are passing near a charted seamount and sure enough, the echo-ranging sonar detects it. We are becoming expert at this operation and it is a reassuring one.

Wednesday, 20 April 1960   0100   Crossed from east to west longitude.

Today is my birthday and also Lt. Sawyer's. After dinner I repaired to my cabin to work on this report.

1900   Chief of the Ship Fitzjarrald came knocking on my door saying, "Something is wrong down in the mess hall, Captain; we need you down there right away." This is a strange message for the skipper of a ship to receive.

"What's the matter, is there a fight?" I asked, starting up from my desk. It was only a jump down the ladder to the lower deck and forward one compartment into the crew's mess hall, where I was greeted by popping flash bulbs, a raucous rendition of "Happy Birthday to You" and a tremendous birthday cake. The cake, prepared by Ramon D. Baney, CS2(SS), was about 2 feet square and 2 inches thick, with great extravagant gobs of frosting all over it. Ray Meadows, Joe Roberts and William R. Hadley were there too, of course, with cameras en echelon.

Earlier that afternoon there had been a cake and coffee ceremony for George Sawyer in the wardroom; I was, quite candidly, looking forward to another cake at dinner, and was caught completely by surprise. It has been a very pleasant day with much good cake eaten by all.

A third birthday for which April 20th used to be remembered in certain quarters went unnoticed: one Adolf Hitler, now deceased.

Friday, 22 April 1960   Our 8th babygram arrived today for Gerald W. Gallagher, IC1(SS), who has an 8 lb. boy born on the 20th. Gallagher, all smiles, informs me delightedly that the child, if a boy, was to have been named Timothy Edward. With Edward in his name and April 20th for his birth certificate, this lad will go far, and in testimony thereof, this calls for a cigar in reverse. Timothy Edward Gallagher's Old Man gets the cigar.

Saturday, 23 April 1960   Tonight we are advised by a message that twenty-five more of our ship's company have successfully passed the examinations for advancement in rate and are soon to be promoted. The news causes excited congratulations throughout the ship. Our statisticians are immediately busy and come up with the following rather remarkable set of figures: excluding the 5 Chief Petty Officers who are designated for commissioned rank, but including the First Class promoted to Chief Petty Officer and the 25 just named, a total of 60% of our men who took the exam have made the next higher rate. Counting only those listed in tonight's dispatch, the percentage is 69%; and if one adds in the 5 new Ensigns, a total of 40 men, or 25% of the crew of 159, are to be promoted. Few ships in the US Navy will equal this performance.

Sunday, 24 April 1960 0436 Completed sealed-ship test, having run sealed for exactly two weeks. Remaining sealed is considerably less strenuous than ventilating once a day, and we are sorry to go back to the earlier routine. When you ventilate, you are attempting to conserve oxygen and at the same time trying to minimize time at periscope depth. It naturally develops that just before you ventilate the ship, her internal atmosphere is at its lowest in oxygen, its highest in carbon monoxide and carbon dioxide. At this time cigarettes are difficult to light, a little exertion sets one to panting, and generally one does not feel in the best of form. On the other hand, with the ship sealed, you maintain a steady atmosphere and set your equipment to keep it that way.

During the sealed-ship test we had replenished our oxygen in two ways. First, there were the oxygen banks—great steel cylinders in which pure oxygen was stored under high pressure. Located external to *Triton*'s pressure hull, in the ballast tanks, they were piped to manifolds forward and aft where we could automatically control the rate of revitalization as the pressure in the banks dwindled.

Our second revitalization system made use of a device borrowed from miners, who had for years employed "oxygen candles" as an emergency oxygen source. Our "candles" were much larger than the miners', but they were made of the same materials and were handled in a very similar manner. Under average conditions, we burned them in a specially designed oxygen furnace at the rate of two per hour, though as previously mentioned, this rate had to be increased on Fridays. Each "candle," when exhausted, produced a large, heavy iron klinker, which in due course found its way to the garbage ejector.

The greatest problem in sealed operations, however, did not lie in maintaining the requisite oxygen content in our ship's internal atmosphere. It was a matter of retaining the atmosphere itself, and this was a problem that remained with us the whole cruise.

To understand this, it must first be appreciated that many of a submarine's mechanisms are operated by compressed air. After it is used, the air simply passes into the interior of the ship, where it becomes part of the ship's internal atmosphere. During the first weeks of the cruise, therefore, the pressure built up slowly during the day and was suddenly vented off every night, when we extended our ventilation pipe to the surface and opened its cap. We discovered immediately that running all the air compressors at maximum capacity during the time we were renewing our atmosphere from outside was not enough to recharge as much air into our air banks as had been used. We were, in effect, slowly losing air. To combat this, we resorted to starting the air compressors well *before* raising our snorkel pipe, thus pumping the precious air back into the high-pressure air banks instead of belching it out when we opened the snorkel-head valve. This had the incidental disadvantage of increasing our "low-oxygen" symptoms and increasing the time we suffered from oxygen deficiency, but, worse, we still were not able to recharge as much air as we had used during the day.

Every night a check of the air banks showed that the maximum air-bank pressure we reached on charge was slightly less than it had been the previous night. Without compressed air a submarine cannot operate, a fact which had lain in my consciousness ever since depth charges had so damaged both of *Trigger's* air compressors that it looked as if neither could be made to run again.

In *Triton's* case, barring a breakdown of our compressors,

we could solve the problem by merely leaving the snorkel up longer and waiting until the compressors had been able to retrieve their position. But to do so would require a sacrifice of speed of advance, since neither periscope nor snorkel tube could withstand cruising speed. And even if we in this manner recovered the air lost, it seemed to me that this would be an admission of our inability to operate our ship properly.

Our real problem lay in the fact that not all the compressed air used during the day was being discharged back into the ship's interior volume. Some of it, somehow, was escaping to the sea. Even after "pumping down" to atmospheric pressure, there was every day slightly less air in the air banks. Obviously, this had to be resolved before beginning the sealed-ship tests.

If there is no leak in an external air line, the most logical place to lose air in a submarine is in blowing sanitary tanks, and this was where, it turned out, we were losing ours. Sanitary tanks, as their name implies, are the collecting tanks for all the waste products from the ship, human and otherwise. Periodically they must be emptied, which is done with compressed air. Considerable pressure of air is required to overcome the pressure of the sea at depth, and when the blowing is finished, all this air must be vented—released—back into the ship. Despite large canisters of activated carbon filters in the vent line, the odor this air brings back with it is pungently distinguishable and fermentedly corrupt. A "good blow" scours the tank, and carries more of the noxious vapor out with the water, and investigation developed the possibility that a little too much "scouring" was costing us a lot of valuable compressed air—not to mention the betraying bubbles thereby sent to the surface.

During the war, we all preferred a little temporary stink to enemy bombs, and sanitary tanks were therefore never blown completely dry when submerged in enemy waters. In our new and modern submarine, this same old smelly lesson had to be learned again, though for an admittedly different reason. Instructions were issued to the tank blowers to keep a sizable water seal in all sanitary tanks at all times and to the rest of the crew to put clothespins on their noses if they were too uncomfortable during the venting periods.

The program was a success. Our air compressors began to gain on the air banks, and every night the final pressure stood a little higher instead of a little lower. And we suffered gamely whenever a sanitary tank was blown.

The man I felt sorriest for was Frank McConnell, the Electric Boat Guarantee Engineer. Good shipmate that he was, Frank never voiced a complaint, but more than once I saw him distractedly jump out of his bunk in the "attic" above the wardroom, unable to stay there longer. It may have been accidental—naturally the sanitary tank vent discharge had to go somewhere—but Will Adams said the vent piping was positively diabolical in its perfect aim at the head of Frank's bunk.

As we ended the sealed-ship period, our air problems were behind us, but the memory remained. I found myself thinking that our first space travelers would have to solve this same problem in even more rigorous measure. Should they, through maloperation or misfortune, be unable to conserve their air supply, there would be no ready replenishment from an inexhaustible source only a few hundred feet away.

From the Log:

We have learned a lot about *Triton* during these two weeks of sealed-ship operations and are extremely gratified with the results. Among other things, we have had no difficulty at all in retaining our precious air inside the ship. But it was a good thing that we recognized the problem, or we might have.

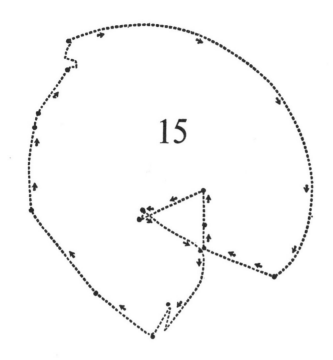

15

The sealed-ship test, by design, had been scheduled to terminate on Sunday, the twenty-fourth of April. It would be a good way to finish off the circumnavigation, Will Adams had suggested, to give us something to think about during the last few days.

But on Sunday, as we resumed normal daily ventilation, I, for one, found it hard to keep from feeling a tingling excitement. Tomorrow, Monday, the twenty-fifth of April, we would have completed the first of our missions. With the return to St. Peter and St. Paul's Rocks, carefully passing on the *western* side this time, *Triton* would become the first ship to accomplish the submariner's dream of traveling, entirely submerged, completely around the world.

It would be on the sixtieth day of the circumnavigation,

254   Around the World Submerged

by our reckoning, but a man perched on the Rocks would have counted the sunrise sixty-one times; for we had lost a day by making the circuit in a westerly direction, following the sun.

On the other hand, we had been forced to set our ship's clocks back one hour twenty-three times. Twenty-three of our days had thus been twenty-five hours in length (the shift to daylight saving time had also occurred, and the twenty-fourth extra hour would be returned to us in October).

The last several weeks of our trip had been singularly free from malfunction of any parts of the ship. It seemed as though we had finally shaken most of the bugs out. As events were shortly to prove, however, our travail might have been almost over—but it was not yet, quite.

From the Log:

24 April 1960, Sunday   2001   Serious casualty in the after torpedo room. The manner in which this develops is illustrative of a point many naval officers are fond of making—there is no sudden alarm, no quick scurry of many people carrying out an expected drill. By the time anyone in authority even knew what had happened, the need for alarm was past. There was left only the correction of the trouble and clean up of the mess, which took some time. What took place is instructive:

The torpedoman on "Room Watch" in the after torpedo room, Allen W. Steele, TM3 (who had only last night been notified of his prospective advancement to Second Class), heard a loud report, nearly like an explosion as he later described it, followed by a heavy spraying noise. Turning, he saw clouds of oil vapor issuing from beneath the deck plates forward on the starboard side. Instantly realizing that this was serious trouble, Steele called the control room on the 7MC announcing system and reported a heavy hydraulic oil leak in the stern plane mechanism; then he plunged into the hydrant stream of oil hoping to find the leak and isolate it.

In the control room, Lt. Rubb was starting to make the routine preparations to bring the ship to periscope depth. His first indication of trouble came when Raymond J. Comeau, Electrician's Mate Second Class, at the stern plane controls, noticed failure to respond to a small movement of his control arm, and called out in a voice edged with concern, "The stern planes are not working right, sir!" At nearly the same moment, the report of a large hydraulic leak in the after torpedo room was received from Steele.

"Whitey" Rubb's action was the one for which we have trained many times: "Shift to Emergency!" Comeau threw a single toggle switch, tested controls and reported them satisfactory. This restored control of the ship, but it did not solve the basic difficulty [the quickness with which this action was taken is demonstrated by the fact that planes and rudder automatically switch to emergency power if the pressure in the main system falls to 1000 lbs; this had not yet occurred].

In the after torpedo room, Steele determined the leak to be in the stern planes' normal power-hydraulic system, and correctly diagnosed it as a massive hydraulic failure. His third immediate decision was also a correct one. Diving into the midst of the high-pressure spray, he reached the two quick-closing valves to the supply and return pipes and shut them. One came shut easily but the other, in the center of the 3000 lbs-per-square-inch oil spray, was very difficult to move because of the pressure unbalance across its seat and an extremely slippery handle. Desperately struggling with the valve, and aided by Arlan F. Martin, Engineman Third Class, who ran to his aid, Steele finally got it also shut. By this time, fifteen to thirty seconds after the onset of the leak, the entire after part of the compartment was filled with oil vapor and visibility was reduced to only a few feet. The fumes were choking; an explosive mixture undoubtedly existed.

With the closing of the isolation valves, the oil flow stopped immediately. Estimates later were that approximately 30 gallons of hydraulic oil had been lost into the after torpedo room bilges out of a 120-gallon system pressurized to 3000 lbs per square inch. Had Steele's action not been so instantaneous and so precisely correct, complete loss of the ship's main hydraulic system must inevitably have happened within a few seconds more. This would have caused a momentary loss of all diving plane control and steering as well. Even with automatic shift to "emergency control," the ship's high speed at the time does not permit this possibility to be viewed other than with deepest concern.

Personnel who behaved with credit were Arlan F. Martin, Engineman Third Class, who ran to Steele's assistance and participated with him in shutting the last and most difficult of the two hydraulic cutoff valves, and Ronald Dale Kettlehake, who had just entered the compartment in process of tracing some system required for submarine qualification. Realizing the possible danger to personnel from the oil spray which was rapidly fogging the atmosphere, he showed presence of mind by waking the dozen or more sleepers and routing them forward into the after engine room.

2002   Things had been happening so swiftly that the first anyone other than those dealing with it knew of the casualty was when Rubb ordered "Smoking lamp out!" "Rig after torpedo room for emergency ventilation." There had been no confusion, no warning, not even any raised voices. Tom Thamm, our Damage Control Officer, quickly got to his feet and strode purposefully aft, followed by Jim Hay, his assistant.

2030   This is far from a pleasant casualty to think about. It should never happen. Our preliminary investigation disclosed that the stern plane control valve, located just underneath the floor plates in the after torpedo room, had broken right through its body at one of the flanged joints. There had been no warning of any kind. The cause may possibly stem from excessive flexing and metal fatigue or from a faulty forging. It will undoubtedly be carefully investigated by qualified metallurgists and design personnel. In *Triton,* this control valve handles hydraulic oil at 3000 lbs pressure in lines 2½ inches in diameter. Steele's swift and decisive action is living proof that if you train for every possible type of casualty, there is a good chance that you can also control the few impossible ones that happen anyway.

Steele has been recommended to receive the Secretary of the Navy Letter of Commendation with Commendation Ribbon for meritorious service. We are preparing the papers now.

2130   Everything is pretty much back to normal so far as the after torpedo room and the hydraulic system is concerned, except that we are still in "emergency" on the planes and shall have to remain so until a replacement is found for the fractured control valve. It turns out there are no spares in stock, and it will be necessary to steal a valve from another system. After due consideration, even this presents no choice; the only hydraulic system in the ship which has an adequately large control valve is the steering system. Steering from now on will have to be in emergency; but after the exchange has been made, we shall have normal stern plane control.

Monday, 25 April 1960   0432   Normal power is restored to the stern planes. The main hydraulic system is back in full commission with a control valve stolen from the steering system. Steering is permanently in "emergency."

0754   Crossed equator for the fourth and final time this cruise at longitude 28°—03′ West.

1200   Position 00°—53′ North, 29°—01′ West. We are within a few miles of St. Peter and St. Paul's Rocks, at which point we will have completed the first submerged circumnavigation of the world.

1330   St. Peter and St. Paul's Rocks in sight, bearing due west.

1500   First submerged circumnavigation of the world is now complete.

We are circling and photographing the islet again, as we did just two months ago. The weather is nice and the sun is shining brightly. Our mileage [Rock to Rock] is 26,723 nautical miles and it has taken us 60 days and 21 hours [days calculated as twenty-four hours each]. Dividing gives an average overall speed of just over 18 knots. No other ship—and no other crew—could have

done better. We are proud to have been selected to accomplish
this undertaking for our nation.

Our total milage for the trip will be a little more than 36,000
nautical miles [including the two thousand-mile mercy mission for
Poole], and it now looks as though our overall time since departure
from New London will be 85 days [New London computation].
We have been instructed to proceed to a rendezvous point off
Cadiz, Spain, where the destroyer *Weeks* is to meet us. *Weeks* will
send aboard the completed bronze plaque we designed in tribute
to Magellan, but it is our understanding it is to be presented at a
later date, possibly by the US ambassador. For the time being we
are to avoid detection, making our rendezvous off Cadiz beyond
sight of curious onlookers.

We earnestly hope *Weeks* will bring mail for us, in addition to
the plaque. Even though we can depend upon our Squadron organization in New London to do everything in its power to assist
our families, there's nothing [except seeing them] which can substitute for a letter from your loved ones. More than this we neither
need nor want. Our provisions are still adequate, though non-
scrambled eggs would certainly taste good, and our personal tobacco stocks have lasted surprisingly well, despite demands placed
upon them by people like Curtis Beacham, who brought a dozen-
and-a-half boxes of cigars with him, then early in the cruise gave
most of them away in an effort to break the habit clean; for weeks
now he has been abjectly relying on the occasional generosity of
the friends to whom he gave them.

We still do not know when—or whether—knowledge of our
submerged voyage will be made public. We therefore shall not surface, will only bring our high conning tower hatch clear of the sea
to pass the plaque and its custodian through, as we did our sick
shipmate nearly two months before.

1645   A congratulatory message has arrived from our Force
Commander. It is read to the crew as soon as decoded and everyone aboard very much appreciates his kind and encouraging words.

1700   Prepared a suitable message on our part recommending

Steele for official recognition and thanking Admiral Daspit for his thoughtful message.

1700 Set course for Tenerife in the Canary Islands. The city of Santa Cruz was the last city of the Old World seen by Magellan. Provisions and supplies were cheaper there than in Spain, and it was therefore customary for voyagers from Castile to top-off there before making their final departure. We shall be coming at it from a direction opposite to Magellan's, but it nevertheless will make a good final port of call. If we have time, we shall make our final photographic reconnaissance there.

2125 William Roy Welch, Machinist's Mate First Class, is re-enlisted in the service of the United States Navy for a period of six years. Since the *Manual of the Bureau of Naval Personnel* specifically prohibits re-enlistments at sea, to re-enlist Welch it was necessary to obtain permission in advance from the Assistant Secretary of the Navy for Personnel and Reserve Affairs. Welch's re-enlistment is a milestone of sorts, inasmuch as it is done at deep depths, at high speed and at the culmination of history's first submerged circumnavigation of the world. All these things we carefully record in Welch's service record and in the ship's Log.

2145 We are not yet home, but we may be considered to have taken a long lead off third base. So tonight, to celebrate completion of the first submerged circumnavigation and our looked-for homecoming, we hold a "third base party" for the crew and officers. There are even several acts of pretty good entertainment. The first is by Fireman Raymond Kuhn, who has been practicing on a home-made French horn. To everyone's amazement it works, and he plays us several fairly recognizable bugle calls on it. Kuhn will never win any Nobel prizes for music, but the fact that he can play that thing at all is astonishing. He gets cheers of appreciation from his shipmates, many of whom throng around asking to try it themselves, and we may use him on the bridge for rendering passing honors to other naval vessels.

Another act is a barbershop quartet consisting of Herb Zeller, EM1; Chief Steward William "Joe" Green; Richard Brown, EM1;

and Wilmot Adair (Mrs. Neptune) Jones, TM2. The quartet are taken aback by their audience's wild insistence upon an encore, for it turns out they know only one song. They needn't have worried; it gets as many cheers the second time.

The hit of the evening, from my point of view, is a skit put on by Jim Flaherty, RM1, and Jones. Flaherty plays a TV announcer and Jones acts the part of "Mother Fletcher," the cooking instructor, who continually samples her sherri-herri [sic] while baking a cake, and slowly drinks herself into a stupor in front of the anguished announcer. Mother Fletcher's delighted audience was particularly convulsed because someone had doctored up the "sherri-herri" bottle with chili sauce; Jones' agonized expression throughout the skit was very real indeed.

We also held a "beard contest," with myself as chief judge. I had already decided who was going to win: he was our ship's barber, Pete Kollar, whose luxurious facial foliage could have competed with any Hollywood actor's, but he fell asleep and no one remembered to call him for the contest. Forced, therefore, to judge honestly from among the other candidates, I finally awarded the prize for the "most glorious beard" to James Bennett, RM1.

0230   Finally wrote finis to the World's First Submerged Circumnavigation Celebration. All hands turned in with the feeling of satisfaction that comes from having finished a big job.

A special Well Done should go to LCDR Bob Fisher, our supply officer, whose cooks kept the party-goers well supplied with a steady flow of pizza, popcorn and punch. Bob also serves as the officer representative on the ship's recreation council, whose members did the planning for the party.

Thursday and Friday, 28-29 April 1960   With a comfortable speed of advance and our circumnavigation complete, these two days were devoted to engineering drills. Like all nuclear ships, we have rigid qualification requirements for officers and men before they may stand certain main propulsion plant watches.

Saturday, 30 April 1960   This is Will Adams' birthday. He has announced everybody else's birthday in his daily "Plan of the Day," but had hoped to avoid mentioning his own. I out-foxed him, however, and wrote it in just before the Plan of the Day went to press.

As an added birthday present, this morning a message arrived with notification that Will Adams is a Commander, US Navy, with a date of rank from 1 February [that is, he will be as soon as he finishes some correspondence courses which are still dogging him]. The same message states that Don Fears is a Lieutenant Commander, also with a 1 February date. We knew both promotions were due, and it is certainly fine to get the news at last; Will and Don have been congratulated all day long.

0430 Periscope depth for approach on Tenerife, Canary Islands. The spectacle on raising the periscope is remarkable. Although we are still quite distant from land, the lights of the city of Santa Cruz are so high above the horizon as to give the appearance of stars. Tenerife, according to the *Sailing Directions,* is an extremely high and mountainous island. The highest peak, Pico de Teyde, is more than 12,000 feet. The chart shows that modern Santa Cruz has a large and efficient-looking artificial harbor formed by a long breakwater. Try as we may, we are unable to locate where Magellan's precipitous cliff-walled harbor could have been.

A historical episode in which Santa Cruz figured was the 1798 attack on the city by an English squadron under Horatio Nelson. Nelson was then 39 years old and had held the rank of Rear Admiral in the British Navy for a year. The attack on Tenerife miscarried in the initial stages, mainly because of indecision among the commanders of the assault troops, and Nelson determined to lead the second attack in person. As he landed, a grape-shot shattered his right elbow, and with their leader out of action, this attack also failed. Nelson's arm was amputated and he was invalided home for several months.

A sketch of the defenses of Santa Cruz and the shore configuration, drawn by Nelson for this campaign, is easily recognized on our chart. The changes wrought by the recent century and a half are not so great, evidently, as those of the previous three.

Apropos of Nelson's arm, shortly before landfall this morning, Chiefs Bennett and Jordan ganged up on our two most junior Electrician's Mates, Franklin D. Caldwell and Ronald D. Kettlehake, with a story to the effect that all ships approaching the Island of Tenerife were required to set a watch for Horatio Nelson's arm, and that they, being junior, had been designated for the first watch. Having been forewarned by the two perpetrators of the joke, I sent separately for Caldwell and Kettlehake in order to brief them on their duties.

Caldwell appeared first, somewhat nonplused at this unusual summons. I carefully explained to him that Nelson's arm had become petrified and greatly enlarged after being tossed over the side from his flagship *Theseus,* and that now, standing vertically in the mud of the channel off Tenerife, it had become a danger to navigation.

Caldwell slowly produced a sheepish grin as I went on with the gag, finally departed to fetch Kettlehake. This engaging young character completely swallowed my long yarn about the huge petrified arm, seemed perfectly willing to believe that it could have become an object able to menace navigation in water many hundreds of fathoms deep. He was, in fact, very interested in all the details of my dissertation of how it came about, and finally blurted out, "It sounds like a grand tradition, sir. How long has it been going on?"

"About an hour," I told him.

But Kettlehake continued with questions about Nelson, and when he departed, he carried off volume one of my precious set of Mahan's *The Life of Nelson.* Now that the fun is over, I am wondering just who was hazing whom, and whether there was a bet in the background involving getting that book away from me.

0830   We are now near enough to begin our "photo-recon" of the outskirts of the city of Santa Cruz on Tenerife island. It is indeed an imposing skyline, though search as we may, we still find no evidence of the harbor supposedly used by Magellan. The scenery is most spectacular, however, far and away the most breathtaking of this cruise.

Behind Santa Cruz towering peaks stretch in both directions. Though vegetation is visible in many places, generally speaking the brown hillsides are similar to the Cape of Good Hope.

The city of Santa Cruz extends back against the hillside in such a way that the whole is laid out before us and presents an extremely imposing view. Many roads can be seen stretching along the hillsides, with automobiles moving back and forth on them. Many new modern buildings, evidently apartments, line the roads and, as at Cebu, march steadily up the hillside and back from the sea. Nearly 300,000 people supposedly live on this island. From the size of Santa Cruz it can be readily believed that about 200,000 of them must live here.

The breakwater is visible. Construction work is going forward to lengthen it and extend the harbor even farther. Sheltered behind are a number of large ships, including some cruise ships. Indeed, Santa Cruz looks like an ideal spot for a vacation.

0933 Departed Tenerife for rendezvous off Cadiz the early morning of Monday, 2 May.

Sunday, 1 May 1960 1330 Our next-to-last church services. Chief Electrician's Mate Hugh Bennett leads. His talk is titled "Success," and it has much food for thought.

The *Triton Eagle* has formally ceased publication, though we shall probably put out one more issue prior to arrival in the United States. The reason is that mail from home will now fill the void the paper has been filling these several months. The entire staff deserve much credit for daily extra duty faithfully performed for the benefit of their shipmates.

Monday, 2 May 1960 0117 Sonar contact identified as USS *John W. Weeks* (DD-701).

0243 Periscope depth. *Weeks* in sight bearing 035.5° true.

A blown tube in sonar equipment prevents communication with

the destroyer. Most annoying to have it take place at precisely this moment. We are however prepared against this eventuality with our homemade method of signaling by light through the periscope. As with the *Macon,* we have to use two periscopes and three quartermasters, but the thing works as well as before. We shall design a more refined apparatus for use at future times.

0302   There are lights of entirely too many ships around our present position. Signal from the *Weeks:* "Follow me." We head out to sea in the direction we'd most like to head, toward the USA.

0554   The *Weeks* is to deliver a SubLant Medical Officer to us for transportation back to the United States and take Commander Roberts with his exposed film to Rota for further transfer by air back to the US. She also carries instructions for us regarding the end-of-cruise rendezvous near the United States.

I remember thinking, at the time, what a good idea this was. All of us were famished for news of New London, not just for personal family news, though that of course figured prominently too, but for general information as well. Occasional news messages had indeed been received, but what I, for one, wanted to know was how Poole had fared, had any of our hydrographic bottle papers been picked up, had there been any repercussions as a result of our encounter with the young man in the dugout canoe in Magellan Bay? Also, I wanted to know which ships were in port and which at sea, what new ships had been launched, which ones completed and commissioned, who had relieved whom in command of what—and a rather considerable list of strictly parochial submariner to submariner professional queries.

A Medical Officer would not be expected to know the answers to all these questions, but if he were anything like Jim Stark, who always tried to keep up with everything going on around him, it was a safe bet he could make a pretty good stab at many of them.

Sparing an officer from SubLant's small staff for a purpose

of this nature would be a problem; no doubt the Medical Officer was a compromise, probably sent for the added purpose of giving us all some sort of physical examination as part of the information needed for the cruise evaluation report. There would be many pleasant hours spent in pumping him for information during the Atlantic crossing, I thought, and I felt like thanking the man who had thought of this kindness.

From the Log:

In broaching we have taken care that the same technique as was used to disembark Chief Radarman Poole two months ago is employed again. That is, the ship as a whole will remain submerged; only a few necessary people will come topside to handle the transfer. We shall use the conning tower as an air lock as before.

0554 With air in safety tank and bow buoyancy, broached ship to 38 feet. I went to the bridge and, after seeing that conditions were suitable, directed that Lt. Sawyer come topside with the boat-handling detail.

0617 *Weeks* had already put her boat in the water and it was alongside almost immediately. As at Montevideo, *Triton* lay dead in the water, rolling gently with her stern submerged. In both cases a slight swell was running. Off Montevideo, it was in the dead of night with a slight rain and relatively little visibility. Here, it was early morning, broad daylight and no rain. Still, this transfer proved more difficult than the previous one.

The boat approached slowly and very cautiously, but clumsily. Alternately, the coxswain gunned his engine too fast, came ahead too fast, then, uneasy, threw it into reverse and backed away too fast. For a period of several minutes, during which he jockeyed alongside, he never approached our sides close enough for our deck hands to reach his bow painter when it was flung over. Finally, acceding to our shouted encouragement, he swept up abreast our bow a foot or so away, rose on a fairly large swell above our main deck—and forgot to cut his engine, with the result that he swept on by, completely missed his landing, and had to circle around for another try.

From the Log:

The first pass failed. The second try was a little better, though the boat came alongside at the wrong time so far as the action of the sea was concerned and rode high up on our side.

In the boat were Commander A. F. Betzel from Washington and Lieutenant Commander Earl Ninow, Medical Corps, from New London. Seizing the right moment, Commander Betzel made a flying leap across to our deck, landed on all fours, was caught and steadied by Fitzjarrald and Sawyer. A line, easily passed over to the boat, brought back with it a sack with a large bulky circular object outlined against the canvas. The coxswain gunned his boat again, brought it up alongside once more, again overshot as the freshening swells lifted it. The boat rode up on our deck and landed right on it with a crash. A moment of pure fear in my heart. Our men on deck reeled back hastily when it became evident that the boat was coming aboard.

As she touched, Commander Ninow leaped out of the whaleboat, landing like his predecessor on hands and knees on deck. As the sea subsided beneath the boat, it slid off our side and plunged drunkenly back into the sea. Two men on the far side of the boat fell backwards into the water. The wisdom of being stopped was now evident; when the men surfaced, being still right alongside their boat, they quickly hooked their arms over the gunwales and in a moment, with the help of their mates, they were back aboard.

In the boat was some mail and gear destined for us, but the coxswain had evidently had enough. He gathered in bow and stern lines and sped off toward his destroyer.

0631   With passengers and part of the cargo on board, *Triton* opened vents and went back down to the comfort of the depths. During the ensuing conference, we will investigate how to transfer

Commander Betzel back to the destroyer and receive the mail and other parcels they have for us.

With the experience of the boat alongside in mind and evidence that the weather is commencing to kick up, it is obviously impractical to attempt another boat transfer. Helicopters are standing by at Rota; we ask the *Weeks* to request their assistance.

0800 Commander Betzel has brought our instructions with him. We are to proceed to the area of the Delaware Capes on the eastern seaboard of the United States, where we shall surface and officially terminate our trip. He has also brought with him the plaque we had left behind to be cast and which we had hoped to present at the site of the statue of Magellan reputed to be at Cadiz.

I recall that my attempts to pump Buzz Betzel during that quick conference were wholly fruitless. And later, during the entire trip back across the Atlantic, I had no better luck with Dr. Ninow. Ninow, in fact, informed us that he had just reported to New London and knew absolutely nothing about submarines. I worked on him all the way across the ocean, but remained hungry for news until we reached the States.

Our memorial to Ferdinand Magellan is about 23 inches in diameter, cast in shiny brass. It depicts the world by general outline of latitude and longitude lines. Around its circumference, in raised letters, are the words: "AVE NOBILIS DUX—ITERUM SACTUM EST," which is translated as "Hail, Noble Captain, It Is Done Again." In the center is an old sailing ship similar to Magellan's, beneath which is inscribed "1519–1960," signifying the dates of his voyage and ours. A laurel wreath with the US submarine dolphin insignia in its base surrounds the ship and dates.

The plaque is symbolic of all we have been trying to accomplish. It is hastily photographed on board and packed away for return to the *Weeks*. It has become an international object. Apparently it is to be presented to Spain by the US ambassador at a formal ceremony!

0807 With helicopters in sight, broached ship once more and

commenced preparations for transfer of personnel. By 0900, Commanders Betzel and Roberts had left the ship, accompanied by all the painstakingly-taken photographs of our nearly three months' journey and the narrative section of our voyage report to date.

Sad to relate, even though there were those who swore there had been several bulging sacks of mail in the *Weeks'* whaleboat when it was swept up on our deck, there was an utterly unsatisfying amount of mail delivered by helicopter. Radioed inquiry to *Weeks* brought the answer that there was no more to be found on board marked for us. Ultimately, it would catch up to us, this we knew, but not until we arrived back home. There is nothing so frustrating in the world as mail which one cannot get one's hands on.

0919   Changed depth to cruising depth and speed to full. We are on the last leg of our trip enroute to the United States.

Tuesday, 3 May 1960   Enroute the United States. Our estimated time of arrival in New London is 0800 on the morning of 11 May, on the 85th day after our departure.

0824   Sonar contact on a merchantman which passed by to north. Even though there might be plenty of time to investigate the contact further, we decide against it in favor of pursuing our homeward-bound passage. Besides, none of us have any time to spare. Working on the cruise report is taking every free moment.

Wednesday, 4 May 1960   Among the papers brought aboard day before yesterday are promotion papers for Robert L. Jordan and Richard N. Peterson, both Chief Interior Communication Electrician's Mates, raising them to the rank of Warrant Electrician. Caught somewhat unprepared, neither had the necessary uniforms or insignia with which to transform his normal CPO dress into that of his newly attained Warrant rank. But once again improvisation comes to the fore. At 1840, resplendent in the fully authorized and correct uniform of Warrant Electricians, US Navy [although closer inspection might show that their rank insignia were made of yellow plastic tape instead of gold stripes and colored, where needed, with blue grease pencil], Bob Jordan and Pete Peterson are promoted to Warrant Officer and move into the wardroom.

Friday, 6 May 1960   One of the mysteries of the cruise has been an anonymous character named "Buck" who occasionally writes a column for the *Triton Eagle*. A particular subject of his misguided wit is usually myself, whom he has irreverently named the "o.m.," and a number of the people on board have wondered who he is and how he can get away with so much. Tomorrow they will find out, as they read the morning edition of the rejuvenated *Eagle* [by popular demand—and the dearth of mail—it had started publication again], for in "The Skipper's Corner" it is revealed that "Buck" and I are one and the same.

1900   There is a rather lively discussion in the wardroom over the suggestion that there has been a let-down in general morale during the past several days. Various reasons are advanced to explain this phenomenon, which all agree is present. A most obvious explanation: we have finished our trip. We have gone around the world submerged, but we still have a long way to go before we get home. Morale had been fairly well sustained all the way to St. Peter and St. Paul's Rocks, which had been our goal. But though our goal was achieved, it was not the end of the line. There were still 6,000 miles to go. Furthermore, we didn't get nearly as much mail at Rota as we had hoped, and many have heard nothing at all from their families. Finally, especially as pertains to the officers, the paper-work problem related to the voyage report, preparation of work items for "post-shakedown overhaul," and necessary revision to ship's procedures resulting from our voyage, has been extremely heavy. It has been a tough trip; the keyed-up attitude with which everyone went into it has, after some 80 days, worn a little thin.

As Jim Hay and George Troffer point out, however, *Triton*'s crew is a highly trained, extraordinarily well-motivated outfit. What we are calling "a low state of morale" would, in most places, be considered a very high state indeed. We really have no right to complain. There is no doubt that we have noticed a drop, but maybe it was inevitable, just a return to normal levels.

At about this time, the conversation turned to some of the privileges which we have not been able to enjoy of recent date. "Here it is dinnertime. How I wish I had a martini right now!" someone mumbles.

This was the cue I had been trying for some minutes to plant somewhere. A surreptitious signal to Green brought him back with a tray containing a dozen deliciously frosted sherbert glasses, each one brimming with a clear liquid in which was submerged a green olive impaled on a toothpick. The effect was magical. We could almost smell the tantalizing odor of vermouth. The illusion lasted until somebody finally could stand it no more—and drank his ice water.

Morale in the wardroom, which had previously hit a new high, touched a new low. Psychology being what it is, I was not sure, afterward, that my little joke had quite accomplished its objective.

2300   A message arrives from ComSubLant which ought to change all this talk about low morale. He announces that upon arrival in New London, *Triton* is to receive the Presidential Unit Citation from the Secretary of the Navy, who will apparently be there in person to present it. Furthermore, although the message itself is received in a highly classified manner, I am specifically authorized to publish the news to the entire crew.

With great pleasure we stop the presses, tear up the front page of the *Triton Eagle* and write a new one, quoting this section of the dispatch in full.

It does, indeed, have the desired effect.

Sunday, 8 May 1960   This is our last Sunday under way on this cruise and, speaking from experience, the last Sunday this crew will be together as a unit. As soon as we arrive in port there will be a number of transfers, some retirements, and of course the inevitable influx of new men. It is ever thus in the Navy and not something that we can really complain about, except to note with regret the dispersion of a fine crew at its highest state of training.

The only man I know who never had to contend with changes in his ship's company was Captain Nemo of Jules Verne's fictional *Nautilus*. Nemo, having isolated himself from mankind, cruised the seas indefinitely with a crew of similar misogynists. But even he was defeated at the end as, one by one, he buried the members of his crew until finally he alone was left.

Today it is my turn again to lead the services of our little Protestant Sunday meetings. It is a good opportunity to deliver some thoughts on homecoming and to point out that although we may have all sorts of preconceived ideas about this, so will the folks at home; for families too have suffered privation while we have been away. We have had the adventure; they the drudgery. We have had change, and the challenge of new things; they the challenge of the same old thing day after day, without ourselves to help.

I also make an effort to point out some obvious dangers. The chance of slowed reaction while driving a car, for instance, or the probability that strong drink will have a much greater and more immediate effect than before. Some medical opinion holds that, having remained cooped up in close quarters for such a long period, our eyes will now find difficulty in shifting from short distances to long distances; thus, for a few hours, there may be greater danger in driving than ever before.

There are one or two other things I should also mention at this stage: Torpedoman Second Class Jones has on numerous occasions drawn the assignment of running the wardroom movies [this is rotated among various movie operators who alternate between showing movies for the crew in the crew's mess hall and for the wardroom. Normally, there are two movies shown each day for the crew and one for the wardroom]. Something of a comic, Jones usually takes a good-natured ribbing as he sets up for us, and has given back as good as he gets. Some time ago, however, after a particularly contrived and illogical movie, I dressed him down severely and decreed that if the next movie was no better, I was going to demote him a grade.

After this, poor Jones had very little luck. Try as he might to tout his movies all were graded "poor," and he successively descended in rating until finally he had been reduced to seaman recruit, as far down the ladder as he could go. At this point, Jones thought he could go no lower and had me whipped, but I held despotic power in our little world and made the rules myself and Jones continued to progress in a negative direction. As of now, he holds the rate of Negative Chief Torpedoman on board this ship, and it has been so announced in "The Skipper's Corner." The crew insists that when we get home he will have to walk down the gangway standing on his hands, wearing a Chief's hat backwards. Others claim he should pay the Navy for the privilege of being in it.

Now that the cruise is nearing the end, however, my duty has become clear and I must perform it. Jones is today promoted back all the way to his original rating of Torpedoman Second. This amounts to a jump of 11 grades, unprecedented in all naval records.

If there has been a sag in morale, it is no longer evident; everybody is cheerful, now that Jones is back in good graces again. Besides, there are only 2 more days to go.

Monday, 9 May 1960   We are rapidly approaching the Delaware Capes, where we are scheduled to rendezvous with helicopters and a weather boat tomorrow morning shortly after daybreak.

Sometime tomorrow we will hold a short ceremony during which 6 of our crew will be awarded the coveted silver dolphins, signifying that they have "qualified in submarines." They certainly have been putting in the extra hours and have gained on this account a great amount of approbation among their shipmates. Qualification in submarines is never an easy task, and we do not intend that it shall ever be. The prospective new dolphin wearers are:

WILLIAM A. MCKAMEY, JR., Seaman
FRED KENST, Seaman

JAMES H. SMITH, JR., Seaman
MAX L. ROSE, Seaman
LAWRENCE W. BECKHAUS,
    Sonarman First Class
WILLIAM R. HADLEY,
    Chief Communications Technician

We had thought of doing this at quarters, upon arrival in New London, but gave up the idea because there will be too many other things to occupy us.

As *Triton* enters Thames River, enroute to her berth in New London, we shall man the rail in traditional Navy style. That is, the members of the crew topside will be dressed in the uniform of the day and will form a solid line from bow to stern, thus creating, we hope, a sharp and military appearance. We are proud of our ship and want her to look her best, despite the scars from her three months contest with the elements.

Flying from our highest periscope will be a rather old and slightly weather-beaten set of colors, and thereby hangs the very personal story which, already partly told in these pages, must now be completed.

In 1916, my father was Commanding Officer of the armored cruiser *Memphis* [ex-*Tennessee*] which, he used to say, was the most responsive ship, the best trained and the easiest handled, of any he had ever served in. On August 29th of that year, lying at anchor at Santo Domingo, capital of the Dominican Republic, while pacing the quarterdeck with the skipper of the tiny gunboat *Castine,* who had come to call, Father noticed a heavy surf along the shore. A look to seaward brought him up with a start; he ordered Commander Bennett back to his ship and directed that both ships be made immediately ready to go to sea. Hurriedly, he sent a message directing the baseball team, then due to return from practice, to stay ashore. Two of the three boats received the message and did indeed wait, but the third either did not see the signal or failed to understand it, for on it came.

Forty minutes later, a tidal wave swept completely over the top of the *Memphis,* swamped the bridge, inundated the entire topsides of the ship. *Memphis* had almost, but not quite, got steam to her engines. [*Castine,* a much smaller ship, did in fact get up steam in time.] Father's anchor chains [all three anchors, in desperation, were down] stretched, then snapped; *Memphis* was swept from her berth, and within half an hour she crashed ashore in 12 feet of water, a total wreck. Until recently, the hulk could still be seen there, placarded with billboard advertisements.

Father survived the catastrophe, although a number of people who were standing on the bridge with him were swept overboard and lost. Several were killed by flying debris below decks, or by burst steam lines; and he watched helplessly as the boat with the baseball party rolled over and over in the gigantic surf. Thirty-three sailors, and a part of Father, died that day.

Not long ago I received a letter from an ex-Navy man who wanted to know, since I bore the same name, if I were related to his old skipper in the *Memphis.* I responded that I was indeed— and after some additional correspondence it developed that Stanley P. Moran of Wilmington, Delaware, one of *Memphis'* quartermasters, had rescued the ensign which flew over *Memphis* that disastrous day.

Sam Worth of Cleveland, Ohio, its present guardian, had no idea, last February, why I suddenly had such need of his cherished flag, but he sent it to me by special delivery immediately upon receipt of my urgent letter. Soon he and Stanley Moran and all the remaining survivors of the *Memphis* catastrophe will know why I wanted it; for when *Triton* enters the Thames River on May 11, next, this same flag will be flying once again, probably for the last time, over a mighty US man-of-war.

The Navy is composed of ships, and men, and long-held traditions—all melded together in dedicated service to their country. It is more fitting that the last sight graced by this old flag should be one of gladness and success, rather than disaster and death.

Father has been gone more than 16 years, but this is something I've always wanted to do for him.

Still from the Log:

Tuesday, 10 May 1960 0430 Surfaced, having been submerged exactly 83 days and 10 hours [figured on twenty-four-hour days], and travelled 36,014 miles.

The rendezvous is still several hours hence, but we are now approaching the shallow water off the east coast of the United States, where *Triton* cannot venture without her fathometer. The long voyage is over.

The men of the *Triton* believe her long undersea voyage has accomplished something of value for our country. The sea may yet hold the key to the salvation of man and of his civilization, for it is the connecting link between all the diverse parts of the world. The sea has given us a means of waging war, but even more, it has given us an avenue to hold the peace. Never have wars been fought for the sole purpose of controlling or annexing the sea. The limitless sea, like the air and space above the air, is free to all who would use it peacefully, in consonance with the principles of international humanity.

That the world may better understand this, the Navy directed a submerged retrace of Ferdinand Magellan's historic circumnavigation. The honor of doing it fell to *Triton,* but it has been a national accomplishment; for the power which propels our ship, the genius which designed her, the thousands and hundreds of thousands who labored, each at his own métier, in all parts of the country, to build her safe, strong, self-reliant, are America. *Triton,* a unit of their Navy, pridefully and respectfully dedicates this voyage to the people of the United States.

EPILOGUE

Our Log ended at sea, ready for pickup on the morning of the tenth of May, its last entry written several hours in advance of the event in order to have it properly typed and ready upon arrival. Tying up loose ends took until the small hours of the morning, and I finally turned in, exhausted, to get a few hours of sleep before the rendezvous. It fell to Will Adams, therefore, to have the honor of bringing *Triton* back to the surface just before dawn. I was awakened by the jolt of high-pressure air roaring into her twenty-two main ballast tanks.

As we slowly steered toward the appointed place off Rehoboth Beach, leaden gray skies gradually replaced the dark overcast of night. With the day came our first visitor, a curious sea bird winging in graceful circles and figure eights overhead, swooping in civilized instinct low over our wake for

the bits of garbage which he and his fellows have long learned
to associate with ships at sea. Land itself was not to be seen,
and we might as well have been in the middle of the Atlantic,
or in the Pacific, half a world away. But this romantic notion
lasted only a short time. Soon our sea bird was joined by another type of bird, a land variety with wheels, a fixed wing, and
a propeller glinting light from its nose. Behaving like its handsome wild cousin, the small plane flew low to pass by our side
at close range. We waved vigorously at its occupants, who
could clearly be seen waving in return. One of them, holding
a large camera, appeared to be taking pictures.

Soon, another small plane joined the first one, and then a
third. And speeding out of the west, where the shadows of
early morning were yet visible in the horizon haze, the bows of
a speedboat pushed a white mustache of water in front of it.
It looked familiar as it came closer, and in a few minutes, as
it turned broadside, I remembered where I had last seen this
powerful craft, or one like it. An experimental postwar PT
boat, it had been based at the old Washington Navy Yard for
the past several years. The Officer-in-Charge was known as
a person whose knowledge of the Potomac River and ability to
handle small craft were second to none in the Navy. I wondered if it was indeed the same boat, if Walter Slye had been
sent to meet us, and indeed whether or not he still held the
post. Binocular inspection brought no answer while the boat
was still bows on, but when it sheared off and presented its silhouette, the interior of the cockpit became visible and revealed
Slye himself, uniform cap, as always, perched squarely on the
top of his head. With delight, I waved my cap to him, and he
waved back.

It seemed only a few minutes, though it must have been
some time later, that one of the lookouts reported the approach of two helicopters lumbering toward us from the hid-
den continent to the west. Radioed instructions had prepared
us; I went on deck with George Sawyer and the helicopter

landing party. When one of the machines hovered over our deck aft to lower a strange inverted mushroom-shaped object to us, I set my hat firmly on my head, ignored the fluttering roar and wind from the whirling blades, and seated myself on it, straddling the center stalk and wrapping my arms around it. To my surprise, the mushroom, which had looked like metal of some kind, felt like foam rubber and was not a bit uncomfortable. I looked down. George was already many feet below me, holding up a signal flag, and *Triton* was receding at a rapid pace. There was suddenly something alongside me —the fuselage of the helicopter and a yawning door into the interior. Friendly faces stared at me and friendly arms reached out to steady the mushroom seat.

Dismounting, I pressed my face against the Plexiglass window of the passenger compartment to see the ship in which I had spent nearly a quarter of a year under water. She looked small, out of her element on the surface. Her sturdy sides were mottled where the paint had been stripped away, and they were speckled here and there with discolorations of rust. A small knot of men stood on her deck—the helicopter handling party whom I had just left—and a group of heads were clustered on her bridge. Slowly, under the command of Will Adams, she gathered way on the leisurely course toward New London which had been directed, holding her speed unaccustomedly low and making only a tiny bow wave. Quickly, she vanished in the distance.

The clattering of the helicopter engine made conversation practically impossible in the passenger compartment, and someone handed me a piece of paper on which was written, "What was your first impression of the world after returning to it?" I wrote back, "It smells fishy!" This was the most immediate sensation, a fishlike odor which had seemed to permeate the entire superstructure of the ship. A number of suckerlike organisms had attached themselves to the bridge area, and there were no doubt many more of them throughout the ship's immense superstructure. There would have to be a pretty thorough scraping, scaling, and repainting job done during our "post-shakedown" overhaul, I reflected.

The grinding beat of the rotating blades brought us over a sandy beach, then some green and plowed farm fields. Here and there were houses. We passed one moderate-sized city, then suddenly were over a bigger one. The helicopter dipped lower. I could see streets and automobiles, and people walking on the sidewalks. There was a surprising number of trees, in many cases almost entirely concealing the streets beneath them. Then we were over a large muddy river. A tall stone obelisk, standing in the midst of a great expanse of grass, reached almost up to us. The helicopter ceased its forward motion, swayed gently fore and aft, swung completely around once or twice, slowly settled. Below us was more grass, a carefully kept lawn dominated by a large building. With a thrill I recognized the White House. The plane landed gently just a few yards in front of the South Portico.

The next two hours were, to say the least, kaleidoscopic. Scores of well-wishers greeted me. I shook hands a hundred times, and suddenly a pair of arms went around my neck from behind and a familiar kiss landed on my ear. There stood Ingrid, looking somewhat breathless but otherwise exactly as I had remembered her these three months.

"How is everybody?" I asked.

"Fine," she said.

"Come along," someone else said—and the next thing I knew I was talking to the President.

In my hand I carried a letter and envelope addressed to President Eisenhower, carefully cacheted with a replica of our circumnavigation plaque which we had printed with homemade ink. There had been a number of experimental inks concocted, but the most successful one—hydraulic oil, ground charcoal, and insulating paint, as I recall—was extremely slow in drying. To protect the envelope from being

smudged, I had wrapped it, along with others for Mrs. Eisenhower, the Secretary of Defense, and the Secretary of the Navy,
in the only readily available highly absorbent paper we had.
Now, standing before the Commander in Chief of the Armed
Forces, I shook his proffered hand, reported successful completion of our mission, and handed him the letter we had so
painstakingly prepared for him. Only then, to my horror, did
I realize that I had neglected to remove the protective paper
covering.

"What's this?" the President asked, with a slightly puzzled
frown.

I froze with the realization of the enormity of my faux pas.
"It's—it's just a little toilet paper we had to use to keep the
ink from smudging," I blurted out despairingly.

I had worked for the President in the fairly intimate capacity
of Naval Aide a few years earlier, but nothing in our relation-
ship had prepared me for this situation. I had never lost my
feeling of great awe for him, and I stood rooted to the rug
in his office, waiting for I knew not what result of this indignity.

People who knew President Eisenhower longer and better
than I might perhaps have been able to predict his reaction.
For my part, it was with the greatest relief that I became
witness to a magnificent set of Presidential "Ha ha's" and
"Ho ho's," delivered as he shook with mirth, steadying himself
with one hand braced on the top of his desk.

"What in the world did you say to the Old Man?" the Press
Secretary demanded, as officials whisked me away again. I
told him, and Jim Hagerty chuckled. "That's probably the
most fun the boss has had all week," he said. "Good for you!"
He said something else, too, and there was an undercurrent of
seriousness in his manner which came back to me later, but
at the time I was too bemused at all that was going on to
catch it.

I had a few minutes chat with Admiral Rickover, and then
found myself in yet another room where a large map of our

route had been prepared, and several thousand newsmen, it seemed to me, had gathered. Each one had a camera, and each used it constantly. Someone had taken care of Ingrid, I saw with relief when I looked around. There were a lot of pictures and many questions, some humorous and some serious, and after a while the President reappeared to pose with us for a few moments. Then Ingrid stood beside me for more pictures, and a large model of the *Triton* was handed to the two of us, so that we stood there helplessly with all four arms gripping the six-foot-long gray-and-black replica.

"Kiss your wife!" someone commanded, and we dutifully obliged.

"This way—do it again!" We turned toward the latest importunator, kissed again.

The smile on Ingrid's face was becoming just a little grim, I thought. She leaned over and whispered, "My heel has come off!" I looked around desperately for a rescuer to take the model. Someone nearby took over *Triton,* junior, and a White House policeman ran off with the shoe for emergency repairs.

Later, riding in a White House limousine toward the Pentagon to call on Mr. William B. Franke, Secretary of the Navy, I had my first sight of a recent newspaper. It was full of stories about the U-2, the high-flying reconnaissance plane which had in some manner been forced down in Soviet Russia, and I read the reports with growing concern and understanding. Ringing through my ears were the cryptic sentences uttered by Hagerty as he ushered me out of the President's huge oval office: "Have you heard about the U-2?" he had asked.

"No," I had answered. "What is it—a new German submarine?"

Hagerty's laugh had not been one of amusement. "Well, you'll find out soon enough. Thank God you made it back when you did!"

This, of itself, might have meant little to me, had it not been supplemented by another comment from another source:

"You've shown the oceans are still free to all. Of all the things we'd planned to prove for the summit conference, you were the only one to come through!"

This was the outcome of the secret we had carried around the world! I had not realized that other efforts were being made at the same time as *Triton*'s, but it figured. A thing this important would not, logically, have been left to the single exertions of a single agent.

Five hours after leaving the *Triton*'s deck, I was delivered back aboard in the same manner—full of news, good and bad information, and the plans for the next day's arrival ceremonies at New London. I took over the ship's announcing system to pass the word to as many people as possible all at once, and then surrendered to the avid questioners in the wardroom.

Next morning, Wednesday, the eleventh of May, *Triton* stood up the Thames River a few minutes before our scheduled arrival at the dock in New London. Except for the temperature, which was considerably warmer, we might have been back in February again. A blustery nor'easter greeted us, with overcast skies and drizzling rain. We had intended to make a grand entrance up the river, with the crew standing in ranks in their whites on deck, the whole ship presenting the formal appearance of spit and polish (except for her weather-beaten sides) traditionally expected of naval vessels home from a long voyage. But not this day. It would have taken a lot to dampen our spirits, and if I had wanted it, I knew the whole crew would willingly have stood on deck, rain or no rain. But there was no point to getting more than the minimum possible number of persons bedraggled and wet. The men in the anchor detail had to be on deck, and a few were needed to break out mooring lines; they wore foul-weather gear and were required to stand in a semblance of ranks when not actually working. Everyone else, except the bridge personnel, was allowed to stay below.

The weather was not bad enough to prevent a number of

pleasure boats from coming out to welcome us and escort us up-stream, however, and on both banks of the river cars stopped, honked their horns at us, and people got out to wave. The Groton Police barracks must have halted all administration of justice, for the windows of the building were full of people waving and shouting.

The rain was fitful and there was very little wind; so as we came near to the berth which had been assigned to us, we had all the hatches opened and all hands who wanted to, who were not occupied below, came on deck to man the rail. Gently, we eased *Triton* into her berth, handling her with affectionate care and minimum speed. At the head of the dock, there was a riot of color amid the somber drabness of the New London "State Pier," and there was no doubt in anyone's mind what that was.

We presented, after all, rather a military appearance as our ship inched her way to her mooring. The rain had stopped —or perhaps it was only that we didn't notice it—and everyone, without orders, stood tall and straight at his post. But it wasn't quite the Prussian military ideal, either, for there was a certain surreptitious craning of necks, of searching the throng of women and children on the dock for a loved face, and now and then a furtive and thoroughly unmilitary signal of recognition. Studiously, I noticed none of this, kept my attention riveted on getting the ship alongside the dock with the least fuss—except that every now and then I, too, found myself checking over the faces under the rain hats and umbrellas.

Finally, I found those I sought. Ingrid had promised to have our three children out of school for the occasion, and there they were, looking rather unhappy and solemn about the whole thing. Ned, Jr., and Hugh were each dutifully holding one of the large "Welcome Home *Triton*" signs with which many of those present were provided—no doubt a contribution of Electric Boat's public-relations outfit.

In a few minutes our visitors were abreast of *Triton*'s sail, as we warped her slowly in, and I picked up a megaphone and made the shortest speech on record. "Hi!" I bellowed to them.

Not far away the Coast Guard Band played martial music for the occasion, blowing with gusto and not caring, evidently, whether the rain filled their horns with water or not. And as I glanced above me, a gust of wind caught Father's old flag, flying from the top of our extended periscope, and straightened its ancient folds in reminiscent glory.

Suddenly my eyes smarted, and I deliberately looked down on deck to make sure that number one line had been properly led around a fair-lead cleat to the forward capstan.

A gangway was standing by, ready as soon as our mooring lines were doubled up and secured, and a battery of news cameras was waiting to record the first tender moments of arrival and greeting. Planned for our arrival was a ceremony in which the Secretary of the Navy, having flown from Washington for the purpose, was to award the Presidential Unit Citation to the ship and thereby authorize the entire crew to wear the Citation ribbon on their uniforms. We had designated the Chief of the Ship, Chief Torpedoman's Mate Chester R. Fitzjarrald, to receive the award in the name of crew and officers. Then the Secretary was to award Allen Steele the Navy Commendation Ribbon for his inspired action in combating the hydraulic oil leak, which had so nearly caused loss of depth control two-and-a-half weeks before.

But here a contretemps developed—one of those things which make gray hairs grow on the heads of aides and public-relations men. As soon as the ship was secured topside and below, Will ordered the in-port watch to be set and summoned all hands topside to fall in at quarters. They were counted off, sized off, told off by rating—officers in one group, chief petty officers in another, "white hats" in a third—and in a short time Adams reported that we were ready for the ceremony to begin. But there was a strange uneasiness on the canopied presentation platform down on the dock opposite our bridge. So far as I could tell everything was ready there—they, at least, could have very little excuse for not having had the public-address systems and all the other details thoroughly checked out—but instead of going forward with the presentation, there seemed to be some sort of a conference being held instead. There was a certain eagerness on the part of the crew to have the program over with as soon as possible, and the officers and petty officers, for understandable reasons, were impatient, too.

After a short time, the explanation came: the Secretary of the Navy was nowhere to be found!

I had directed that no one was to be allowed aboard or off the ship until the ceremony had been completed; we couldn't take a chance on lousing things up for the Secretary, I had thought, and this seemed little enough sacrifice at the time. But now *Triton*'s crew stood eagerly and uncomfortably on deck; our wives and families equally uncomfortably—and no less eager—on the dock. No one knew how long the Secretary would be delayed. Apparently, the plane bringing him had been diverted to the Naval Air Station at Quonset Point because of the bad weather, and he was driving to New London. If so, he should arrive at any moment; but the moments came and the moments went, and the Secretary of the Navy remained absent. As we later found out, fate was not quite through with us even yet. The driver of the lead car of the group assigned to bring the Secretary of the Navy and his party to New London, with Mr. Franke himself riding in the back seat, did not know the way!

I don't remember anyone putting the idea into my head, but a single wave of thought must have been going full blast that day. When the word arrived that no one knew where the Secretary was, and that for some reason he had entirely missed the police guard waiting for him at the Rhode Island border, I asked Admiral Daspit whether it would be permissible to dismiss the men from their quarters.

"Certainly, send them below," said the Admiral. But then he had a better idea, and we announced "dockside liberty," all hands to remain within earshot and get back aboard in a hurry when the Secretary finally showed up. Thus it was that the first reunion of our crew with their loved ones took place before, rather than after, the official reception of our ship. And it's a pleasure to record that the Secretary of the Navy finally did arrive, and, so far as I knew, not a soul of our crew abused the trust by going AWOL that day!

One man, however, was not affected by any of this protocol; Franklin Caldwell had been expecting a babygram, but none had arrived for him. In vain, he had haunted our radio room those last few days under way, and in vain, he had searched the smiling faces on the dock for that of his wife. She was not to be seen, and when he finally got ashore and to a telephone, it developed that she had one of the best excuses in the world for not being present to welcome her husband. Once informed of the situation, Will had Caldwell off the ship and, legitimate trip or not, into an official car within minutes. An hour or so later, a baby girl named Sandra swelled *Triton*'s dependent population by one.

With all the goings on, it was quite a while before I was able to have that quiet communion with my own wife and family which is the traditionally most cherished reward for the sailor home from a long voyage. There were a hundred things to talk to her and the children about, and a number which had to wait until the youngsters had said their prayers and gone to sleep.

"Sounds to me," I said, when we were at last alone, "that you make out better when I'm not here than when I am."

Ingrid sighed and put her head on my shoulder. "You'd

better not put me to another test for a while," she said. "The children kept me pretty busy, and I got quite a few calls toward the end from some of the wives who were getting rather anxious. . . . The worst time was when Admiral Rickover called on the telephone."

"What's this?" I asked. "Nobody told me about that."

"Well, I've not had a chance to until now, sweetie. I had a party for all the officers' wives, and right in the middle of it the phone rang. It was long distance. So I said yes, this was Mrs. Beach on the phone, and then a voice said, 'This is Admiral Rickover. I want you to know privately that your husband is all right. Everything is fine. Don't worry about him.'

"I must have let out a yelp or something, and I said, 'That's wonderful!' and I could hear all the conversation in the living room suddenly stop dead. Everybody was listening, and everybody was hoping it was some kind of news about the ship.

"I thanked the Admiral, and he said good-bye and hung up. Then I remembered that in the past you had cautioned me against passing on information from calls such as this, and I had missed my chance to ask the Admiral if it was all right to tell the other wives. You said I could never know what might be behind the call, so I was never to let anyone even know that I *had* been called.

"There wasn't a word I could say, but still I had to go back into the living room and face all those girls. They all just looked at me, and I thought fast and said, 'That was my father's doctor calling from Washington, where he's had to come from California for a meeting, and he said that Father has been much better recently.' I really felt terrible, lying to them like that. They all looked so dreadfully disappointed, and I wanted so much to tell them."

I hugged her. "Good girl," I said. "It was a lot tougher on you than on them. Anything else happen?"

She chuckled. "You had said that you didn't know when you'd be able to get mail, so I didn't write this time, except a little while ago, when I thought maybe I should have at least one letter in the mail for you just in case—did you get it, by the way?"

I shook my head.

"Well, I suppose it will catch up to you here at home. Anyway, one of your crew didn't get the word to his wife. A couple of weeks ago, this girl called up, and she was nearly in tears. She had written seventeen letters to her husband, and he hadn't answered a single one!"

"Why did she call you?" I asked. "We had put out the dope that anyone with a problem should call up the Squadron. . . ."

"I'm glad she did, of course," Ingrid interrupted. "Women understand these things better than men do. She knew I couldn't write the letters for her husband. All she wanted was some womanly comfort. Besides, I told them all to call up if they felt like it."

"You what? How did you do that?"

Ingrid smiled. "I forgot that my letter never reached you. It tells about it. I gave a coffee for all of them—it was a lovely warm day, and we had it outside, and that's when I told them. Mrs. Poole came, too, and she never said a word about her husband being home."

"You had 183 women, here?" My voice must have had an incredulous tinge.

"All your crew isn't married, silly! Besides, some couldn't come. But the garden is big enough, and all the officers' wives helped."

Ingrid sighed again. "They were all extremely nice. The only bad time was just before they came, when the telephone operator got me all excited about a long-distance call coming in, and I waited around thinking it must be about your arrival at last. But when the call finally came through, it was just a polite girl's voice saying she was sorry she couldn't come."

We had been home for two days, when all at once I had occasion to recall the intuitive warning I had ignored when we designed and ordered our commemorative plaque. Lieutenant John Laboon, Chaplain Corps—a 1943 Naval Academy graduate who had resigned to enter the Jesuit priesthood after the war and had subsequently re-entered the Service as a Chaplain —was responsible. This onetime All-American lacrosse player and decorated submarine combat veteran, now the Catholic Chaplain for our nuclear submarine unit in New London, had come aboard to see if there were anything he could do for us. Over a cup of coffee, he confessed that although he could translate most of the words in our plaque's Latin inscription, one of them was too much for him.

"What word?" I asked, my stomach experiencing a precipitant sinking feeling.

"*Sactum,*" said Laboon. "If it were *'Factum,'* now, the phrase would literally mean 'It is again a fact.' But I don't know the word *'Sactum.'* "

Hasty investigation restored Father Laboon's faith in his preordainment schooling. There simply was no such word as *"Sactum"!* It turned out that in receiving and reading back the Latin inscription over the telephone, the letter "F" in the word *"Factum"* had been erroneously taken down as "S," and the plaque as delivered to the US ambassador had therefore contained a misspelled word!

The hopelessness of the situation was enough to make one despair, but there was one thing we could do: we could get a new plaque—with the word "FACTUM" spelled correctly— over to Spain immediately; even though the original one might have contained an error, at least all posterity would not have the opportunity to criticize America's lack of erudition.

So ran my thoughts on that black Friday, the thirteenth of

May, as *Triton* went to work. A new plaque was cast forthwith. It was still cooling as final arrangements were made with a trans-Atlantic airline. In the meantime, I placed a telephone call to the Naval Attaché in Madrid, to insure that the situation would be properly taken care of in Spain.

By Sunday morning the plaque was ready and packaged. Jim Hay took it by automobile directly to New York's Idlewild Airport, where it was delivered into the hands of the pilot of a TWA plane bound for Boston and thence Madrid, nonstop. At 8:00 A.M., Monday morning, the jet rolled to a stop at the Madrid airport and was met by a US naval officer who took custody of the weighty package; and in due course the replacement was made and the mistake rectified insofar as it lay in our power.

The correct plaque is now mounted on the wall of the city hall of Sanlúcar de Barrameda, the port city near the mouth of the Guadalquivir River from which Magellan left on his historical voyage. Beneath it is a marble slab, installed by the Spanish government, memorializing the fact that it had been brought by the United States submarine *Triton*, first to circumnavigate the world entirely submerged, in homage to the first man to circumnavigate the globe by any means. The plaque originally delivered, bearing the word *"Sactum"* instead of *"Factum,"* is now held by the Mystic Seaport Museum at Mystic, Connecticut. A copy from the same mold is mounted in the ship. Four others have been presented to the Naval Academy, the Naval Historical Association in Washington, D.C., the Submarine School in Groton, Connecticut, and the Submarine Library at Groton within arrow shot of the launching ways where the *Triton* first took the water.

For the next month or so I dreaded the receipt of mail, for the Log of our journey had been made public by the Navy Department, and, of course, our error was plain for anyone to see. But only one person, a woman Latin teacher, very courteously and tactfully wrote to point out the mistake.

There were, of course, several other loose ends to wrap up: Poole, thoroughly examined aboard the *Macon* and later at a hospital in Montevideo, needed no operation. His third attack, which had precipitated our decision to seek medical assistance, had been his last—even as he himself had predicted. He had had a pretty rough time from curious friends in New London, and to his credit had said nothing to anyone.

Our fathometer, when inspected, brought an embarrassed frown to the faces of *Triton*'s builders. The cables connecting its head, in our bulbous forefoot, to the receiver in our control room, had been laid in an unprotected conduit through our superstructure which by mischance was subjected to severe water turbulence when the ship made high speed. Exposed thus to constant buffeting from the water, one by one the cables had ruptured. This will never happen again.

The return of our hydro papers to the Navy Oceanographic Office (to give it its new title—our Navy is constantly changing the names of things) has been rather disappointing. Only a few of the 144 we launched have come back. Possibly their finders are keeping them, in their pretty orange bottles, as souvenirs of *Triton*'s voyage.

So far as Carbullido was concerned, *Triton* kept her promise. The problem was broached to Pan American Airways, and, aided and abetted by various company officials with a warm heart for the Navy, a magazine article about our cruise was sold for exactly the cost of a round-trip ticket to Guam. Carbullido got home on Christmas day, 1960, with sixty days' leave in his pocket. His father had recently purchased a gasoline station; so the dutiful Carbullido spent his time on Guam pouring gasoline into the gas tanks of automobiles.

The concern I had about the young man who saw our periscope in Magellan Bay is still not completely dissipated. There were no repercussions from the Philippines awaiting us in New London, but after a few months the National Geographic Society believed our friend in the dugout canoe had been located. His photo did not, however, greatly resemble the lad our photographic party snapped on the other side of the world, and his name was the same as that of the local Chief of the Constabulary. Rufino Baring, if it was indeed he, thought he had seen a sea serpent that day, and, in terror, had kept his entire encounter with us a secret.

Commander Will Adams has his own command, the brand-new *Plunger,* under construction at Mare Island, California, and I expect we shall hear more of her in due course. Les Kelly, also a Commander, has another year or so in command of *Skipjack.* As this is written, the only one of *Triton*'s circumnavigation wardroom still in the ship is Tom Thamm, now a Lieutenant Commander and no doubt destined to become the Old Man of the Ship, the oldest plank-owner, as I was of my long-dead *Trigger.*

As these final words are written, *Triton* is again at sea, under a different Commanding Officer. In a few more months, she will no longer hold the title of being the world's biggest submarine, for the first of the new and heavier Lafayette-class ballistic-missile submarines will soon be commissioned. But for a very long time to come, *Triton* will continue to serve our country to the best of her tremendous and versatile capability, wherever the need may arise. As is true with all naval vessels, she will have a succession of skippers, and a succession of different people will form her crew. Time will slowly erode her newness and freshness, and the diverse requirements of the national policy will send her hither and yon throughout the waters of the world, charting new courses or following courses charted by others, as the case may require.

The members of *Triton*'s crew who made the voyage with her are already largely dispersed to other assignments, many of them to other submarines. Some of them are, at this very moment, on patrol in ballistic-missile submarines, helping to safeguard America's ideal of freedom and humanity. Some, having served long and faithfully in the Navy and the Submarine Force, have retired to civilian life.

As time goes on, more and more of us will retire, but in future years, all of us, like myself—though perhaps no one so much as I—may have occasion from time to time to reflect upon the events of this first voyage of the *Triton*. As we do, we will no doubt find our accomplishment pale beside far greater deeds as yet unaccomplished on or beyond this earth. For as soon as the capability is there, man will do what needs to be done so that earth and the spirit of man will both benefit therefrom.

USS *TRITON* (SSR(N)586)

Data Sheet Appendix to
First Submerged Circumnavigation Certificate

Exact mileage—nearest mile and nearest hours—(All "days" calculated on 24 hour basis) for:

  a. Rock to Rock—Statute miles   30,752
                Nautical miles   26,723
                Time   60 days, 21 hours

  b. EB Dock to Helicopter pick-up off Rehoboth Beach
                Statute miles   41,553
                Nautical miles   36,102
                Time   83 days, 18 hours, 56 minutes

  c. Dive 1737, February 16th to 0430, May 10th, 1960
                Statute miles   41,411.9
                Nautical miles   35,979.1
                Time   83 days, 09 hours, 54 minutes

  d. EB Dock, February 16, to State Pier, May 11, 1960
                Statute miles   41,821.7
                Nautical miles   36,335.1
                Time   84 days, 19 hours, 8 minutes

  e. Time spent at Rehoboth on surface before *Triton* left for New London:
      5 hours, 41 minutes from surfacing point to Helo pick-up
      19 minutes at Helo pick-up point

ADMINISTRATIVE REMARKS

USS Triton (SSR(N)586)

CROSSING THE EQUATOR

Know ye that on this 24th day of February 1960, as TRITON set course southwestward on the first leg of her submerged circumnavigation of the world,

(crewman's name)

appeared in the realm of Neptunus Rex, on board USS TRITON (SSR(N)586) as she crossed the equator in the vicinity of St. Peter and St. Paul's Rocks, mid-Atlantic Ocean, Longitude 29°—32'.8 West; and

WHEREAS,

after due ceremony and examination he was found worthy to be reckoned as a member of the Ancient Order of the Deep and the Royal Order of SHELLBACKS; and

WHEREAS,

during this historic, record-setting submerged cruise of more than 36,000 miles, he crossed the equator thrice more . . . viz:

At Longitude 155°—54'.8 West, mid-Pacific, near Christmas Island.

At Longitude 119°—05'.1 East, Makassar Strait, between the Celebes and Borneo.

At Longitude 28°—03'.0 West, mid-Atlantic, again near St. Peter and St. Paul's Rocks; and

WHEREAS,

on each crossing and visit to my realm, he was found still worthy to be my subject, now

THEREFORE,

I, Neptunus, Ruler of the Raging Main, do solemnly command all my loyal subjects to honor and respect this trusty SHELL-BACK, for he is one who has received special favor in my sight for having crossed the equator submerged four times on this First Submerged Circumnavigation of the World.

	LOYD L. GARLOCK
Authenticated:	Chief Fire Control Technician
Wm. ADAMS, JR.	United States Navy
LCDR, USN	NEPTUNUS,
Executive Officer	REX

About the Author

Generally known as the author of *Submarine!*, a vivid account of submarine action during World War II, and *Run Silent, Run Deep,* a best-selling novel, Captain Edward L. Beach, USN, is nevertheless one of the most experienced submarine commanders in our modern Navy. Since 1939, when he was commissioned upon graduation from the United States Naval Academy, he has served as executive officer of the submarines *Trigger* and *Tirante* during World War II, and as Commanding Officer of the submarines *Piper, Amberjack, Trigger,* and *Triton,* as well as the fleet oiler, *Salamonie.*

Born in New York City and raised in California, the son of an equally famous naval officer and writer, he has served additionally as Aide to the Chief of Naval Personnel and, from 1953 to 1957, as Naval Aide to the President of the United States. He holds six decorations for combat, among them the Navy Cross and two Silver Stars. He was awarded the Legion of Merit for *Triton*'s circumnavigation.

He and his wife, the former Ingrid Bergstrom Schenck of Palo Alto, California, have three children, two boys and a girl.